DATE DUE

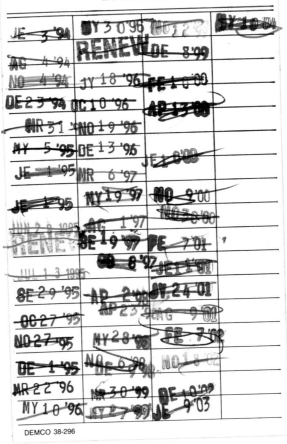

JE 3 '94	MY 3 0 '96	NO 2 0
	RENEW	DE 8 '99
AG 4 '94		
NO 4 '94	JY 18 '96	FE 1 0 '00
DE 23 '94	OC 10 '96	AP 13 '00
MR 31 '95	NO 19 '96	
MY 5 '95	DE 13 '96	JE 1 0'00
JE 1 '95	MR 6 '97	
JE 1 '95	MY 19 '97	NO 8 '00
JUN 2 9 1995	AG 1 '97	NO 30 '00
RENEW	SE 19 '97	FE 7 '01
JUL 1 3 1995	OC 8 '97	JE 1 1 '01
SE 29 '95	AP 2 '98	OV 24 '01
OC 27 '95	AP 23 '98	AG 9 '01
NO 27 '95	MY 28 '98	FE 7 '02
DE 1 '95	NO 6 '98	NO 1 8 '02
MR 22 '96	MR 30 '99	DE 1 0 '02
MY 1 0 '96	MY 2 7 '99	JE 9 '03

DEMCO 38-296

PITT SERIES IN

Policy and Institutional Studies

Affirmative Action

AT WORK

LAW, POLITICS, AND ETHICS

Bron Raymond Taylor

University of Pittsburgh Press

Published by the University of Pittsburgh Press,
Pittsburgh, Pa., 15260
Copyright ©1991, University of Pittsburgh Press
All rights reserved
Eurospan, London
Manufactured in the United States of America

Library of Congress Cataloging-in-Publication Data

Taylor, Bron Raymond.
    Affirmative action at work : law, politics, and ethics / Bron
Raymond Taylor.
        p.   cm.—(Pitt series in policy an d institutional studies)
    Includes bibliographical references (p. 00) and index.
    ISBN 0–8229–3674–7 (cloth).—ISBN 0–8229–5453–2 (paper)
    1. Civil service—California—Personnel management.
2. Affirmative action programs—California.   3. California—
Officials and employees—Attitudes.   4. California.   Dept. of
Parks and Recreation—Officials and employees—Attitudes.
5. Affirmative action programs.   I. Title.   II. Series.
JK8760.A33T38   1991
353.9794001′04—dc20   90–24450
                                                                CIP

A CIP catalogue record for this book is available from the British Library.

To the memory of my father,
James Carlton Taylor

CONTENTS

List of Tables   ix

Foreword   xi

Preface   xv

I THE CULTURAL AND ETHICAL BACKGROUND

Introduction   3
1 The Cultural and Legal Context of
   Affirmative Action   5
2 An Ethical Analysis of Affirmative Action   34

II THE EMPIRICAL RESEARCH

Introduction   73
3 Research Theory and Methodology   75
4 Impressions from the Workplace and Interviews   88
5 Survey Responses: Approval and Disapproval
   of Affirmative Action   113
6 Survey Responses: Moral Arguments About
   Affirmative Action   136
7 Conclusions and Implications   172

Appendixes   205

Notes   217

Glossary   235

References   239

Index   247

LIST OF TABLES

1. Race and Gender of Questionnaire Respondents   85
2. Ideological Self-Identification of Respondents   87
3. Agreement with Survey Statements, by Race
   and Gender   116
4. Agreement that Affirmative Action Is Morally
   Right, by Ideology   122
5. Agreement that Affirmative Action Is Wrong and
   Should Be Changed, by Ideology   125
6. Agreement with Use of Hiring Goals to Promote
   Work Force Parity, by Ideology   130
7. Support for and Opposition to the Overall Morality
   of Affirmative Action   134
8. More Concern with the Common Good over
   Personal Advancement, by Ideology   137
9. Agreement that Doing Well Financially Is More
   Important than Overcoming Financial Inequality in
   Society, by Ideology   138
10. Agreement that Affirmative Action Violates the
    Rights of White Men, by Ideology   141
11. Agreement that Strict Antidiscrimination Enforcement
    Is Better than Affirmative Action, by Ideology   142
12. Agreement that Affirmative Action Helps Many
    Who Do Not Need Help, by Ideology   146
13. Agreement that White Men Should Be Satisfied
    with Fewer Job Opportunities, by Ideology   149
14. Agreement that It Is Usually Possible to Identify
    the Best Qualified Applicant, by Ideology   151
15. Agreement that It Is Morally Right Always to Hire
    the Best Qualified Applicant, by Ideology   152
16. Agreement that Affirmative Action Promotes Equal
    Opportunity, by Ideology   153

17. Agreement that Affirmative Action Is Needed to
    Overcome the Effects of Discrimination, by Ideology   156
18. Agreement that Affirmative Action Is Needed to
    Ensure that Women and Nonwhites Get Serious
    Consideration for Jobs, by Ideology   158
19. Agreement that Affirmative Action Should Be
    Broadened to Include All Disadvantaged People,
    by Ideology   163
20. Agreement with Use of a Deontological Approach
    to Affirmative Action, by Ideology   164
21. Agreement that Affirmative Action Benefits Society,
    by Ideology   165
22. Agreement that Affirmative Action Reduces
    Employee Quality, by Ideology   167
23. Agreement that Affirmative Action Harms the
    Mission of the California State Department of Parks
    and Recreation, by Ideology   168
24. Support for and Opposition to Affirmative Action
    Rationales and Practices   169

FOREWORD

THE MOST unfortunate aspect of the behavioral revolution was the chasm it created between empirical and normative researchers in the social sciences. This was especially true in political science. From the 1950s through the mid-1970s, political science departments throughout the country were torn apart over different approaches to the study of politics. Discussions at faculty meetings and colloquia were often heated, pitting political behaviorists against political theorists over questions such as whether the scientific method could realistically be applied to the study of politics and whether analysis of writings in political philosophy could be used to acquire knowledge.

Heinz Eulau and other prominent behaviorists argued that political theory contributed little to our conceptualization of politics and political systems in the "real world." At the same time, Sheldon Wolin and other distinguished theorists questioned the premises and assumptions on which empirical inquiry in the social sciences was based. Graduate students, even at the most prestigious universities, were drawn into the conflict and were often forced to take sides. Support for one side over the other usually meant that students took certain courses, worked with particular professors, and wrote either empirical or normative seminar papers and dissertations. As a consequence, empiricists graduated with little knowledge of normative theory, and normative theorists with little knowledge of empirical research. The pursuit of knowledge was severely hampered, and the development of political science was substantially retarded as a result of the rivalry between the two groups.

The postbehavioral revolution, which took hold in the late 1970s, was supposed to usher in a new tolerance for empirical and normative approaches to the study of politics. In addition to calls for behaviorists and theorists to put aside their long-held differences, it was hoped that empirical and philosophical pursuits would complement one another, thus leading to a rich, holistic understanding of politics. Some thought that public policy, a relatively new and emerging subfield, would take the lead in integrating the two approaches in a meaningful way. Although the behavior-theory controversy has not built a high wall between faculty in the policy area, a handful of researchers are still fighting old battles against behaviorism (whatever that means now) and continue to insist that empirical inquiry is inferior to philosophical inquiry in the study of political science and public policy (for example, Davis Bobrow and John Dryzek). At the same time, several scholars repeatedly overlook the potential value of incorporating central concepts and principles of political theory in their quantitative work (for example, Richard Hofferbert and David Nachmias). Many if not most postbehaviorists believe there is much to be gained by consolidating quantitative and normative approaches in investigations of politics and government activities, but they rarely do so themselves.

The postbehavioral revolution also led to increased interest in interdisciplinary studies. Political scientists attracted to the "new politics" of the 1970s and 1980s, such as women's rights, environmental protection, and disarmament, quickly realized that they had to go outside their discipline for important theoretical insights into the types of research issues they wished to examine. While political scientists can learn a lot more from other disciplines, movement in this direction has allowed students to add greatly to their knowledge and comprehension of politics and public policy both in the United States and abroad.

In sharp contrast to traditional methodological practices followed by mainstream political scientists, Bron Taylor effectively combines empirical and normative approaches in his study of the moral and ethical values underlying the formulation and implementation of affirmative action policy in the California State Department of Parks and Recreation. Writings by prominent social theorists are used to identify and explore central empirical concepts and questions concerning affirmative action. With this knowledge as a guide, Taylor relied on participant observation and in-depth personal interviews with carefully selected individuals to develop a standardized questionnaire for Parks Department employees. Using sophisticated sampling, survey research, and data analysis techniques, the author finds surprising patterns of support and opposition to many of the Parks Department's affirmative action policies and guidelines. One of the most surprising findings, for example, is the apparent opposition to affirmative action voiced by American Indian men. By delving into the attitudes and values of Native Americans and other employee groups at all levels in the department's hierarchy, Taylor presents a comprehensive picture of the cross pressures at work in the minds of agency personnel. While learning about people's responses to the attitudinal items in the questionnaire, one begins to appreciate the push and pull of racial prejudice, moral and ethical values, and individual self-interest.

Taylor relies upon his empirical findings rather than subjective perceptions to critically examine conventional thinking concerning important philosophical and normative issues regarding the rights of minorities in the workplace. At the end of the book, he returns to the moral and ethical considerations of social theorists. In the end, policy researchers are rewarded with a deep and broad understanding of the highly complex normative and empirical issues surrounding affirmative action in public agencies. Taylor's book is the breath of fresh air we have been waiting for in the policy field.

The interdisciplinary nature of the study also deserves to be noted. Taylor draws heavily from such diverse fields as philosophy, religious ethics, political science, sociology, and psychology to help readers comprehend the social, moral, ethical, and political complexities underlying affirmative action. His analysis carefully navigates the incredible maze of complicated issues that have made affirmative action programs difficult to formulate and implement. Along the way, we are forced to confront our own feelings about other racial and ethnic groups and about equality, equity, fairness, and justice.

Despite the passage of important federal and state laws concerning civil rights and affirmative action, the issue is likely to continue to be debated for quite some time. While most now agree that discrimination in terms of gender, race, religion, ethnicity, and disability should not be allowed in the workplace, it is not clear to what extent, if at all, past discriminatory acts must be addressed and compensated. As Taylor's exhaustive review of the history of affirmative action and related antidiscrimination law points out, the question of quotas and the desire to base hiring and promotion strictly on minority status have been addressed by the courts and various legislative and administrative bodies without resolution.

Where citizens, leaders, and political parties stand on the application of affirmative action guidelines depends upon their moral and ethical convictions involving social justice and equality. Given recent rulings by the Supreme Court and its continuing shift to the political right, the issue of affirmative action is likely to be hotly contested for some time to come. Taylor's book, therefore, has important implications for hiring and promotion practices in both the private and public sectors, making it required reading for law and policy analysts and nonacademics in business and government. Clearly, this study could not have been published at a more fitting time.

As Taylor's book demonstrates, there is much to be gained by fusing empirical and normative perspectives in the analysis of public policy. Alone, each orientation tells only a partial story of how and why certain issues reach the government's agenda and are addressed by legislators and executives. Students can greatly benefit from Taylor's analysis by simultaneously learning the ethical and moral values behind certain government actions and the intricacies of the policy formulation and implementation processes. This line of inquiry is clearly suitable for research on other social policy issues, including abortion, euthanasia, and surrogate parenthood. Before this approach can be adopted, however, students of public policy must become familiar with alternative research perspectives. Perhaps by learning from the deleterious effects of past discriminatory actions on minority groups in the workplace and society, Taylor found it easy to put his own analytic biases aside and produce a study of high quality. This result is a book that is theoretically and methodologically on the cutting edge of the discipline and makes a significant contribution to the literature on affirmative action and antidiscrimination policy.

Sheldon Kamieniecki

PREFACE

AFFIRMATIVE ACTION is a battleground for competing values, especially competing concepts of distributive justice. But both advocacy and criticism of affirmative action is often characterized by idealism or self-interest, neither of which is grounded in a careful analysis of the actual impact of such policy. The research presented in this volume is an attempt to integrate such analysis into moral deliberations over affirmative action.

Both qualitative and quantitative sociological techniques (participant observation, interviews, and survey research) were used to analyze and compare the attitudes of different groups of individuals in the California State Department of Parks and Recreation toward the idea, practice, and typical rationales used to justify affirmative action policy. This population was chosen because its members had firsthand experience with an aggressive affirmative action program. The views of four subgroups were examined especially closely: white men, white women, nonwhite men, and nonwhite women. The qualitative and quantitative methods complement each other: the former facilitated an in-depth archeology of respondent attitudes; the latter made it possible to test the research hypotheses that were generated qualitatively.

Part 1 provides a legal history of antidiscrimination and affirmative action law, as well as an ethical analysis of the typical ways that social philosophers have evaluated principles of distributive justice in general and affirmative action policy in particular.

Part 2 establishes a theoretical framework for the empirical research and describes its methodology. It then provides an in-depth analysis of respondent attitudes. This analysis includes discussion of the extent and nature of respondent approval and disapproval of affirmative action. The analysis concludes by focusing on the different beliefs about distributive justice that underlie the attitudes of the various groups toward affirmative action and compares these beliefs with the typical approaches to affirmative action taken by social philosophers analyzed in part 1. The research concludes by discussing the ways in which the data illuminate the most common arguments for and against affirmative action, with suggestions as to the implications of the research for organizations with affirmative action programs.

This work is grounded in a discipline known as *social ethics,* which concerns itself with diverse issues at the intersection of morality and society. Thus the discipline is necessarily interdisciplinary—dependent equally on the humanities and social sciences. In this interdisciplinary spirit, I have written this book for a wide audience: for nonspecialist citizens as well as for policy makers and academicians who are concerned about civil rights, social justice, and the impact of public policies on race and gender relations. The research is also intended for those charged with the difficult task of enforcing antidiscrimination laws or implementing affirmative action programs. Often such people do not have adequate knowledge of the premises upon which these policies are based or the attitudes of individuals who are affected by the policies.

I have not assumed that readers know much if anything about antidiscrimination and affirmative action law, nor have I assumed that they are well acquainted with philosophy or ethics. Part 1 provides primers into the legal and ethical dimensions of these controversies. The purpose of part 1 is not to provide the definitive treatment of either the legal or ethical issues but rather to illuminate the central issues involved in the controversy and, thereby, provide the necessary background for the empirical research, and the normative reflections, in part 2. The expert in either area might find it more rewarding to move directly to the empirical research found in part 2.

I am indebted to many who helped me accomplish this work. Andrea Patterson, Steve Kann, Dan Abeyta, Denise Murphy, and Ginny Lindstrand were especially helpful, along with others too numerous to mention. Gerald Weil and Kirk Sturm and several other friends commented on the early drafts of the interview protocols and the survey; and Sturm commented helpfully on early drafts of the manuscript. Glen D. Nagle and Theodore Shaw helped me in interpreting the law; any remaining errors are due to my own unwillingness to become as much of a legal expert as they are.

I am also deeply grateful to all the department employees who freely shared their views.

Several professors have been especially encouraging. Donald Heinz inspired me while I was still an undergraduate, while John Crossley, Jr., Don Miller, Mark Kann, and Sheldon Kamieniecki posed fascinating questions and pushed me to focus on the critical issues.

Other colleagues who have provided intellectual and moral support include Paul Bube, Matthew Glass, Lois Lorentzen, Mark Ridley-Thomas, Mark Kowaleswki, Carlos Piar, Bob Pierson, Fredi Spiegel, and Beth Virgili. Bube's comments on some of the earliest drafts deserve special thanks. I am also grateful to my colleagues in the Religious Studies Department at the University of Wisconsin, Oshkosh, for supporting interdisciplinary work such as this is, as well as the Faculty Development Board of the University of Wisconsin for a research grant which enabled the research into antidiscrimination and affirmative action law.

I am most grateful of all to my wife Beth, who provided me more time to write than I could reasonably have asked for, and to Anders, Kaarin, and Kelsey, who all too often have had to do without me while I traveled or wrote. I am even more grateful for the humanizing diversions they continually provide.

Part I

THE CULTURAL AND
ETHICAL
BACKGROUND

INTRODUCTION

THIS RESEARCH *focuses on the moral and religious attitudes toward affirmative action policies held by individuals from groups who are favored and unfavored by such policies and who have experienced such policies firsthand. A key premise of this study is Max Weber's insight that moral and religious values are important and perhaps even the decisive factors in the matrix of variables that produces social stability and social change. The purpose of this undertaking, however, is not to make predictions about the direction of U.S. culture (although it may provide some clues as to this direction). Instead, this study employs two major types of ethical analyses, each of which has a distinct purpose.*

The first purpose of the research is to answer questions from the perspective of descriptive ethics. Through participant observation, interviews, and a survey, I have attempted to understand the attitudes of people directly affected by affirmative action. I particularly focused on differences among four groups of people: white women, nonwhite women, nonwhite men (all of whom presumably benefit from affirmative action), and white men (who probably seldom benefit). Most basically, I tried to uncover what norms of action and what values these people hold that inform their views of affirmative action.

The research addresses a number of questions, including: To what extent and in what ways do individuals from favored and unfavored groups apply moral sentiments and reasoning to the affirmative action issue? Do the ways these people think about affirmative action parallel recognizable patterns of moral thought?

To what extent is there a backlash against affirmative action, and does it reflect a strong cultural tendency to retreat from commitment to moral principles of compensatory and distributive justice? What are the moral and religious values that contribute to attitudes about affirmative action? Are the values that provided the impetus for policies such as affirmative action in decline, making it difficult for our society to sustain such policies? Has individualism become so pronounced in the United States that people are incapable of affirming the principles of justice that engender policies that, while promoting the common good, also require individual sacrifice?

The second purpose of the research is to address issues from the perspective of normative ethics. The first normative aim is not to advance a particular comprehensive normative ethical judgment of affirmative action; rather, the aim is to contribute to the ongoing dialogue over the moral permissibility of such policy, by suggesting which arguments against and for affirmative action are supported by the data generated by this research. The second normative aim is to address the implications of the data for organizations with affirmative action programs.

Chapter 1 discusses the importance of affirmative action in the context of the Liberal culture, provides background definitions, and concludes with a primer of affirmative action law. Chapter 2 provides an ethical analysis of affirmative action and reviews the ways in which social philosophers have approached this issue. In short, part 1 provides a backdrop for examining the empirical research discussed in part 2.

1

THE CULTURAL AND LEGAL CONTEXT
OF AFFIRMATIVE ACTION

DURING A BREAK in a training session on affirmative action, a frustrated middle-management woman asked, "What can I do to deal with this good-old-boy network? I just can't seem to break into the group." Moments later, a crusty, middle-aged, white, male manager, in a parody of the woman's statement, joked to several other white men, "What are we going to do about the good-old-boy system? Nothing, that's what we are going to do about it. We like it just the way it is!" Appreciative chuckles greeted his candid affirmation of the good-old-boy network.

A young, white, male employee, who believes he almost did not get into the California State Parks Department because of affirmative action and who has seen friends excluded because of such programs, said emphatically, "If I ever get to a place where I have any power over hiring, I will do everything I can to thwart this affirmative action bullshit."

A black male rank-and-file employee argued that if it were not for affirmative action the department would still be "lily white."

A middle-aged, white, woman manager said that at one time she was a clerical worker, without self-esteem or hopes of advancement, but affirmative action opened up possibilities for her. Some years ago, her supervisor, a white man supportive of affirmative action efforts to promote women and nonwhite men, told her that she had potential and encouraged her to go back to school to get management training. Now, although she has some negative feelings about affirmative action, she sees it as a lesser evil to the loss of talent and dignity that occurs when women and nonwhite men are not encouraged to develop their potential.

The above stories are about employees of the California State Department of Parks and Recreation, which provided the setting for this research into attitudes toward affirmative action. The stories illustrate how deeply held are the feelings that surround this issue. Affirmative action has become a critical locus of the tensions between racial groups and between men and women. From the workplace to legal, political, and philosophical literature, impassioned debates rage about the prudence and morality of affirmative action law and policy. Some politicians defend affirmative action, while others attempt to dismantle it. Given the origins of affirmative action in the civil rights movement, the rallying cry of opponents to affirmative action is a cry heavy with irony: affirmative action betrays civil rights; instead of producing new freedoms and opportunities, it has produced the tyranny of "quotas" and "reverse discrimination."

What is this phenomenon that has produced such intensity of feeling? To what extent has there been a backlash against affirmative action? Why has this backlash been so vehement in some quarters? What are the stakes involved in the affirmative action issue that contribute to the intensity of reaction, especially among those who feel directly affected by it? This chapter begins to address these questions.

The Importance of Affirmative Action in the Context of Liberal Culture

Given its grounding in the premises of philosophical Liberalism, affirmative action provides analysts a window through which to examine many of the critical moral dimensions of contemporary Liberal culture. Affirmative action is controversial largely because it represents and reflects several of the most critical unresolved moral conflicts within the Liberal culture. Some of these conflicts are grounded in the unresolved problems of nineteenth-century Liberalism. When I speak of Liberalism, I include conservatives, liberals, and libertarians of contemporary parlance. Despite real differences, all share the key tenets of Liberalism: rights naturally inhere in the individual, people are self-interested, acquisitive consumers (usually unchangeably so); these people compete in political and economic markets; and this competition produces at best a good society, or at least the best society people are capable of producing, and this society generally is characterized by economic growth and political freedom.[1]

Affirmative Action and the Legitimacy of Liberal Culture

Affirmative action proponents and opponents often rest their arguments on one of Liberalism's central principles, namely, its version of distributive justice: the idea that preferred jobs and rewards ought to be distributed according to talents and qualifications (or *merit*) in a social context characterized by equality of opportunity. (This conception of distributive justice is often referred to by the terms *equal opportunity* or the *merit principle.*) It is possible, however, if the social context were to be characterized by increasing social scarcity, declining overall opportunities, and increasing conflicts over affirmative action policies, that the equal opportunity principle itself could be called into question. Since the equal opportunity version of the distributive justice principle is itself a fundamental premise of the Liberal culture, such a reevaluation could raise questions about the legitimacy of that culture.

Some Liberal theorists have argued that social scarcity and declining opportunities are increasing, that there are two factors involved in this dynamic, and that these factors exacerbate certain tensions, which have not been resolved by Liberalism. The two factors are resource scarcity and social or positional scarcity. Social scarcity is defined by Hirsh (1977, 27) as the scarcity of preferred jobs, services, opportunities, and other goods that accrue to those with preferred positions (cf. Daly, 1980; Thurow, 1980).[2] Daly emphasizes the problem of resource scarcity. Hirsh and Thurow emphasize social scarcity: the problem of limits to the growth of positional goods and opportunities. Taken together, these analysts suggest that Liberalism cannot deliver on its promise to provide ever increasing growth, however such growth is defined. This is important, because a central tenet of Liberalism is that growth is the best way to deal with poverty and the inequalities of distribution—it is better to expand than to redistribute the pie. But if growth proves not to be an easy way to ameliorate inequalities, then other principles of distribution not grounded in the premises of Liberalism may deserve serious consideration. (While Liberalism does have a principle by which to distribute scarce resources—merit—it generally has assumed that in the long term, there would be more, not fewer, opporunities. If it becomes clear that the promise of expanding opportunities is exaggerated, under a situation of decreasing opportunities, the merit principle may not appear as attractive as under expectations of increasing opportunities.)

If there were widespread agreement that scarcity and limits on growth and opportunities are serious problems, then the affirmative action controversy could take on an additional dimension. This would be especially true if it were to become clear that the gains being demanded by women and nonwhites cannot all come from an expansion of material and positional pies, but that such gains inevitably require some sacrifice by (or coercion of) those people in positions of relative privilege. One of the questions the research addresses is whether people think that the gains made by previously excluded persons can come without requiring sacrifices from those who have traditionally been included. Another question the research addresses is how people perceive market competition and the stakes involved in this competition.

While the stakes of the competition over jobs seem to be increasing (winners seem to be reaping larger rewards, losers seem to be marginalized increasingly), some Liberal theorists are agonizing over the inability of Liberalism to make the difficult decisions necessary to reduce the stakes of market competition.

The point relevant to the affirmative action issue is that Liberalism (with its view of human nature as individualistic, self-interested, and acquisitive) seems ill equipped both to increase opportunities for those traditionally excluded and to reduce the vast differences in deserts that accrue to the winners and losers of market competition. Some philosophical Liberals are concerned that without some supplemental principle of social justice, an increasing redistributional compulsion will threaten the very stability of Liberalism's market society. They then suggest that some supplemental principle of social justice is needed that would keep the equal opportunity principle as axiomatic while reducing the stakes of the competition, so that those who do not win will still have enough material goods to insure they are content with their share of the pie (Hirsh 1977, 10–12, 152–77, 182–87).[3] In various ways Hirsh (1977, esp. 177), Lowi (1979, 67, 236–37, 293, 296) and Thurow (1980, 17–18) all express such concerns.

While these concerns are understandable from those sympathetic to the premises of Liberalism, there is another implication beyond the reality of increasing scarcity, which further illustrates the importance of the affirmative action issue. Affirmative action functions as one important contemporary legitimating strategy for

Liberalism's market society. This strategy asserts that through reforms such as affirmative action, market competition can be made increasingly fair.[4] But when people cite evidence which suggests that equal opportunity does not exist or is in decline, this can suggest that perhaps other non-Liberal principles of distribution ought to be considered. Liberal culture has achieved an amazing degree of consensus in favor of equal opportunity as its principle of distribution. But a serious threat to the legitimacy of this principle could also lead to questions about the other key tenets of Liberalism. If such questions are taken seriously, the legitimacy of a Liberal market society itself could be questioned (although such a reexamination seems unlikely, at least in the short term, in view of recent events in Europe, and subsequent self-congratulatory rhetoric within Liberal culture).

While scarcity contributes to and makes more clear the significance of the affirmative action issue, this discussion shows that the underlying issue is not scarcity but the equal opportunity principle itself. This principle underlies affirmative action policy, as well as the dominant streams of liberal thought in the United States.

This section began by asserting that affirmative action is controversial primarily because it represents and reflects several of the most critical unresolved moral conflicts within the Liberal culture, conflicts grounded in unresolved problems of nineteenth-century Liberalism. The affirmative action issue is important because it is based on the equal opportunity principle, and because of this, the affirmative action controversy could invite a reevaluation of this principle and its premises.

Affirmative Action and the Future of the Liberal Culture

Whether or not the struggle over the principle of equal opportunity causes a reevaluation of the premises and legitimacy of Liberal market society, the affirmative action conflict remains important. It remains important because it presents the various options from contending Liberal perspectives concerning which principles of distribution—principles at issue since the beginning of Enlightenment thought—are morally warranted.

Since the Enlightenment, the type of individualism the equal opportunity principle represents has been a critical issue. Some libertarians and conservatives argue that this principle does not do enough to protect individuals, while some left-leaning liberals and leftists believe this principle is excessively individualistic and erodes the basis for social solidarity and cooperation.

Underlying this debate is the perpetual tension between concern for the general interest and concern for individual rights. Liberal thought has asserted both that individual, acquisitive, self-interested behavior is justified by its efficiency in producing collective benefits (promoting the commonweal) and that individuals have some inviolable rights against the group. But Liberalism has had problems in resolving tensions and conflicts between social welfare goals and individual rights.

Related to the basic issue here of how individual rights ought to be balanced against the commonweal are a variety of additional problems, the resolution (or nonresolution) of which will be important to the future of liberal culture. Some of these problems include: How to define terms such as *rights* and *justice*, *liberty* and *equality* and how these concepts are related to each other. Are individual rights absolute? Can criteria of economic efficiency be squared with principles of freedom and justice? Which of the premises from the variant forms of Liberal theory (for example, premises about human nature, market dynamics, and economic growth) hold up under analysis?

To summarize, the controversy over affirmative action is a battleground for conflicting values. The outcome of this battle may be decisive in determining which principles of distributive justice will guide public policy in America. The affirmative action controversy asks the perennial question regarding the proper relationship between individual rights and social justice, on the one hand, and the various principles of distributive justice that provide competing perspectives on rights and justice, on the other. The affirmative action issue, grounded as it is in the currently dominant equal opportunity principle, provides an appropriate window through which to examine moral meaning in our culture. The immediate task, however, is to provide some background definitions and history to the affirmative action controversy.

Background Definitions:
Equal Opportunity and Affirmative Action

Definitions are important because they often promote a particular perspective on controversial issues. For example, the different connotations of terms such as *protection against discrimination, compensatory redress, preferential treatment,* or *reverse discrimination* often do more to indicate the bias of the speaker than the meaning of the term. Not surprisingly, it can be difficult to define objectively the terms surrounding the affirmative action issue. I will attempt to clarify the terms and the issues at stake by providing objective working definitions that avoid prejudging the issue.

To a great extent, Americans have come to affirm equal opportunity as their central principle of distributive justice. It is not, however, easy to define this principle precisely. For some, equal opportunity means equal *legal* access to market society and strict enforcement of antidiscrimination law. Some opponents use this definition to deny, a priori, the legitimacy of affirmative action programs based on a more comprehensive definition of equal opportunity. This version of equal opportunity as equal legal access, combined with an uncompromising adherence to the idea that the "best qualified" ought always be hired, I will call *pure equality of opportunity.*

For others, the meaning of equal access includes an additional criterion of developmental access. Here the idea is that all persons should have equal access to whatever goods are needed to develop their natural talents so that persons with equal natural talents have equal opportunities and resources to develop their talents and compete in the market economy. I call this version the *equal opportunity principle* or the *merit principle.* Using this definition of equal opportunity, rather than the pure equal opportunity definition, as the central definition of equal opportunity for this study is justified, because most people recognize that more is needed than the absence of *legal* barriers to equalize people's opportunities to develop their talents and competitive abilities.

Equal *employment* opportunity refers to situations in which characteristics of persons (like gender and ethnicity) that are not relevant to the job are not considered in personnel decisions. With equal employment opportunity, only traits relevant to the job (such as education, training, experience, and character) are considered in personnel decisions.

In general, affirmative action refers to specific steps, beyond ending discriminatory practices, that are taken to promote equal opportunity and ensure that "discrimination will not recur" (Maguire 1980, 28–29). The goal of affirmative action is to eliminate nonlegal barriers to equal employment opportunity, including intentional discriminatory practices and nonintentional (structural or systemic) discrimination.[5] Proponents of affirmative action assume that these types of discrimination hinder the ability of persons from *target groups* or *affected groups* (terms for groups identified as having been negatively affected by discrimination and, therefore, targeted for concern by affirmative action programs) from competing equally. Proponents argue, for example, that past discrimination leads to inferior education and training, which hinders affected group members from gaining the traits and skills necessary to compete with those not disadvantaged by discrimination.

More specifically, affirmative action is best understood as a diverse continuum of (more or less severe) responses that attempt to overcome discrimination. Some affirmative action programs are limited to the attempt to protect individuals belonging to targeted groups from personal or structural discrimination. For example, these programs may provide review procedures to double-check personnel actions, root out intentional discrimination through *discrimination complaint processes* and other procedures, and examine practices in the attempt to eliminate nonintentional discriminatory practices, such as those based on nonrelevant job qualifications.

Other affirmative action programs are explicitly preferential. They establish minimum qualifications and, once these are met, give preference in employment decisions to individuals from affected groups, even if those individuals are, overall, less well qualified than others being considered. Preferential treatment is usually tied to affirmative action timetables, or goals. Affirmative action law and policy has evolved to the point where goals are established in an attempt to bring the representation of minorities in the workplace into parity with the work force in the local population or the society at large. Where it is useful to distinguish these types from affirmative action in general, or from each other, I call these two types *protective* and *preferential* affirmative action, respectively.[6]

Some proponents of affirmative action believe that only the protective type is justifiable, because the goal is to get the best qualified individual for the job or promotion (Blackstone and Heslep 1977; Goldman 1977). Some of these people base their view of protective affirmative action on the idea of pure equal opportunity and believe that whenever preferences enter in, affirmative action is no longer justified.

Another group of affirmative action proponents believe that some preferential treatment is necessary and justifiable but that it is misleading, and perhaps strategically unwise, to apply the term *preferential treatment* to affirmative action, because all that such treatment really does is counteract the massive preferential treatment the culture imparts to white men.[7] There is some merit to this line of thought. It is understandable why proponents of affirmative action would have such strategic concerns; preferential treatment is a term that seems to indicate unequal treatment and unfairness and is used by the opponents of affirmative action to frame the debate in a way that ignores many important issues. Yet my experience leads me to conclude that the attempt by proponents of affirmative action to excise the term *preferential* from the conceptualization of affirmative action is often disingenuous and obscurantist. It seems disingenuous because such proponents usually favor not only protective affirmative action but also forms of affirmative action that ensure minimum qualifications are met and then (at least relative to the affirmative action continuum) wish to promote rapid progress toward specific numerical goals.[8] It seems obscurantist because attempts to define affirmative action only in protective terms underplays the various ways affirmative action programs usually do lead to preferential treatment, and this in turn inaccurately focuses the discussion on whether affirmative action is really preferential, after all—instead of illuminating the debate over whether such preferences are morally justifiable and, if so, under what circumstances.

While it is at times helpful to distinguish between protective and preferential forms of affirmative action, the distinction ought not be overdrawn. There are preferential aspects even to the forms of affirmative action that, on the affirmative action continuum, are close to the protective forms described above. For example, the attempt to expose and eliminate inappropriate barriers to blacks and not those to whites is preferential, not merely protective: there may be inappropriate cultural barriers to whites, which, if focused upon, could be exposed and eliminated. Given such preferential dynamics related to the so-called protective affirmative action, when I refer to affirmative action in this research, I assume that some preference is involved, unless the affirmative action practice is specifically labeled protective.

Another reason I do not excise all preferential aspects from this book's working definition of affirmative action is that the institutional context of this study has a strongly preferential affirmative action program. The California State Parks Department has had a poor record of hiring women and nonwhites. As a result, in part because the state feared lawsuits claiming discrimination (under the laws discussed in the next section), the California State Person-nel Board (the state agency responsible for eliminating discrim-inatory practices in state government) pressured the Parks Depart-ment into entering a sanctions agreement. The two sides agreed on goals and timetables for bringing the work force up to proportional representation or work force parity—terms that refer to an institu-tional work force approximately proportional in ethnic and gender representation to the work force available in the state. When man-agement places a high priority on such goals, preferential treat-ment almost inevitably results.

Within the Parks Department, this is true notwithstanding pro-tests from some affirmative action proponents, who deny the pro-grams are preferential or say that they are uncomfortable with the use of the term *preferential treatment*. And it is true despite fre-quent disclaimers by some of these proponents that the purpose of the department's affirmative action program is to ensure simply that the "best qualified" person is hired. In short, it is best to be clear that affirmative action involves some degree of preferential treatment, because not to do so is to beg the question—it is to force the most crucial issue into the background: the issue of whether preferential treatment for women and nonwhites can ever be morally justifiable.[9]

A Primer of History and Law Related to Affirmative Action

Before I discuss specific developments in the legal history of affir-mative action and related antidiscrimination law, it will be helpful to give a broad overview of the range of possibilities available for such legislation and the related issues at stake. These possibilities are discussed within five, related dimensions.[10]

First and most fundamental is the question: Is it ever permissi-ble to discriminate (namely, to make decisions, in whole or in part), based on race, ethnicity, gender, or any other trait that groups of people share, such as age, disability, sexual orientation, religious tradition, or political ideology? (Beyond this, ought the *moral* standard be different from the *legal* standard? For example, are race-dependent decisions morally repugnant, while state judicial sanctions are even more objectionable on other grounds, such as the nonfeasibility of enforcement, or some moral "right" to free association?) Specifically, which individuals should be protected by antidiscrimination law or should benefit from preferential affirmative action? (The importance of this question should not be underestimated. For instance, the Taft-Hartley Act makes legal discrimination against those believed to hold communist ideas, and only recently have the civil rights of homosexuals, the disabled, and the elderly been given serious consideration.)

Second, if race-dependent decisions are sometimes permissible, how should such decisions be evaluated? Specifically, when race-conscious decisions are permitted under affirmative action laws or antidiscrimination remedies, what standards should be applied to insure that these decisions are truly benign? -

Third, when dealing specifically with antidiscrimination law, what sort of proof would be sufficient to establish discrimination and to trigger remedies? The answer depends on the answer to other questions, namely, questions concerned with how discrimination is understood. Is it simple, based on human prejudice, or hatred, or discomfort with individuals from certain groups? Or is it subtle and complex, assuming structural forms unrelated to human intentions? Or is it both? Can systemic discrimination exist in the absence of discriminatory intent?

Fourth, with regard to affirmative action and antidiscrimination laws, what sorts of enforcement mechanisms are needed to promote compliance, and what sort of remedies should those responsible for enforcement be empowered to impose? Specific questions include: Should those caught discriminating, or those who do not comply with affirmative action laws, be subject to criminal trials and punishment? If so, which specific illegal acts would be subject to criminal charges? If, rather, enforcement actions are restricted to civil remedies, should the civil remedies available include punitive monetary damages, designed to punish the wrongdoer? Or rather, should civil remedies promote conciliation between victim and perpetrator and therefore be limited to nonpunitive damages, which attempt to "make whole" victims, by awarding them back pay, for example, or by restoring them to their "rightful place" (their place in the absence of discrimination), while enjoining the wrongdoer from continuing the discriminatory actions? If there is a difference between intentional and nonintentional discrimination, is such a difference relevant to the types of remedies deemed appropriate? And who should benefit from enforcement or compliance efforts—identifiable victims or all members of the group illegally discriminated against? Finally, who are the enforcers to be? Can such cases be handled by standing courts, or would special government agencies need to be established to assume responsibility for certain aspects of the enforcement and compliance efforts?

Fifth, who is prohibited from discriminating? All individuals? All institutions? Only government agencies and contractors? Only some government agencies? Labor unions? Private institutions and companies? Private institutions and companies of a certain size? Private clubs? May religious individuals or institutions prefer members of their own traditions and discriminate against others?

Beyond the above possibilities for antidiscrimination and affirmative action legislation and enforcement, other stakes are revealed by a review of the history of such legislation. Among the most important is: Who will have the last word when it comes to such law and related policies: Congress, or the Supreme Court (and, of course, the presidents, who cast their shadows over the Court's decisions through their judicial appointments to it)?

These issues frame the discussion of the legal background. They also illustrate, when combined with the following legal history, the complexity of this area of law and show that not all of the possible choices have been considered seriously.

The Fourteenth Amendment and the Emergence of Antidiscrimination Law

The history leading to the implementation of affirmative action programs is largely the history of the civil rights movement, beginning with the abolitionists. It showed brief but frustrated promise during the period of reconstruction after the Civil War, followed by a gradual awakening of conscience, beginning especially during the late New Deal period. It gained momentum after the Second World War and got a decisive impetus in 1963, when over 200,000 people gathered in Washington, D.C., in for what was then the largest civil rights demonstration in U.S. history, a demonstration that expedited passage of the Civil Rights Act of 1964.

Several specific legislative events stand out during the above periods. The Civil Rights Act of 1866 seemed "to prohibit a broad range of private as well as public acts of discrimination" (Burstein 1985, 16).[11] This act was followed by the all-important Fourteenth Amendment to the Constitution, ratified in 1868, section 1 of which guarantees to all citizens "equal protection" under the law, "due process" of all laws, and the right to life, liberty, and property. Equal protection of the laws to all citizens is expressed in legal literature as the "antidiscrimination principle" (Brest 1976, 1–4). This principle disfavors decisions dependent on racial classifications (at least if they hurt individuals from oppressed groups), and is the ground of subsequent civil rights law.

But despite the apparently obvious intent of these laws (preventing discrimination against black citizens), they were construed so narrowly by the Supreme Court (in *Civil Rights Cases of 1883*, 101 U.S. 3) that these legislative achievements were essentially nullified. These cases made it appear impossible for the federal government to do much about discrimination in the private labor market on the basis of the Fourteenth Amendment (Burstein 1985, 16, summarizing Gunther 1975).

But while the practical effect of these rulings was to nullify, for decades, the apparent purpose of early civil rights legislation, the interpretation of the contract protections within the 1866 Act (section 1981), and the equal protection clause of the Fourteenth Amendment have emerged as important if not crucial issues in the struggle over civil rights law in the second half of this century. For example, in 1968 the Supreme Court decided the case of *Jones v. Mayer*, 392 U.S. 409, by resurrecting the 1866 Civil Rights Act as a remedy for private racial discrimination. In 1989, however, the Court decided, in *Patterson v. McLean Credit Union*, 87 U.S. 107, to narrow significantly the application of the act. This decision contributed to the widely held belief among the civil rights lobby that the Court was reversing civil rights gains and thereby contributed to the urgency with which this lobby pressured Congress to enact the Civil Rights Act of 1990. (This bill was passed by Congress, but President Bush's veto was sustained by a margin of one vote in the Senate.) This proposed act had been designed, in part, to insure a broader interpretation of the purposes of the 1866 act. When assessing the future of antidiscrimination law, I will return to the issues posed by these cases and recent civil rights legislation.

But a prior question now requires attention: Is it ever permissible to make race-dependent decisions? Three options are possible when considering this question: (1) race-dependent decisions are always dangerous—color blindness must be an exceptionless rule; (2) the risks inherent in race-dependent decisions are justified only in the case of extraordinarily important government interests; (3) the dangers of race-dependent decisions must be weighed against the government interest on a case-by-case basis (Brest and Levinson 1983, 442f.). In *Korematsu v. United States*, 323 U.S. 214 (1944), the wartime ruling on Japanese-American internment, the Court forbade race-dependent decisions unless they were necessary to promote important or "compelling" government objectives (Brest 1976, 15). The Court made the general ruling that classifications based on race are "suspect" and subject to "strict scrutiny" by the courts. As for the specifics of the case, the Court concluded that the internment did pass such "strict scrutiny," given the wartime circumstances. An important implication of this ruling is that racial classifications could be utilized in the interest of the commonweal—a principle that became important when classifications that benefit racial minorities and women were considered.[12]

Twenty years later, in *McLaughlin v. Florida*, 379 U.S. 184 (1964), the Court required a higher level of review than it did in *Korematsu*. It held that a decision based on a racial classification will be subject to the "most rigid scrutiny" and that such classifications were "in most circumstances irrelevant" and "will be upheld only if it is necessary, and not merely rationally related, to the accomplishment of a permissible state policy" (Brest and Levinson 1983, 446–47).

The *Korematsu* and *McLaughlin* cases helped frame much of the subsequent legal debates over affirmative action and antidiscrimination law: What level of review, or scrutiny, would be required? Were race-dependent decisions permissible in the interest of the commonweal, or were "important" or "compelling" government interests required? But after *McLaughlin*, the question soon shifted from whether racial classifications that adversely affect racial minorities should be permitted to whether race-dependent decisions are permissible that benefit women and racial minorities as a means for promoting the common good. Put briefly, after *McLaughlin*, the debate shifted to the legitimacy of race-conscious decision making for *remedial* purposes.

What does the foregoing analysis have to do with affirmative action? During May and June 1990, I interviewed policy makers and lobbyists in Washington, D.C., about the proposed Civil Rights Act of 1990. Technically, this act had to do with antidiscrimination law, not affirmative action. Indeed, one important proponent of the bill insisted that the bill "had nothing to do with affirmative action." Similar language found its way into the bill itself. This proponent was understandably sensitive about this, because the major objection to the bill was that it would force employers to engage in preferential quota hiring as insulation from charges of discrimination. Since the common perception of affirmative action is that it involves goals and even quotas (and given the fact that affirmative action is less popular than equal opportunity as a policy goal), proponents did not want the bill linked to affirmative action. Technically and conceptually, as a matter of law, antidiscrimination law can be separated from affirmative action law. But in my judgment, for two reasons, the distinction between them is overdrawn.

First, the courts have blurred the distinction between them (Fullinwider 1980, 163). Second, as a practical matter, antidiscrimination law contributes probably as much as or more than affirmative action law toward the legal and quasi-legal pressures on employers to diversify the work force. In fact, I have found that within the workplace legal distinctions between antidiscrimination law and affirmative action law are rarely made. In the ordinary manager's mind, pressure to diversify one's workplace was related *both* to "affirmative action" laws, and also to the perception that the department was trying to avoid the appearance of continuing discrimination, in part to prevent class action discrimination lawsuits. On the other hand, attorneys who litigate discrimination lawsuits have said that many decision makers in institutions do not blur the distinctions between antidiscrimination and affirmation action law, although subordinates may. The origins of the two types of law can be clearly distinguished.

The Civil Rights Act of 1964 and the Birth of Affirmative Action

The landmark Civil Rights Act of 1964, Public Law 88–352 (1964), definitively prohibits discrimination in voting, public accommodations, public education, and employment. Title VII of the act prohibits job discrimination, and places a priority on equal employment opportunity.[13] The legislators never seriously considered criminal penalties for persons who discriminate, nor do the civil remedies they established include punitive damages or compensation for pain and suffering.[14] They chose, rather, to establish a "conciliation process," through which victims can be restored to the economic status and job situation they would have enjoyed in the absence of discrimination. In the language of the law, victims are to be "made whole" (economically) and restored to their "rightful place."[15]

The act also established a new federal agency, the Equal Employment Opportunity Commission. The EEOC's role is to facilitate the conciliation process between private employers and plaintiffs and to pressure employers who discriminate into providing victims with back pay, restitution, and equitable relief (Greene 1989, 44). The act enables plaintiffs to initiate discrimination complaints and request mediation through the EEOC, or through the federal courts, or both. The EEOC can support litigation initiated by a plaintiff.

In two crucial areas the act is ambiguous or subject to different interpretations. It speaks only of intentional discrimination and does not even mention nonintentional (structural or systemic) discrimination. It thereby provides no guidance as to whether these types of discrimination should be treated differently. This is probably because in 1964 most people assumed discrimination was intentional. The effect of this omission is to leave it to the Supreme Court to decide what to do in the case of discriminatory practices that are "fair in form but discriminatory in operation" (Greenhouse 1990b).[16] (An example of a practice that is fair in form but discriminatory in effect is requiring a high school diploma for menial jobs, consequently screening out more minority persons than whites.)

Just as important, Title VII is subject to differing interpretations with regard to the remedies it does permit. It leaves open to debate whether the directive to make victims whole permits courts to order preferential treatment benefiting victims (or, for that matter, benefiting minority individuals who have not been discriminated against). Three major interpretations regarding the remedies permitted by Title VII have been advanced: (1) courts may order only those remedies that benefit (and make whole) the actual victims of discrimination (no preferential treatment is permitted); (2) courts may order preferential treatment that extends beyond demonstrable victims to redress statistical imbalances between the discriminating employer's work force and the available work force; (3) courts may order preferential treatment as a remedy to social discrimination (Fullinwider 1980, 124–42). Whatever the intent in 1964, by the time Congress enacted the Equal Employment Opportunities Act of 1972, 92 U.S.C. 261 (1964), Congress clearly did intend to authorize preferential, results-oriented affirmative action (Greene 1989, 46–53). (This act is discussed more fully later.)

By analyzing presidential directives, administrative actions by the Labor Department and the EEOC, Supreme Court decisions, and civil rights legislation subsequent to the enactment of Title VII, one can begin to grasp the importance of the struggle to resolve the ambiguities over intentionality and preferential treatment. One can also begin to grasp the stakes involved in these struggles, understand the nature of affirmative action, and wonder about the nature of antidiscrimination law and affirmative action law in the future.

One year after Title VII was enacted, Lyndon Johnson signed Executive Order 11246, which requires federal contractors to "take affirmative action to ensure that applicants are employed, and that employees are treated during employment, without regard to their race, color, religion, sex, or national origin." The order specifies: "Such action shall include, but not be limited to the following: employment, upgrading, demotion, or transfer; recruitment or recruitment advertising; layoff or termination; rates of pay [and] selection for training."

The order left it to the Labor Department to define the specifics of affirmative action and its enforcement. The Office of Federal Contract Compliance Programs (OFCCP) was given enforcement responsibilities over federal contractors and subcontractors, and the EEOC over private employers. The Labor Department's guidelines state that affirmative action applies to a wide range of minority groups and women and consists of results-oriented actions, such as goals, timetables, back pay, and retroactive seniority, designed to ensure equal employment opportunity.

So it is to these guidelines that the most controversial aspects of affirmative action programs—goals and timetables—can be traced. By 1968, the Labor Department had developed "utilization analysis," namely, statistical analysis comparing the proportion of minorities and women in an organization to the work force at large. This analysis was designed to determine if employment practices had produced an "underutilization" of or "disparate impact" on women and minorities. These terms refer to situations where women and minorities (or "affected classes," in affirmative action discourse) are not being hired in proportion to their availability in the qualified applicant pool. The underlying assumption here was that in the absence of discrimination, persons from affected classes would be hired in roughly the same proportion as they are qualified and available. Based on this assumption, the Labor Department viewed disparate impact as strong evidence of discrimination. The Labor Department, the EEOC, and the OFCCP used such evidence to demand that goals and timetables be established to reduce the "underutilization" of affected groups.[17] Now the government *officially* recognized discrimination as systemic (not necessarily intentional), and the result-oriented goal of proportional representation became part of U.S. public policy. Thus affirmative action law and antidiscrimination strategies began to be linked together—as a result of Johnson's executive order and its implementation.

The Development of Affirmative Action Law: 1971–1988

In 1971, the controversial nature of these shifts in interpretation led to the landmark Supreme Court ruling in *Griggs v. Duke Power Co.*, 401 U.S. 424 (1971). (The discussion of *Griggs* and *Albemarle* draws on U.S. Congress 1990, 14–16.) The Griggs decision held unanimously that "Title VII forbids not only practices adopted with a discriminatory motive, but also practices which, though adopted without discriminatory intent, have a discriminatory effect on minorities and women." This decision was the beginning of a legal framework for bringing "disparate impact" cases. The Court ruled that employers cannot use nonrelevant job requirements to screen applicants when such requirements disproportionately and adversely affect black applicants. (Specifically, it prohibited Duke Power Company from requiring intelligence tests or a high school diploma as a prerequisite for low-level jobs.) The Court concluded that employers must be able to demonstrate that challenged job practices are required by "business necessity." In other words, practices that adversely affect minorities or women must be related to (or be good predictors of) job performance.

Shortly after the *Griggs* decision, Congress enacted the Equal Employment Opportunities Act of 1972, 92 U.S.C. 261 (1964). This act amended Title VII of the 1964 act in several significant ways, some of which reinforced the direction that affirmative action policy had taken under Johnson's executive order, under the subsequent Labor Department guidelines, and under the *Griggs* decision. What was most significant, Congress expressed the idea that discrimination is often complex and systemic and that current manifestations of it are often not tied to the personal prejudice of individuals. This recognition can be seen in the act's stress on class action lawsuits as necessary for effective enforcement. Systemic discrimination could not be eradicated through the complaints of a few aware, brave individuals spoiling for a fight. "Congress sought to retain the class action lawsuit because the nature of discrimination is such that it cannot be attacked simply by addressing isolated acts of discrimination" (Greene 1989, 54).

The act retained the individual's right to file suit (and thus the idea that discrimination is also intentional, but it also enhanced the EEOC's enforcement power, enabling it to initiate litigation. This also reflected the assumption that discrimination is systemic and that eradicating it is, as a congressional report states, a "major public interest" beyond the interests of any individual person. The major rationale advanced for the bill was results-oriented: it stressed the need to improve the economic status of blacks. Moreover, the Senate defeated weakening amendments to the act, including one that would have prohibited preferential treatment, by a vote of sixty to thirty (Greene 1989, 52–53). It is not surprising, given the act's strong results-oriented rationale, that the courts would construe the law broadly, in an attempt to secure measurable results.

After *Griggs* and the 1972 amendments to the 1964 act, it was left to the courts to refine further the legal processes in disparate impact cases. The 1975 decision in *Albemarle Paper Co. v. Moody*, 422 U.S. 405 (1975), set out the legal principles in detail. First, the complaining party must establish a prima facie case of discrimination by showing that the employment tests adversely impact *qualified* affected group members. (It was the decision in *Hazlewood School District v. United States*, 433 U.S. 299, that insisted that the comparison group include only *qualified* individuals.) Second, when such a prima facie case is established, the burden shifts to the employer to offer evidence that the test or practice is required by business necessity. Third, even if the employer can show that its tests predict job performance, or otherwise meet the standard of business necessity, plaintiffs can still prevail by showing that other tests, also good predictors of job performance, do not have a discriminatory effect. Proving intent was not required.

By prohibiting practices unrelated to job performance that have an adverse impact, the *Griggs* decision brought results oriented affirmative action remedies into antidiscrimination law. This had the effect of blurring the distinctions between them—even though differences remained. The first way it blurred the distinctions was by recognizing that discrimination can be systemic and not necessarily intentional; therefore, intention need not be proven for remedies to be ordered. The *Griggs* ruling appropriated the ideas of disparate impact and the method of utilization analysis into the legal processes of antidiscrimination cases.

The second way the ruling blurred the distinction between antidiscrimination and affirmative action law can be seen by examining the moral value premise underlying the adverse impact theory of discrimination. Indeed, there is a moral assumption about what constitutes a proper distribution of jobs that is

> implicit in the adverse impact theory of discrimination. Adverse impact is identified by racial imbalances in employment categories, i.e., the absence of minorities in relation to their percentages in the labor market. Therefore, it is clearly concerned with [and has an opinion about the] proper distribution of workers through the work force. This concern with distribution when identifying discrimination is followed with a concern with redistribution when considering remedies for that discrimination. Affirmative action is a natural outgrowth of adverse impact theory since adverse impact theory is based on racial imbalances and affirmative action is a means of remedying those imbalances. (Greene 1989, 64)

Such analysis shows that once adverse impact theory is accepted, goal-type, results-oriented affirmative action might be a rational remedy for a court to impose, in response to proof of discriminatory practices. And goals and timetable remedies did become one of the major forms of "equitable" relief that the courts came to order in subsequent disparate impact cases. Just as important, these notions led many employers on their own to scrutinize their employment practices and implement voluntary goal-type affirmative action. A Senate report in 1990 underscored the importance of the *Griggs* decision, calling it "the single most important Title VII decision, both for the development of the law and in its impact on the daily lives of American workers." The majority view in this report praised the impact of this decision, arguing that, as a result, "in hundreds of cases, federal courts have struck down unnecessary barriers to the full participation of minorities and women in the workplace, and employers have voluntarily eliminated discriminatory practices in countless other instances" (U.S. Congress 1990, 15).

So Johnson's affirmative action executive order, combined with subsequent interpretations of Title VII, led to a wide range of responses to discrimination, including goal-type, results-oriented affirmative action programs. Challenges to the resulting policies led to further rulings dealing with both affirmative action and antidiscrimination law. In general, later rulings have limited the circumstances under which affirmative action measures are permitted.

Perhaps the best-known affirmative action case is *Bakke v. Regents of the University of California*, 438 U.S. 265 (1978). Bakke was a white male who was denied entry to medical school, even though he had higher scores than some minorities who were admitted. This was the first major test of the permissibility of "benign purpose," voluntary, race-dependent decisions. Would the Court permit preferential treatment in favor of affected classes for *remedial* purposes, even in the absence of a finding or admission of discrimination? In its ruling, the Court reiterated previous cases which stated that race-dependent policies are inherently suspect and must therefore be subjected to a level of review characterized by "strict scrutiny."[18] The strict scrutiny standard requires consideration of the purpose of the race-dependent policy, whether the decision utilizing the classification can reasonably be expected to promote the purpose intended, whether the means are the least intrusive possible, and whether the measures are such as to insure that people are treated as individuals (Fullinwider 1980, 7–8; Brest and Levinson 1983, 515–29). It should be noted that the individual treatment requirements, here and in *United Steelworkers of America v. Weber*, 443 U.S. 193 (1979), were inconsistent with the findings in cases in which "considerations of the common good can override the right to . . . individualized treatment" (Maguire 1980, 45). Here is the tension between individual rights and the common good that underlies much of the controversy over antidiscrimination and affirmative action laws.

In any case, in its ruling the Supreme Court acknowledged the value of racial diversity (the purpose of the racial classification was permissible), and then addressed the particular type of race-dependent decisions that were being challenged (Brest and Levinson 1983, 6). The Court made two rulings in the case, one about the specific program under review, and one about the general permissibility of affirmative action. The finding of long-term interest holds that race can be a factor considered in admissions policies, as long as the policies do not involve fixed quotas, the means chosen are among the least intrusive available, and, of course, the purpose is not invidious. The ruling thus enabled universities and professional schools to design affirmative action programs to increase their enrollments of minority students (Schwartz 1988, 152–53). Bakke won his own case against the University of California, however, because the Court ruled that the university's program did not meet these criteria.

In 1979, in *United Steelworkers of America v. Weber*, 443 U.S. 193 (1979), the Supreme Court ruled that employers and unions may voluntarily agree to give minority workers preferences (in this case, for a training program).[19] This case establishes that racial classifications are not per se illegitimate, that is, violating Title VII (Neill 1981, 161–67). Then the Court, without defining the limits of permissible affirmative action plans, ruled that such plans are permissible under certain circumstances. Such plans should be remedial, but social discrimination alone is insufficient to justify such programs. (No formal finding of discrimination was made in this case, even though 39 percent of the local work force was black, compared to less than 2 percent of the employer's skilled workers.) The challenged program planned to admit 50 percent whites and 50 percent blacks until blacks approximated their representation in the work force (Newman 1989, 36).

The plan should also be of temporary duration, of a voluntary nature, and should not preclude whites from getting or advancing in jobs. The Court found that the plan in question, which set proportional representation as the goal, met such criteria. This decision established that proportional representation remedies are permissible, even though such remedies are not tied to "making whole" and restoring to their "rightful place" actual, identifiable victims of discrimination. This decision provided more latitude for affirmative action programs than did the *Bakke* decision.

After this ruling, a series of decisions in 1987 and 1988 solidified the permissibility of policies setting proportional representation as a goal. The decision in *United States v. Paradise,* 480 U.S. 149 (1987), narrowly approved of a municipal police department's program awarding to black officers 50 percent of all promotions to the next rank. The Court allowed these promotion goals even though the relief benefited nonvictims, because the goals were flexible, temporary, required no layoffs, and because "pervasive, systematic and obstinate" racial discrimination had been proven (Savage 1987a, 1987b; Newman 1989, 40–41).

This case was followed by a six-to-three decision in *Johnson v. Transportation Agency,* 480 U.S. 616 (1987), which established that "an employer may, [through a *voluntary* preferential plan] promote a woman or minority over a better qualified man to remedy a 'statistical imbalance' in its work force" even in the absence of proven discrimination (Savage 1987b). While this decision seemed to go even further than the *Weber* decision in not requiring that a voluntary affirmative action program be based on demonstrable discrimination, at the very least, it affirmed the *Weber* decision. The majority reasoned, "Because Congress had not amended Title VII after the *Weber* decision, its interpretation could be presumed correct" (Newman 1989, 41).

Antonin Scalia, Ronald Reagan's second Supreme Court appointee, registered a strenuous dissent against this decision, complaining that it "inverted" the obvious purpose of Title VII, "from a guarantee that race or sex will not be the basis for employment determinations to a guarantee that it often will. Ever so subtly . . . we effectively replace the goal of a discrimination-free society with the quite incompatible goal of proportionate representation by race and by sex in the workplace." The confirmation of Ronald Reagan's third appointee, Anthony Kennedy (who joined the Court in February 1988), brought the Court much closer to Scalia's view than previously, and the confirmation of Bush appointee David Souter may complete the Court's transition into one strenuously against any results-oriented policies involving preferential treatment or those which value proportional representation. But Kennedy's appointment was not enough to prevent the 1988 ruling in *Watson v. Fort Worth Bank and Trust* (86–6139), which continued the Court's string of decisions approving affirmative action programs. This decision extended the use of statistical analyses to support claims of sex discrimination in promotions. However, the ruling did not establish a way to prove such cases (Savage 1988b).

The momentum through most of the eighties produced a narrow, fragile majority that supported affirmative action: statistical data were used to support claims in favor of voluntary affirmative action goals promoting proportional representation, even when employers were not charged with discrimination (although such goals could not be used to override seniority rights). With some clarifications, the *Griggs* standard governed discrimination litigation, permitting, even in the absence of proven discriminatory intent, policies utilizing affirmative action goals; and the *Weber* decision (as extended and modified in the cases just summarized) governed voluntary affirmative action programs.

But in 1989, the tide appeared to turn. The Court began to issue opinions narrowing the scope of affirmative action and antidiscrimination laws. Affirmative action goals and timetables might continue to be permissible, but certainly under stricter conditions. Many in Congress and most within the civil rights lobby saw these rulings as reversing years of positive legal developments. As a result, they initiated the Civil Rights Act of 1990 to reverse many of these 1989 decisions and to buttress perceived weaknesses in civil rights laws. This act was making steady progress through Congress, despite the threat of a presidential veto, when in June 1990, in the most watched affirmative action case of the term

(Metro Broadcasting v. FCC, 89–453), the Court surprised almost everybody by narrowly approving a challenged affirmative action program and, even more surprisingly, by advancing a new, nonremedial rationale for this program!

1989 and Beyond: Supreme Court Rulings and the Congressional Response

One form of preferential affirmative action initiated by governments are set-aside programs, which involve awarding a percentage of government contracts to minority-owned or minority dominated firms. In January 1989, the Supreme Court issued a six-to-three decision striking down a 30 percent set-aside program for minority contractors (*Richmond v. Croson,* 448 U.S. 469, 1989). The Court held that such programs (when initiated by municipalities or the state) are "constitutionally suspect"—even if they are purported to be for benign purposes. The Court declared that such programs require a finding of intentional discrimination and argued that, otherwise, such programs violate the rights of white men, who are also covered under the Equal Protection Clause of the Fourteenth Amendment.[20]

The ruling narrowed the Court's approval in *Fullilove v. Klutznick,* 448 U.S. 448 (1980), of a minority set-aside program, thereby casting doubt on such programs in thirty-six states and hundreds of cities (Savage, 1989a).[21] Shortly afterward, the courts began to undo many such programs throughout the country. Some cities commissioned studies to meet the required finding of discrimination, while others simply abandoned such policies (Pear 1990a). The *Croson* decision, then, seemed to indicate that all voluntary, preferential, affirmative action programs, whether private, municipal, or state, would have to demonstrate the existence of intentional discrimination in order to pass muster at the highest level of judicial review, namely, "strict scrutiny," which views all racial classifications as "constitutionally suspect." But it is still unclear what types of evidence—statistics, documentary or firsthand testimony—will suffice as evidence of discriminatory intent.

The *Croson* decision did not address affirmative action by private employers, nor did it affect preference plans by the federal government because, as Sandra Day O'Connor wrote for the majority, "Congress has more power than the states [and municipalities] under the Constitution to remedy racial discrimination" (Savage 1989a).

This interesting aspect of the ruling presaged the next important affirmative action ruling. On 27 June 1990, in *Metro Broadcasting v. FCC* (89–453), the Court voted five to four to bolster race preferences by upholding two federal affirmative action programs designed to increase minority ownership of broadcast licenses. The ruling was based upon three important judgments. First, the Court reiterated that Congress has greater authority to order preferences than private employers or other government agencies (given its co-equal status with the other two branches of government). Second, the Court applied a much more lenient standard of review for race conscious programs when such programs are enacted by Congress. It held that such programs are constitutional to the extent they "serve *important* Government objectives and are substantially related to the achievement of those objectives" (my emphasis). Third, the "important" government interest endorsed by the Court was "broadcast diversity." The Court reasoned that the welfare of the public depends on "the widest possible dissemination of information from diverse and antagonistic sources."

It is this third element of the decision that is most striking, and it could prove the most significant development in antidiscrimination and affirmative action law. This rationale provides, for the first time since Bakke—which rested in part on educational interests such as diversity—a forward-looking rather than a backward-looking remedial rationale for affirmative action policies (Greenhouse 1990a). Future use of this rationale to justify affirmative action preferences, either in Court rulings or through congressional legislation, would entail the most significant shift in years, because with such a rationale affirmative action could be endorsed without requiring a finding of past discrimination. This is because such a rationale is based on considerations of the public welfare, rather than on backward looking, compensatory notions. (One finding of the empirical research in part 2 of this book is not surprising, that backward looking, compensatory rationales are not popular. This underscores the potential importance of this rationale articulated by the Court. If broadened to where diversity is seen as an intrinsic good, crucial to the welfare of the nation, such notions could provide a rationale for racial and gender preferences well into the next century.)

The decisions in *Croson* and *Metro Broadcasting* would seem to establish affirmative action programs, but two complicating realities suggest that such a conclusion may be premature. In 1989, a series of cases, based primarily upon reinterpretations of Title VII's antidiscrimination provisions, placed significant barriers before preferential affirmative action programs.

Aside from the *Croson* set-aside case, the 1989 Court decision viewed with the greatest alarm by the civil rights lobby is unquestionably *Wards Cove v. Atonio* (87–1387). This ruling reversed important elements of the *Griggs* standard for disparate impact cases, making it more difficult for plaintiffs to win Court-ordered remedies, including affirmative action preferences.

As I have described, *Griggs* and its progeny interpreted Title VII to endorse a specific framework for resolving disparate impact cases. After a prima facie case of discrimination is established, by showing statistically that the employer's business practices have had an adverse impact on qualified members of affected minority groups, the employer must prove that its employment practices are good predictors of job performance. The *Wards Cove* decision, however, puts the burden of proof back on the plaintiff for the duration of the litigation.[22] Rather than employers having to produce proof of the job relatedness of their employment practices, plaintiffs have to identify a specific discriminatory practice and show how this practice caused the disparate impact. Having accomplished this, to prevail, the plaintiff then has to prove either that this practice is not job related or that the practice is a pretext for discrimination and that there are other employment criteria available with less adverse racial impact.[23] But unless the plaintiff shows discriminatory intent, the employer does not have to respond to claims that there are criteria available which do not have an adverse impact. In short, *Wards Cove* made it easier for employers to prove "business necessity" to the satisfaction of the courts.[24]

Wards Cove, then, made it significantly more difficult for plaintiffs to prevail in disparate impact cases, and very possibly it reduced employer incentives to pursue voluntarily affirmative action. The five-to-four decision in *Martin v. Wilkes* (87–1614) further undercut affirmative action precedents (Savage 1989d). The decision extends to white men the protection of Title VII. It deals with consent decrees—court-approved agreements between litigants in a discrimination case—which mandate affirmative action benefiting minorities or women. The Court held that such decrees could be challenged in Court by people affected by them but who had not been party to them, even if these people had known about the original litigation and had not entered into the dispute. This decision opened thousands of consent decrees to legal challenge; many lawsuits have already been filed by white men alleging reverse discrimination. "At least one [already] resulted in awards of back pay and seniority rights to white men (Pear 1990b). Thus *Wards Cove* and *Martin v. Wilkes*[25] have reduced employers' fears of discrimination litigation. Concomitantly, they have reduced employers' incentives to use affirmative action plans preemptively to prevent the effective use of disparate impact analysis against them. These rulings, however, would have been nullified, at least temporarily, if the Civil Rights Act of 1990 had been signed into law.

What then is the current status of antidiscrimination and affirmative action law, and what are the likely future prospects for such law? The five dimensions summarized at the beginning of this legal history provide the focus for the answers to these questions.

Race-dependent decisions continue to be sanctioned by law, although only under certain circumstances. With the addition of the Americans with Disabilities Act of 1990, antidiscrimination law now addresses discrimination according to race, gender, color, national origin, religion, and disability.

There has been a legal and judicial tug-of-war over what level of scrutiny should be applied when evaluating the permissibility of using any of the above characteristics as a basis for employment decisions. In the period since World War II, the law has concluded that no invidious race-dependent decisions are permissible. (Gender-based programs are not covered under strict scrutiny.) State and municipal set-aside and goal-type affirmative action policies are now considered "constitutionally suspect" by the Court and are subject to the "strictest scrutiny," requiring a clear finding of intentional discrimination. The Court recently applied a lower level of review to such programs mandated by Congress; such programs must serve an "important" government interest, and the means chosen must be "substantially related" to the important government interest.[26] It remains to be seen what government interests beyond "broadcast diversity" will be considered important or if the Court will tighten scrutiny requirements at a later time with regard to federally mandated programs.

Speaking generally, Johnson's executive order mandating affirmative action is still the dominant affirmative action law (along with the Labor Department's purpose of promoting proportional representation through goals and timetables). The *Weber* ruling is still the central guide in such programs; currently goals must be tied to qualified members of the available work force, must be limited in duration, and must not evolve into rigid quotas (they must not be too "intrusive"). Moreover, at least for now, the federal government's prerogative to use racial preferences has been vindicated in *Metro Broadcasting*.

With regard to antidiscrimination law, *Griggs*, as modified by *Wards Cove*, guides disparate impact cases. Class action discrimination lawsuits are still permitted, the Labor Department's EEOC (and other offices) can still initiate them, and a fairly broad range of remedies are still available. Limited-time, goal-type affirmative action may also be ordered, and it may extend its benefits beyond identifiable victims, as long as it is remedial (in other words, as long as intentional discrimination has been demonstrated). The law has gradually extended the range of who is prohibited from discriminating, so that now virtually all who employ more than fifteen employees are covered under antidiscrimination law.[27] Given the *Croson* decision, however, state and municipal affirmative action programs are declining in number and scope.

Despite these characterizations of the current state of affirmative action law, the history reviewed above reveals that the law is fluid, if nothing else. The Court is still struggling to come to a firm consensus on many important issues, such as the appropriate level of scrutiny for race-conscious decisions. And the struggle to define these policies continues beyond the Court. Several interesting, recent political developments illustrate how much these areas of law are still controversial battlegrounds. Some proponents of affirmative action, for example, encouraged by the Court's decision in *Metro Broadcasting*, have discussed initiating a congressional attempt to overturn the *Croson* decision (limiting municipal and state affirmative action set aside programs; Lewis 1990). Such an effort has been sidelined by the failure of the Civil Rights Act of 1990 to be enacted. Meanwhile, conservative business interests, mindful of yet another conservative appointee to the Court, are preparing to challenge the constitutionality of Johnson's original affirmative action executive order (Kilborn 1990). And muddying the water further, even though Bush vetoed the Civil Rights Act of 1990, arguing that it was a quota-promoting bill, at the same time Secretary of Labor Elizabeth Dole was publicizing her initiative attacking job bias at the top levels of industry—an area heretofore largely ignored by antidiscrimination efforts (Kilborn 1990). The department's efforts will be grounded in Johnson's executive order and will attempt to avoid promoting the quotas objected to by conservatives. Dole herself, however, will not be a part of these efforts; she resigned her post shortly after the defeat of the civil rights bill.

The reconstitution of the Court after Justice Brennan's departure also underscores how volatile this area of law will likely be in the 1990s. Brennan wrote many of the crucial decisions approving affirmative action law and disparate impact analysis in discrimination cases. He was also known for his skills of persuasion and ability to fashion compromises. He was largely responsible for preserving the slim majorities endorsing affirmative action in *Bakke, Paradise, Johnson,* and *Metro Broadcasting.* It seems unlikely that in future cases the Court will continue to look as favorably at such policies as it has with Brennan's presence.

The only thing that can be said with certainty is that the future of affirmative action remains in doubt, and the tug-of-war over these policies will continue, both in Congress and in the courts. Having discussed such laws in detail with many key players in upcoming legislative battles, and after analyzing the Court logic to this point, I think it is likely that preferential, goal-type affirmative action will be further narrowed by judicial rulings but will remain a permissible remedy for specific cases of demonstrable discrimination. Certainly, the civil rights lobby will fight hard to retain such policies, through the Congress if need be.

The history of this area of U.S. law underscores several reasons that research into this issue is important. Affirmative action is capable of having a significant impact on U.S. society, and this society has not yet approached a consensus as to whether such policies are morally permissible and socially desirable. The continuing legal and political battles over affirmative action show that people believe the stakes are high. These struggles make public awareness and discussion of these issues particularly important. Such a discussion requires an understanding of the *ethical* arguments undergirding the most controversial part of these programs, namely, goal-type affirmative action. This is provided in chapter 2. Such a discussion also requires an understanding of the impact of such policies on the attitudes of those affected by them: the chapters in part 2 focus on the impact of *goal-type* affirmative action in the workplace. This study does not beg the real question by examining some nonexistent "ideal" form of affirmative action found only in the minds of theorists. It is real-life affirmative action that is explored.

2

AN ETHICAL ANALYSIS OF
AFFIRMATIVE ACTION

THIS CHAPTER has three parts. The first discusses how ethical analysis works and clarifies why most of the ethical debates about affirmative action have to do with principles of distributive justice. The second analyzes four major post-Enlightenment theories of distributive justice, focusing on how public policy issues in general and affirmative action policies in particular look in the light of such theories. The third provides a summary discussion of the problem of justice posed by affirmative action. The overall purpose of this chapter is to provide a background understanding of the ethical dilemmas posed by the affirmative action controversy as well as the arguments about affirmative action expressed by average Americans. This is necessary background for focusing (in chapter 3) on the theoretical questions that underlie the empirical research.

How Ethical Analysis Works

An overview of the discipline of ethics provides the background necessary to understand how ethical analysis works. Ethics as a discipline is generally divided into two branches: non-normative ethics (which includes metaethics and descriptive ethics) and normative ethics (which has both theorical and applied aspects). (This review is indebted to Beauchamp and Walters 1982, 1–31; Velasquez 1982, chap. 1; Frankena 1973, chap. 1).

The two types of non-normative ethics (metaethics and descriptive ethics) share a descriptive and analytical purpose and attempt to do so without making moral evaluations of the subject under scrutiny (Beauchamp and Walters 1982, 1).

Metaethics analyzes the ways in which people arrive at, reason about, and justify their moral values and decisions. Descriptive ethics also analyzes and describes, but it has different foci, including which moral theories, principles, and rules (judgments) are held by people; and what effects such ethics have on culture. Of the two types of non-normative ethics, the present inquiry is concerned more with descriptive ethics than metaethics.

Normative ethics drives at making moral evaluations about moral theories, principles, rules, and values (theoretical normative ethics) and about particular issues or actions (applied normative ethics). The analysis (in the second part of this chapter) of the four major approaches to distributive justice and affirmative action depends on an understanding of the two major branches of theoretical normative ethics.

Deontology and consequentialism are the two types of normative theories of obligation. Both theories commonly reflect on three moral *principles:* autonomy (which has to do with human freedom), justice (how burdens and benefits are distributed), and beneficence (having to do with the common good and the promotion of good over evil). Various *rules* are derived from these principles, including laws, policies, and moral guidelines. Finally, numerous *actions* or specific *judgments* are enjoined based on the principles and rules. Normative ethics, then, involves evaluation at several different levels, from the general (theory) to the specific (action). Beauchamp and Walters (1982, 12) summarize:

> Different kinds of discourse are involved in moral reasoning and argument. A moral *judgment,* for example, expresses a decision, verdict, or conclusion about a particular action or character trait. Moral *rules* are general guides governing actions of a certain kind; they assert what ought (or ought not) to be done in a range of particular cases. Moral *principles* are more general and more fundamental than such rules, and serve (at least in some systems of ethics) as the justifying reasons for accepting rules. . . . Finally, ethical *theories* are bodies of principles and rules that are more or less systematically related.
>
> The different kinds of moral discourse can also be developed as a theory of *levels* of justification. Judgments about what ought to be done can be viewed as justified . . . by rules, which in turn are justified by principles, which then are justified by ethical theories. . . . This thought can be diagrammed as follows (where the arrow indicates the

direction of *justification*, the particular or less general moral assertion being justified by appeal to the more general): Judgment → Rule
→ Principle → Theory.

Interpretations of fact play a crucial role at each level of moral discourse. Such interpretations are especially important at the level of
judgments, and the interpretations function to confirm or discon-
firm the legitimacy of the judgments/actions, the rules, the principles, and the theories upon which the actions depend.

The decisive difference between the two main normative theories of obligation is that consequentialist theories require the deter-
mination of the *Good*, or what is to be valued (for example, what
the common good is), before one can be expected to decide the
Right, (that is, what right actions are). Thus, with consequentialist
theories, the Good is *determinative* of right and wrong principles,
rules, and actions: Right principles, rules, and actions are those
which promote the Good, and wrong principles, rules, and actions
are those which detract from the Good. With deontological theories, on the other hand, the Right is prior to the Good: principles,
rules, and actions of a moral nature are intrinsically right or
wrong, and the Good need not be determined in order to justify the
principles, rules, and actions.

Consequentialist theories tend to have greater trouble incorporating and dealing with principles of justice; justice principles usually appeal to some notion of intrinsic rightness instead of consequentialist, common good notions. Deontological theories tend to
play down principles of beneficence and give priority to some principle of the Right over the Good. In spite of the difficulties, each
type of normative theory must come to terms with the role of each
of the three common principles of ethics: autonomy, justice, and
beneficence.

As theories of ethics grapple with the role of the principles of
autonomy, justice, and beneficence, they must also agree upon the
precise content of these terms. For example, how should equality
be understood? It usually is understood in either a formal or substantive sense. Formal (or procedural) equality has to do either
with whether procedures are fair (for example, is due process provided) or with whether persons have equal legal access to some benefit. Here, equality is a *principle*, in the sense of a rule of action.
Substantive equality refers to material conditions: For example, to
what extent are material goods or positions distributed equally?
Here, equality is a *value*, in the sense of a desired good or a condition worth pursuing. It is important to keep these different senses

of equality in mind; attention must be paid to what different theorists mean when they speak about equality.

Four Theories of Justice and Affirmative Action

Just as theoretical normative ethics must come to terms with each of the three principles of ethics, so must applied normative ethics, when evaluating specific policies such as affirmative action. Since the affirmative action controversy ultimately boils down to the question of how preferred jobs and incomes ought to be distributed, principles of distributive justice are clearly at the center of the affirmative action controversy. At the same time, some theorists tend to place a premium on principles of autonomy or beneficence, and their principles of justice are influenced (or determined) by these principles.

Specific attempts to apply normative ethical theory to affirmative action can be broken down into four basic approaches: justice as freedom, justice as fairness, justice as productive freedom, and justice as the greatest good. The following discussion first analyzes these approaches by examining the normative ethical theory of a major figure who has advanced each approach, and then examines how contemporary theorists, allied with each approach, tend to apply such theories to affirmative action.[1] The discussion focuses on how justice principles look within each of these four perspectives: first in general, and then as applied to affirmative action. The first three approaches to be analyzed are grounded in deontological theory, the fourth in consequentialist theoretical premises.

Justice as Freedom: Libertarian and Conservative Approaches to Affirmative Action

While on some issues, true philosophical libertarians differ from conservatives, the premium both place on the principle of autonomy leads to a similarity of approach on the issue of affirmative action. This section first analyzes the general approach to justice in Robert Nozick's libertarian theory, and then analyzes contemporary conservative analyses of affirmative action.

ROBERT NOZICK: FREEDOM OF CHOICE AND AFFIRMATIVE ACTION

The following discussion of Nozick's deontological theory involves four steps: first, it summarizes his overall theory, paying particular attention to his priority of the principle of autonomy (or freedom) and how it relates to justice and beneficence principles; second, it analyzes how a case in favor of affirmative action policies can be built on Nozick's theory; third, it explains why his theory is unlikely to provide a moral rationale for preferential affirmative action; and finally, it analyzes problems with Nozick's approach to justice in general and affirmative action in particular.

Nozick analyzes the development of human "protective associations" and concludes that only a "minimum state" (one with a monopoly on coercive power and whose purpose is to assure that individual freedom is not violated) is morally justified because only it protects human autonomy. On the one hand, the "ultraminimal" state does not protect freedom—it provides no protection from coercion for those unable to pay for protection. On the other hand, any state more extensive than the minimal state violates freedom by treating people as means to some socially desirable end, not as ends in themselves (1974, 27–32).[2]

The role of the minimal state is to assure that burdens and benefits are distributed according to what Nozick calls the "Theory of Justice in Holdings" or the "Entitlement Theory" (1974, 149–82). Nozick prefers to use the phrase "Justice in Holdings," because he believes it is a more nearly neutral concept than the more commonly used notion of distributive justice (1974, 150). Nevertheless, his entitlement theory contains his own principles of distributive justice, and it is the core of his autonomy-grounded ethic.

Nozick rejects all "end-result," "prepatterned," or "allocative," principles of distribution, which base the justice of distributions on "who has what" (1974, 153) instead of on a historical analysis of whether goods were fairly acquired. For Nozick, three elements are necessary for the just distribution of material goods: (1) The original acquisition of holdings must be done in accordance with the *principle of justice in acquisition.* (2) Transfers must be done in a way consistent with the *principle of justice in transfer.* (3) Any goods held by virtue of violations of 1 and 2 above are subject to *the principle of rectification,* which returns the goods to the person whose rights were violated (1974, 151–53). Nozick declines to specify what constitutes fair procedures of acquisition, although he applauds socialists for specifying such procedures, pointing out that socialists assess the justice of holdings by analyzing how such holdings came to be possessed (1974, 153, 155). He criticizes, however, the processes that socialists believe constitute fair acquisition (1974, 250–65). (For Nozick, fair transfers involve voluntary exchanges, gifts, payments for contacted services, and the like.)

But when it comes to acquisition, what he would expect is that acquisition of holdings would usually occur in a way that has some affinity with Liberalism's central principle of distributive justice— the idea that preferred jobs and salaries ought to be distributed according to merit in a context characterized by equal opportunity— except for Nozick, such distributions would be based less on moral principle than economic rationality and the requirements of competitiveness. (Although Nozick would probably say that the owner of a company could hire anyone for whatever reason, libertarian assumptions suggest that economic rationality requires merit hiring. So while Nozick might not insist on merit hiring on moral principle, as a practical matter he would expect such hiring to be the norm in a market economic system.)

Nozick clearly rejects the sentiments of liberal theorists who include in their conceptions of equal opportunity all the social conditions needed to guarantee *actual equal chances* for individuals to develop their talents and compete in market society. Nozick believes that people are entitled to what flows from their natural talents (1974, 226) but that it would be wrong to try to equalize actual opportunities by taking resources from a privileged person and giving them to one less privileged. "Holdings to which people are entitled may not be seized, even to provide equal opportunity for others" (1974, 235).

Nozick argues that distributions based upon prepatterned or end-state principles violate human autonomy by overriding free choices made in most transfers. He asserts that it is usually free choice that leads to inequalities. (He uses as an example the case where many people pay to see Wilt Chamberlain play basketball, making Wilt richer and his fans poorer.) He concludes that to then reverse the outcomes of these free choices violates freedom of choice. With Nozick's entitlement theory, therefore, the focus of his principle of distributive justice is on free choice. He writes that his principle of distributive justice can be abbreviated in a somewhat oversimplified way into the maxim: "From each as they choose, to each as they are chosen" (1974, 160).

Clearly, Nozick's principle of distributive justice is concerned with formal (or procedural) fairness. Freedom requires a specific type of formal equality: every individual is equally entitled to acquire goods according to processes affirmed in the entitlement theory. This can allow great material inequality, because such a view of freedom precludes the redistribution of goods except in those limited cases where the principle of rectification applies. Nozick recognizes that the question of paramount importance with his principle of rectification is: How far back must this principle reach to rectify present holdings based on past injustices? (1974, 152). This is one important question for determining how Nozick would evaluate the morality of affirmative action. But Nozick does little to answer specifically this question (1974, 152–53).

Nevertheless, it is possible to utilize the rectification principle to build a case for affirmative action. Nozick says that when the entitlement theory is violated, a more extensive state may be necessary to implement the rectification principle (1974, 231). He even suggests that the policies of such a state may sometimes distribute goods by prepatterned principles of justice. He writes that such justice principles may provide a useful rule of thumb in implementing the rectification principle:

> Perhaps it is best to view some patterned principles of justice as rough rules of thumb meant to approximate the general results of applying the principle of rectification of injustice. . . . [The key question is,] given *its* particular history, what operable rule of thumb best approximates the results of a detailed application . . . of the principle of rectification? (1974, 231)

It could then be argued by libertarian principles that a temporary expansion of the state in order to implement and enforce affirmative action is justified as the best means of applying the rectification principle. This argument would be strongest, under libertarian theory, when the discrimination to be rectified has recently occurred, and specific victims and perpetrators can be identified and compensated or forced to bear the burden of compensation. Nozick's key concern remains protecting each individual's rights, as he sees them.

Under certain circumstances, Nozick's discussion of the "Lockean Proviso" could also be used as a basis for an argument in favor of redistributive policies such as affirmative action. This proviso limits property rights when such rights are used to exclude others from the most basic material requirements of liberty (1974, 178–81). For example, one may not monopolize any of the requirements of liberty, such as food or water. If combined with a rejection of classical economic assumptions about the potential for ever increasing economic growth, this proviso could be used to support various redistributive policies such as affirmative action. Nozick himself does not make such a move. He does not seem to be worried about limits to growth and states that the proviso only applies if *subsistence* conditions would be worsened by a property right—

the proviso cannot be used simply to improve someone's relative position (1974, 181). This limits his theory's application to affirmative action, because such policies usually address relative opportunity, and not survival itself.

While there may be grounds within Nozick's theory to argue for affirmative action policies, the overall thrust of his theory makes it likely that Nozick would endorse protective but not preferential affirmative action. Nozick's priority of freedom (autonomy) over any principle of justice or beneficence is the most basic reason that Nozick's theory cannot easily provide support for preferential affirmative action. Nozick's autonomy principle limits the reach of the rectification principle by placing two conditions on it: it can reach back only as far as it is possible to force actual violators of the entitlement theory to compensate actual victims; and it can only apply to those cases where it is reasonably possible to calculate what the distribution of goods would have been had the violation not occurred.

It is unlikely, then, that Nozick's rectification principle could compensate for wrongs done more than a generation or two ago. It is also unlikely Nozick would countenance preferential affirmative action, which extends preference to some individuals over others regardless of any personal culpability in violating entitlements. For Nozick and libertarian thought, such preferences violate an individual's right to her or his justly gained holdings. Nozick rejects the formal distributive principle upon which affirmative action is usually based and therefore rejects affirmation action—it violates the individual rights guaranteed by the entitlement theory (1974, 235–38). Nozick would be likely to support only those forms of protective affirmative action that are limited to identifying specific individuals whose entitlement rights have been violated by discriminatory practices and where the compensation can be extracted from the individual violator. It is also unlikely under Nozick's theory that a corporation could be held liable for discrimination by its employees, since it would be "innocent" stockholders who would have their entitlement rights violated in order to compensate for such discrimination. Nozick certainly would have no problem with policies designed to compensate actual victims of discrimination when the compensation is provided by the actual perpetrators of the discrimination.

A final question has to do with the strengths and weaknesses of Nozick's solution to the problem of justice. To summarize his view: when individual freedoms are upheld (when people's entitlement rights are not violated), then justice is done. Certainly, Nozick's priority of freedom resonates with many people in a culture so heavily influenced by Liberalism. But one central problem remains unresolved: Nozick restricts the definition of freedom to free legal access to market society—with the caveat that one's freedom also requires that people have access to the means of subsistence. But free choice, even if understood in the limited terms of Nozick's entitlement theory, depends on material conditions other than having legal access and the means to survival. The problem remains that if one does not have enough material resources (beyond survival needs) to compete and choose in market society, then one's entitlement rights are violated. And the resulting disparity between those who do and those who do not have the material resources to choose freely and to compete boils down to a competition between the freedom or entitlement rights of those with such resources—and thereby *actual* access to the market and the entitlement rights of those without such resources or real access (choice). This analysis suggests that if free choice requires actual access, which in turn at least partly depends on one's material resources, then the situation of competing entitlement rights again raises the central issue of distributive justice: how goods, in this case freedoms (of choice), ought to be distributed. Nozick leaves the problem of distributive justice unresolved.

It is logically necessary to develop explicit principles of distributive justice in order to arbitrate the competition between people with competing claims to freedom. But Nozick sidesteps this necessity in two ways. First, his analysis of facts plays down the lack of access that many people have owing to past and present discrimination. For example, he states that although there are unequal opportunities due to differences in natural assets and social privileges, there still is access, and the social situation remains competitive (1974, 236). But Nozick's attempt to demonstrate this with cute but stretched analogies is not convincing. (An exegesis of Nozick's analysis of the facts concerning free access and free choice available to a social underclass is beyond my current task, but if he is right in this analysis, then the analysis in the preceding paragraph is based on a faulty premise.)

The ironic and fundamental problem is that Nozick insists that his entitlement theory is inviolable—it is grounded in basic human rights—but the application of this theory will always produce and perpetuate vast inequalities that ultimately overwhelm and make meaningless his idea of freedom. Second, Nozick avoids articulating specific distributive principles through a strategy of Kantian absolutism. He argues that one ought never abrogate a right in the quest to maximize rights in the culture (see note 2). Even if he were to admit that inequality can overpower human freedom, this absolutism makes it difficult for him to address the distributive justice problem of how to distribute such "rights."

In summary, Nozick's evaluation of social issues through the lens of his priority of autonomy may provide a basis for protective, but not preferential, affirmative action. This is not surprising, since his entitlement theory is really concerned with equal opportunity (understood to include equal legal access to market society but not necessarily actual equal chances to develop one's natural talents). The tendency of libertarian theory, to endorse protective but not preferential forms of affirmative action, therefore makes it unlikely that libertarian theory will provide a moral argument for affirmative action, at least as this policy is currently practiced.

CONTEMPORARY CONSERVATIVE ANALYSES OF AFFIRMATIVE ACTION

There are two types of conservatives in the United States, those in the tradition of philosophical Liberalism, and those from the civic republican tradition. The latter evaluate affirmative action based on whether the facts show that it promotes their own particular conception of the common good. These types of arguments are included in the discussion of contemporary consequentialist analyses of affirmative action. (Arguments about affirmative action that fall broadly within one type of approach are not necessarily exclusive to that approach. Those who evaluate affirmative action focusing on its impact on individual rights may also strongly consider its social consequences.) Conservatives broadly within the Liberal tradition, however, commonly discuss affirmative action in terms of the idea of compensatory justice. This notion of compensatory justice has a great deal of affinity with Nozick's rectification principle.[3]

Compensatory justice is one aspect of distributive justice: it is concerned with righting wrongs through some form of redistribution. How *right* and *wrong* are defined varies and depends on how principles of autonomy and justice are defined. Compensatory justice usually includes several conditions which must be met before it is approved as a morally appropriate remedy. First, an injury must be inflicted that is morally wrong. Second, the victim and perpetrator must be identifiable, and the compensation must be from the perpetrator to the victim. Third, the compensation must be proportionate to the injury. The similarity to Nozick's thought is obvious.

Some Liberal theorists think preferential affirmative action can be justified in terms of compensatory justice. Much of the debate in the legal and philosophical literature deals with whether compensatory justice principles provide grounds for affirmative action. For example, in his defense of affirmative action, Sher (1977) combines the distributive justice principle of equal opportunity based on merit with the idea of compensatory justice. Anticipating objections, he focuses not on compensation for *past* wrongs but argues that affirmative action rightly compensates for the loss of *present* competitive ability—a loss that results from both past and present discrimination. This discrimination is morally wrong because it violates the principle of equal opportunity based on merit.[4] Sher argues that in the context of competitive market society this is the best justification for affirmative action, because such preferences provide a compensation "closest to actually replacing the lost good" (1977, 53). Since deprivation harms the ability to compete for jobs, affirmative action directly addresses the harm that is done (Sher 1975, 54; see also Thomson 1977). Sher's argument is similar to Nozick's rectification principle in its focus on the loss of a good in the present: competitive ability. But he differs in not insisting that the guilty be forced to provide the compensation.

However, those who reject compensatory rationales for affirmative action raise three major objections. The first complains about a dynamic labeled *overgeneralization*—that is, affirmative action either does not help the people who have suffered the greatest harm, or it helps those not in need. The second raises a culpability objection: affirmative action often demands that those not personally culpable compensate the victim. Blackstone asserts that this is partly due to the recent overturning of the individual focus of Aristotle's own compensatory principle. Groups, not individuals, have become the focus of compensation. With this shift in focus, the actual wrongdoer is not required to provide the compensation (Blackstone and Heslep, 1977, 54). The third objection suggests that there are better alternatives to deal with discrimination than affirmative action. These arguments are analyzed below.

Overgeneralization occurs in two ways. First, affirmative action is *overinclusive*, because it grants preferences to those minority persons who are the most marketable—the very people who have been harmed the least by discrimination and do not need help. Second, affirmative action is *underinclusive* in its failure to provide significant compensation to those who are currently the most disadvantaged as a result of discrimination (see Gross 1978, 94–95, 112). Simon puts it this way: affirmative action violates the requirement that there be proportionality between the amount of compensation and the degree of harm, by awarding one victim a prestigious position, another victim just a position, and another victim nothing at all—where actually "those with the strongest compensatory claims should be compensated first (and most)" (1977, 44). Simon concludes that another reason affirmative action is unfair as a means of compensation is that even though a person's marketability is not morally relevant from the perspective of compensatory justice, marketability nevertheless becomes the critical distributive principle (1977, 48).

Those who raise the culpability objection argue that not all white males are equally liable for discrimination and that preferential affirmative action does not take this into account. They argue that as a result affirmative action is arbitrary and unfair "in assessing the costs of compensation" (Simon 1977, 47; See also Heslep 1976; Blackstone and Heslep 1977). The burden tends to fall on young people who are least responsible for the wrongs imposed on minorities (Gross 1978, 100; see also Thomson 1977, 38–39). (Some of these critics do not want to abandon the idea that compensatory justice demands a response to discrimination but believe that, in light of the above dynamics, the burden of compensation ought to be placed on the entire society, not just on those who happen to be approximately as marketable as persons targeted for affirmative action preferences; Simon 1977, 47; Taylor 1973; Bedau 1972).

In any case, the objections about overgeneralization and culpability make it difficult to sustain compensatory arguments for affirmative action. While notions of compensatory justice have a long heritage in Western culture, and are incorporated by Liberalism, the premises of compensatory justice principles tend to be individualistic—concerned more with protecting individuals than groups. This individualism makes it difficult for any theory grounded in Liberalism, whether libertarian, conservative, or liberal, to find in compensatory justice principles a compelling rationale for affirmative action. Some theorists observe that the individualistic way in which compensatory principles are usually conceived in the Liberal culture tends to lead to these kinds of objections to affirmative action. Freeman argues that focusing on the individual guilt of a perpetrator, and making the identification of a specific perpetrator a prerequisite to any compensatory program, creates an emphasis on fault, which leads to complacency and a "class of 'innocents,' who do not feel any personal responsibility for the conditions associated with discrimination, and who therefore feel great resentment when called upon to bear any burdens in connection with remedying violations" (in Brest and Levinson 1983, 513).

Compare this with the argument in the legal literature. Looking at the individualistic, Liberal, antidiscrimination principle upon which the courts have grounded their approval of compensatory affirmative action programs, Fiss states that the individualism of this principle ultimately erodes support for preferential treatment (1976, 136). This result, where people do not feel any responsibility, is grounded in an emphasis on purely procedural notions of distributive justice (such as Nozick's), when substantive principles of distributive justice are needed to promote effective compensatory remedies.

Finally, arguably, there are much better alternatives than affirmative action to provide compensation, alternatives that limit overgeneralization and do not require blameless individuals to bear the burden of compensating victims. After all, race- and gender-based classifications are not the most accurate indicators of injuries and damages sustained by people. It would be more accurate to base compensation on direct measures of disadvantage (such as low income and poverty) than to use racial classifications.

To summarize, then, while for many people it seems intuitively right to compensate people for damages resulting from discrimination, the problems of overgeneralization, culpability, and the existence of alternatives not based on race and gender classifications make it difficult to sustain arguments for affirmative action based on principles of compensatory justice. If this is true, and neither libertarians, conservatives, nor liberals (using purely compensatory arguments) are likely to approve of affirmative action, then the next step is to examine liberal ethical analyses of affirmative action to see if more compelling grounds for affirmative action can be found.

Justice as Fairness: Liberal Approaches to Affirmative Action

Conservatives and libertarians strongly tend to reject preferential affirmative action largely because of their view that affirmative action violates individual rights. On the other hand, liberal theorists, who also believe rights inhere in the individual, tend to approve of affirmative action (although often not based on compensatory justice rationales). The following analysis suggests that a major reason that liberals and conservatives (and libertarians) cannot agree is that for liberals, disadvantaged individuals take precedence, while for conservatives and libertarians, already dominant individuals take precedence. (Although conservative and libertarian theorists may contend that under their theory no individual takes precedence over another, already dominant individuals do take precedence because their privileges are left in place—privileges that help insure their continued dominance.) This analysis begins by discussing the relationships among the principles of beneficence, autonomy, and justice in John Rawls's theory of justice as fairness. The immediate purpose is to assess how preferential affirmative action would look in light of his overall ethical theory, and particularly his principles of distributive justice. A summary of Liberalism's approaches to affirmative action follows.

JOHN RAWLS: JUSTICE AS FAIRNESS AND AFFIRMATIVE ACTION

Rawls promotes a social contract theory of justice: fairness or justice is that which people will freely agree to in a context in which they do not take into account their own actual interests—he calls this context the "original position." He says that people want a society characterized by equal opportunity and the maximum possible equal liberty, where inequalities are permitted only because such inequalities promote an expanding economy, which improves the well-being of the least advantaged (1971, 299). Rawls supplements these ideas with two priority rules: a "priority of liberty" stipulates that an individual's liberty ought to be restricted only when people agree (in the original position) with such restrictions and only when a restriction on liberty increases the overall sum of liberty in society; and (2) there ought to be fair equality of opportunity unless inequalities of opportunity enhance the opportunities of those with lesser opportunities.

It is not an easy task to determine how Rawls would apply his theory to evaluate affirmative action morally. Different theorists have come to opposite conclusions. On the one hand, Greene (1976) asserts that the priority of the principle of liberty in Rawls's theory does not permit preferential forms of affirmative action, because this would violate the freedom to pursue one's rational plan of life. On the other hand, Fullinwider thinks there are grounds for interpreting Rawls as favoring affirmative action. He says that general justice theories like Rawls's are usually too vague to be helpful when it comes to specific social policies such as affirmative action. Nevertheless, he concludes that Rawls's second priority rule (inequalities of opportunity might be acceptable if they enhance the opportunities of the least advantaged) could possibly justify preferential treatment (1980, 118–24).

Much of the problem in interpreting whether Rawls would support affirmative action is due to ambiguity in Rawls's use of the term *liberty*, which he defines in terms of what human rights ethicists call negative liberty: freedom *from* the coercive power of the state and from intrusions against one's person (including one's conscience), or property (1971, 201–05). Rawls does not define as liberties the so-called positive liberties, which refer to the entire complex of conditions necessary *for* the full development of human capabilities, beginning with food, clothing, and shelter. Instead, he rejects definitions of liberty that include positive notions, and says that such notions refer to the "worth" of liberty, but not to liberty (understood as negative liberty) itself (1971, 204). Rawls thinks that the worth of liberty (positive liberty) may be different from the degree of liberty (negative liberty), because as a result of disparities of wealth and power, people may have different actual opportunities to advance their ends (different actual opportunities are related to differences in the worth of liberty, or positive liberty), while at the same time they may have equal (negative) liberty from the coercive power of the state (1971, 204).

This distinction between liberty and the worth of liberty, however, leads to confusion. Throughout the rest of his book, the distinction is not emphasized, and it becomes increasingly untenable. For example, his discussions of natural liberty, liberal equality, and democratic equality do not recognize a distinction between liberty and the value of liberty. Blurring the distinction between his two conceptions of liberty makes it difficult to discern exactly what is precluded by Rawls's "priority of liberty." For example, is state action in the form of affirmative action precluded by the priority of liberty, as Greene (1976) asserts? It would be if freedom were defined in a strictly negative sense. Or does the second priority rule—Inequalities of opportunity are acceptable only if inequality of opportunity for some enhances opportunities for the least advantaged—recognize such inequalities as threats to liberty? If so, the attempt to counter these threats, in the effort to promote the most extensive system of liberties for all, might conflict with a priority on strictly positive liberty. Thus, Rawls's second priority rule questions his distinction between liberty and the worth of liberty (and between negative and positive liberties). (Rawls tries to "leave aside" the controversy between proponents of positive and negative liberty by providing a simple definition of liberty as freedom from limitations and freedom to do something or not. But with his distinction between liberty and the worth of liberty he reintroduces this distinction so commonly made by social philosophers [1971, 201–05].)

The confusions grounded in the above problems make it difficult to discern a clear verdict on affirmative action policies from the perspective of Rawls's theory. Nevertheless, it seems to me that the overall thrust of his theory supports policies such as affirmative action. This is especially true when, upon analysis, it becomes clear that his initial definition of liberty, and his distinction between liberty and the worth of liberty (between negative and positive liberties), is not as clear-cut as it may appear upon an initial reading.

The suggestion that Rawls's theory overall tends to support policies such as affirmative action can be illustrated through a discussion of how his principles of autonomy, justice, and beneficence are related and how they arise out of the process of moral discernment.

Deontological theories such as Rawls's place priority on principles of Right over principles of value or of the Good (or beneficence). Yet in important ways, for Rawls, assumptions about values related to the Good are prior and decisive. Rawls divides his thoughts on beneficence into the "thin" and "full" theories of the Good (1971, 395–439). He believes that some concept of the Good (a thin theory of the Good) is needed before people can discern principles of justice. Rational people desire to increase their primary goods—liberties, opportunities, and wealth—and these goods are the means to all rational aims.

> Rational individuals, whatever else they want, desire certain things as prerequisites for carrying out their plans of life. Other things equal, they prefer a wider to a narrower liberty and opportunity, and a greater rather than a smaller share of wealth and income. That these things are good seems clear enough. . . . The thin theory of the good which the parties are assumed to accept [in the original position] shows that they should try to secure their liberty and self-respect, and that, in order to advance their aims, whatever these are, they normally require more rather than less of the other primary goods [including income and wealth]. (Rawls 1971, 396–97)

In order to arrive intuitively and rationally at Rawls's principles of justice, people in the original position must already value these primary goods and also be knowledgeable about other "basic facts" of human psychology and economics (1971, 137).

Implicit in Rawls's thin theory and explicit in his discussion of basic facts is an anthropology positing that (1) people have tendencies toward acquisitive behavior (because income and wealth are a means toward rational ends) and (2) inequalities in market society can work to the advantage of the least advantaged. Rawls's view of acquisitive human behavior is implicit even in his thin theory of the Good. People in the orignal position, he says, are assumed to accept his notion that people "desire greater liberty and opportunity, and more extensive means for achieving their ends" (1971, 433). For inequalities to work to the advantage of the least advantaged, it must be possible to have ongoing economic growth, some of which trickles down to the disadvantaged, improving their station in life. Clearly, Rawls believes this is possible: he sees the "zero-sum society" (Thurow 1980)—where one person's gain must come at the expense of another—as a tragic, unnecessary situation (1971, 545).

Rawls then asserts that people in the original position, who know these basic facts and the thin theory of the Good and are ignorant of their own degree of privilege, will agree on two principles of justice. First, everyone has a right "to the most extensive total system of equal basic liberties compatible with a system of liberty for all" (1971, 61, 302). By *liberty*, he is referring especially to equal liberty to seize opportunities, but also to negative liberties such as political liberty, freedom of thought and speech, and freedom from arbitrary arrest (1971, 61). Second is his principle of distributive justice which he calls the "difference principle"—where inequalities are to be tolerated only if they benefit the least advantaged and are "attached to offices and positions open to all under conditions of fair equality of opportunity" (1971, 302). To these principles Rawls adds the priority rules mentioned above. Once the people in the original position (with the basic facts and the thin theory of the Good) agree on the principles of justice, they can use these principles to help develop a "full" theory of the Good.[5] The full theory can be used to evaluate the morally good person and society (1971, 435).

The full theory of the Good conceives of the Good as rationality. For individuals, the Good is any rational plan of life (1971, 424). For social systems, the Good is conceived of as a well-ordered society characterized by a system of "pure procedural justice" (1971, 545). Here, two procedural principles of justice govern the distribution of material goods, and no end-state allocative principles are used to determine distributions (1971, 545). This is rational because such a system does not hinder the efficiency of the market (assumptions about market efficiency were included in the "basic facts"). Rawls concludes that when principles of justice, autonomy, and beneficence are conceived of in this manner—with procedural principles, the Right, and a formal notion of the Good as rational plan all included—these principles are congruent (1971, 513–77).

How then does this analysis illuminate the question as to whether Rawls would support affirmative action policy? At first glance, the difference principle (which requires inequalities to benefit the least advantaged) seems to encourage redistributive programs such as affirmative action. But this would not be true if any of the priority rules were to override the difference principle. (And, as discussed earlier, some think the priority of liberty overrides affirmative action policies.) The second priority rule—which includes the statement that "fair opportunity is prior to the difference principle" (1971, 303)—could also be interpreted to preclude preferential forms of affirmative action. The following discussion, however, analyzes specific elements of Rawls's theory that contradict the idea that his priority rules preclude policies such as preferential affirmative action.

Rawls qualifies the second priority rule by stating: "An inequality of opportunity must enhance the opportunities of those with the lesser opportunity" (1971, 303). Rawls recognizes that there will always be inequalities of opportunity (this recognition is behind his discussion of the worth of liberty). With this explanation, Rawls insists that efforts to insure that inequalities benefit the disadvantaged are fair. (Again, by *fairness* Rawls refers to things that people will consent to in the original position.) Since Rawls believes that people will agree that any fair inequality of opportunity must enhance the opportunity of those with less opportunity, it is unlikely he would see preferential programs designed to enhance the opportunities of the disadvantaged as a violation of fair opportunity.

Rawls's rejection of distributive justice schemes based on natural liberty and liberal equality further demonstrates that his concern for fair opportunity does not preclude preferences. Rawls reflects on Nozick's view of freedom as natural liberty (which asserts that liberty is achieved when distributions result from the working of market mechanisms where careers are open to talents—in other words, when there are no *legal* barriers to opportunity). Rawls rejects this concept of justice based on natural freedom (or liberty), arguing that it is improper to allow distributions to be influenced by factors such as natural and social assets and circumstances, because these are undeserved and therefore are "arbitrary from a moral point of view" (1971, 72). The notion of careers open to talents only perpetuates and exacerbates previous inequalities based on differences in natural and social advantages. Here again, Rawls blurs his own distinction between the worth of liberty and liberty itself, by stating that natural and social advantages (which affect the worth of liberty) are as important as liberty itself. Here Rawls rejects natural liberty because this concept of justice permits distributions according to morally arbitrary circumstances. But Rawls's rejection of natural liberty makes no sense if Rawls means that the worth of liberty can never override liberty itself. Rawls's rejection of natural liberty suggests that his concern for fair opportunity would not preclude preferential affirmative action policies.

Rawls also rejects distributive schemes of liberal equality. The idea of liberal equality, Rawls states, "is that positions are to be not only open in a formal [and legal] sense, but that all should have a fair chance [namely, similar life chances] to attain them" (1971, 73). Liberal equality therefore requires structural changes to mitigate the influence of unequal wealth on educational and cultural opportunities. Rawls critiques this as addressing only one of the arbitrary effects involved in natural liberty. Liberal equality addresses unmerited social station but not the arbitrary effects of the "natural lottery." Rawls is concerned that this leads to meritocracy, that is, to rule by the naturally gifted (1971, 74).[6] Here again he emphasizes the importance of overcoming dynamics that negatively affect what he earlier defined as the worth of liberty. His attempts to enhance the worth of liberty further show that his priority principles do not preclude affirmative action.

In place of natural liberty and liberal equality, Rawls advocates his own notion of democratic equality, which adds the difference principle to the principle of fair opportunity (1971, 75). The difference principle mitigates the effects of natural and social privilege by requiring that inequalities work to improve the situation of the least advantaged. If inequalities cannot be made to benefit the least advantaged, "an equal distribution is to be preferred" (1971, 76). If Rawls intended to have a theory where nothing could override negative liberty rights (as is true with Nozick), he could never make such a statement, because if a prepatterned equal distribution were ever required by these criteria, some negative liberty would have to be restricted. And one liberty that might have to be restricted is the right to compete for positions on an equal basis.

Rawls's priority rules, then, do not preclude efforts resulting in greater state action and the restriction of some individual freedoms. Affirmative action can be seen as an attempt to implement Rawls's view of justice as democratic equality, by increasing the worth of liberty for the disadvantaged and by applying the difference principle to the effects of unequal social and natural privilege.

This interpretation is reinforced by Rawls's own summary of his theory of justice: "All social primary goods—liberty and opportunity, income and wealth, and the bases of self-respect—are to be distributed equally unless an unequal distribution of any or all of these goods is to the advantage of the least favored" (1971, 303). Although Rawls prefers to emphasize formal (procedural) principles of justice, here he holds in reserve an allocative principle of distribution, in case the institutional structure is not able to make inequalities work to the advantage of the least favored.

This is particularly interesting because it is his assumptions about the basic facts of socioeconomic life—assumptions such as (1) economic growth can continue, (2) wealth trickles down, and (3) there is a potential harmony of interests among economic classes—that make two critical things possible for his theory. It makes it possible for him to believe that social inequalities can work to benefit the disadvantaged, and this in turn makes it possible for him to promote purely formal principles of justice instead of allocative ones. But if these basic facts are false (for example, if zero-sum or scarcity theorists are or become convincing), then Rawls's theory itself, since it is committed to an egalitarian concept, must fall back on his egalitarian allocative principle. If this were to occur, preferential affirmative action could be affirmed as one (imperfect) means to promote a redistribution consistent with such a concept.

One final piece of evidence supports this interpretation. Rawls explicitly condones race and gender as potentially appropriate identifiers of disadvantage in the application of the difference principle (1971, 96–99). So when Rawls says he wants to promote a system of basic liberties, he leaves room for policy that takes groups into account, if and when individuals are being denied equal liberty because they are members of a particular group. This contradicts those who believe that the priority of (negative) liberty precludes policy from ever infringing on the liberty of an individual, even in the interest of enhancing liberty for the group. Grounded in his difference principle, which emphasizes the rights of disadvantaged individuals, Rawls's theory can permit group-sensitive affirmative action programs, in which group membership serves as an (admittedly imperfect) indicator of individual disadvantage.

In conclusion, while there are some elements in Rawls's theory that would seem to disapprove of policies such as affirmative action, the overall thrust of Rawls's theory supports such policy. Although he distinguishes between liberty and the worth of liberty, his theory does not suggest that one can be abandoned completely for the sake of the other.

CONTEMPORARY LIBERAL ANALYSES OF AFFIRMATIVE ACTION

Proponents of affirmative action express two major arguments for it. Some argue that affirmative action benefits the workplace or society at large. These types of arguments are discussed later under consequentialist analyses of affirmative action. Other arguments for affirmative action are grounded in principles of justice similar to those Rawls has labeled *liberal equality*.

To reiterate, liberal equality refers to principles of distributive justice where goods are to be distributed according to merit in a social context characterized by equal opportunity, where equal opportunity refers not only to the absence of legal barriers (which is what libertarians want) but also to the absence of barriers grounded in unequal social conditions (such as unequal educational and cultural opportunities), which might prevent persons with similar natural talents from having equal life chances to develop their talents and compete in market society.

This concept of equality is behind Sher's argument, first mentioned during the discussion of compensatory rationales for affirmative action, that since past and present discrimination harms present competitiveness and thereby violates the equal opportunity principle, preferential treatment of those whose competitive potential has been damaged is morally right because it comes close to replacing that which was lost, namely, competitiveness related to innate talents (1977, 54–55).

Dworkin's theory of rights and justice provides another example of a liberal defense of affirmative action, which shares premises about distributive justice similar to liberal equality. Dworkin's principle of justice is grounded in his concept of human rights:

people have the right to be treated as equals (meaning with equal respect, by which he means either equal consideration or equal concern). Included within this principle is the idea of equal opportunity—people ought to be treated as equals when competing for jobs.

Dworkin's thinking is in part a reaction to Nozick and Rawls. He rejects Nozick's notion of autonomy as liberty, because there is no right to liberty. And he rejects Rawls's priority of liberty, because laws inevitably compromise liberty in order to protect equality (1977, 266–78). In his construction of a liberal basis of rights, he proposes that the only basis for rights is treatment as an equal, which in turn is grounded in the idea that all persons deserve equal respect. While this could lead to actual equal treatment (for example, pure equal opportunity and hiring the best qualified), for Dworkin, unequal treatment (or unequal opportunity) may actually be necessary in order to create a society where treatment as an equal (or equal opportunity) is more nearly possible (1977, 223–39). Dworkin uses the example that if I have two children and one is sick, then I can treat them as equals (with equal respect) while unequally giving the sick child the last of the medicine (1977, 227). Dworkin concludes that the unequal treatment involved in preferential affirmative action policies may be warranted if it serves the goal of respecting the right of all persons to be treated as equals, or the long-term objective of true merit hiring (1977, 238–39). Dworkin is concerned with specific distributive allocations only to the extent that they can be shown to be necessary to fulfill the right to treatment as an equal (1977, 273–74).

Here, then, is a carefully reasoned theory, grounded in premises of distributive justice similar to liberal equality, that suggests that preferential affirmative action is necessary, even though it might compromise the ideal of equal opportunity in the short term, in order to promote this ideal in the long term. Many supporters of affirmative action, basing their views in similar premises, agree with Dworkin that promoting equal treatment (equal opportunity) in the long term may require some actual unequal treatment (unequal opportunity) in the short term.

In summary, advocates of justice as liberal equality, with its particular version of equal opportunity based on merit, tend to conclude that affirmative action is morally permissible as an attempt to overcome the unfairness of unequal actual opportunity resulting from unequal social conditions and opportunities.

Summary: Liberalism and Affirmative Action

Rawls's discussions of natural liberty, liberal equality, and his own preferred concept of democratic equality provide a framework for summarizing two approaches to distributive justice and affirmative action grounded in the premises of philosophical Liberalism: justice as freedom and justice as fairness.

Rawls's concepts of natural liberty, liberal equality, and democratic equality belong to a broadly conceived philosophical Liberalism. All three give at least conditional approval to the distribution of goods and positions according to merit and assume that market competition is generally an efficient way to distribute jobs and rewards. But the differences are such that these three concepts of distributive justice can accurately be grouped into two overall approaches to affirmative action: conservative and libertarian, and liberal.

Libertarian and conservative thinkers tend to restrict the idea of equal opportunity to a strictly formal equality of opportunity, where no legal or quasi-legal barriers (such as nonrelevant job classifications) hinder careers open to talents. Their principles fit the concept of equality that Rawls calls natural liberty. Such opponents of affirmative action focus on the individual (and in particular, the individual who already has access and choice in market society) and often justify their objections to affirmative action with Kantian ideas about the inviolability of the individual. Pure equal opportunity is the axial principle: an individual ought not have his or her opportunities enhanced at the expense of another. Influenced by this version of equal opportunity, conservatives and libertarians tend to oppose affirmative action.

However, some conservatives also recognize that there are cultural barriers to equal opportunity and express support for protective forms of affirmative action, as long as the measures taken are neutral with regard to the treatment of individuals.[7] For example, measures may be taken to counteract inequalities of opportunities due to disparities of wealth or educational and cultural experiences, and attempts can be made to eliminate non-job-relevant requirements that may disproportionately hold back individuals from disadvantaged groups. But overall, conservatives and libertarians believe that preferential affirmative action's focus on disadvantaged individuals contradicts the fundamental premise of Liberal society, which stresses the importance (even the sanctity) of every individual and her or his right to treatment as an individual.

On the other hand, most liberal critics agree with Rawls's criticism that the conservative and libertarian principle of natural liberty, at least in its application, ignores the social reality that inequalities of wealth prevent equal opportunity, even when formal law prohibits discrimination. These liberals agree with libertarians that careers ought to be open to talents but also insist that social conditions must promote actual equal opportunity. Such liberals tend to agree that affirmative action is a morally permissible means to enhance the conditions of equal opportunity for all. They also suggest that in light of the social bases of variations in competitiveness, it is wrong to take pure equal opportunity (or the actual equal treatment of individuals at the point of hiring) as an inviolable human right, because at the point of hiring, privileged individuals have an unfair advantage, which is grounded in unequal opportunity. Liberal theorists, then, are usually more willing than conservatives and libertarians to let disadvantaged individuals take precedence. Once this priority is allowed, preferential treatment can be seen as providing some balance to the total complex of societal inequality of opportunity faced by individuals from traditionally disadvantaged groups. (Of course, many liberals, probably Rawls included, prefer public policies such as remedial education and training programs to preferential programs. The question remains, however, whether—despite its imperfections—affirmative action is better than nothing, especially when nothing is the likely alternative.)

The principle of liberal equality has not, however, provided an adequate solution to the problem of justice posed by affirmative action policy. Rawls pinpoints the central weakness: distribution according to liberal equality still allows great inequality resulting from differences in natural talents. His preferred principle of democratic equality adds the difference principle, so that even inequalities grounded in natural talents would be required to help the least advantaged.

While Rawls's concept could reduce such talent-based inequalities, it is not likely that his concept would really prevent the differences in natural talents from producing a meritocracy. Under his theory, positions would still be allocated largely according to merit and market forces, that is, ultimately—as with liberal equality—according to natural talents (as such talents are developed by personal effort). Thus Rawls's idea of fair equality of opportunity would reduce but not eliminate meritocracy or inequalities of rewards earned by more talented rulers and less talented subjects.

Thus, while there are differences between principles of justice related to the ideas of liberal equality and Rawls's democratic equality, there is less that distinguishes these two principles than Rawls seems to think: thus both can accurately be called liberal theories of justice.

Both liberal equality and democratic equality express several similar, critical ideas. Both express formal principles of distributive justice: distributions are acceptable if the competition is fair, when fairness includes the requirement that the results of the competition work to the advantage of the least favored, because people would agree to this in a situation of uncoerced bargaining. Both address actual inequality of wealth—not because distributive principles indicate such inequality is wrong, but because inequality can create differences in competitive ability not due to talent and effort. Both advocate public policies that focus on groups, in order to protect and promote the fulfillment of individuals. And both leave market society free to award positions to the most talented, as long as social policies exist that reduce the effects of disparities of wealth on competition. In addition, neither liberal nor democratic equality concepts wish to eliminate market competition or to promote allocative, prepatterned principles of distribution for their own sake. Instead, both seek to insure a formally fair competition. There is, then, more that unites than divides advocates of liberal equality and democratic equality.

There is also more that unites than divides conservatives and libertarians: both tend to place a premium on the individual (expecially the relatively privileged individual) over the group; and both tend to be unwilling to extend concern for equal opportunity beyond "protective" measures designed to overcome legal (and perhaps quasi-legal) barriers to equal opportunity. For all these reasons, Liberalism's approaches to affirmative action fall into two groups: libertarian and conservative approaches and liberal approaches.

The ethical analysis thus far finds that the greater the emphasis on the individual who already has access and choice, the more likely the opposition to affirmative action. It also finds liberal theorists such as Rawls refining the idea of equal opportunity to the point where the problem raised by distributions based on unearned natural talents is of central concern. As the preceding analysis suggests, Rawls's notion of democratic equality mitigates but does not eliminate the inequalities and resulting meritocratic tendencies of Liberalism's equal opportunity principle. The next section analyzes Liberalism's equal opportunity distributive justice principles from Marxist perspectives, discusses the alternative principles of distribution advocated by Marxist thought, and concludes by speculating on how affirmative action would look in light of these Marxist principles of distributive justice.

Justice as Productive Freedom: Marxist Approaches to Affirmative Action

The following discussion is interested not in Marx's revolutionary rhetoric but instead in his fundamental criticisms of Liberal culture and its principles of distributive justice. The purpose here is to analyze the implications of this Marxist critique for the moral evaluation of affirmative action policy.

KARL MARX, MARXISM, AND AFFIRMATIVE ACTION

Marx was no ethicist, yet his writings contain reflections on the three major principles of ethics. These reflections have established a tradition critical of the principle of equal opportunity and merit upon which affirmative action programs are usually based. Marx's central problem with equal opportunity is that it delivers a false promise: people do not succeed based on their natural talent, because the power of money overwhelms natural talent (Tucker 1978, 103–04). Marx writes that Liberal freedom really means only the "right to the undisturbed enjoyment, within certain conditions, of fortuity and chance" (Okin 1981, 249, 250). For Marx, formal (procedural) law—which today, for example, prohibits discrimination and tries to assure formal equal opportunity—merely permits the powerful to protect their interests (Tucker 1978, 51).

Marx's ethics is grounded in a principle of autonomy or freedom different from those found in Liberalism. Freedom requires that people become free from the enslavement that results from the division of labor (Tucker 1978, 160): the capitalist division of labor separates people from each other, from the products of their labor, and from their own creative nature. This division of labor thereby deprives them of their true humanity as social beings who find fulfillment in noncoerced, creative production with others. Freedom and authentic humanity are found not in consumption but in this type of creative coproduction. There is no human need to maximize acquisition, because the increasing desire for money is not grounded in human nature but is created by the capitalist economic system (Tucker 1978, 93). Under capitalism, freedom boils down to free trade, which really means freedom only for capitalists (Tucker 1978, 486). Marx believes that Liberal, individualistic notions of rights misunderstand the social nature of human beings and, thereby, misperceive society as external and threatening to the individual's independence (Tucker 1978, 43).

For Marx, as for Nozick, principles of distributive justice are heavily influenced by principles of autonomy. It is more important to examine how goods are acquired and to see if human freedom is violated in the process than to apply allocative principles of justice. The only time Marx refers to the French socialist distributive principle, "From each according to his ability, to each according to his need" (Tucker 1978, 531), he states this principle will only be appropriate to a high stage of communist production, when the division of labor has been overcome. He denies it is appropriate to focus on this principle of distribution. What is needed first is attention to production, because this is the real root of unfreedom *and* unequal distribution (Tucker 1978, 531, 532). In a free society, unequal distribution will cease to be a problem. People will have enough material goods to fulfill their natures, and they will have no desire to maximize their wealth or consumption.

Marx's principle of beneficence is also grounded in his autonomy principle. The Good is a truly human society of people who are not alienated from their social and productive natures. The division of labor will be eliminated, and people will be able to do many things without becoming identified with one function. Marx looks forward, therefore, to a society where he would be able to "hunt in the morning, fish in the afternoon, rear cattle in the evening, criticize after dinner, just as I have a mind, without ever becoming hunter, fisherman, shepherd or critic" (Tucker 1978, 160). While the ultimate ground of Marx's ethics is in his view of human freedom, because such freedom requires the full flowering of interdependent, social, creative, productive relationships, collectivism is also central to his ethics—both as a means and as an end to human freedom. His autonomy principle, therefore, does not reflect an individualistic view of freedom, because, ultimately, there can be no free, isolated individual—all human beings are social and can become free only in a community where they are simultaneously subject and object in their own self-creation.

Marx would critique affirmative action policies on the same basis that he rejects socialist programs that focus on redistribution: a focus on distribution obscures the real origins of these distributions—a system of production that violates human freedom. For Marx, Liberalism's notions of freedom and equality and even distributive justice are an illusion; they hide the interests they help to protect. If Marx were alive today, he would admit that affirmative action increases interclass mobility, while insisting that it does nothing to overcome the class system itself and its dehumanizing processes. For Marx it is the overthrow of this dehumanizing class system that is the important task of history. While Marx advises against revolutionary violence when the conditions are not ripe, he clearly does not want Liberal reform to bring equal opportunity closer to reality: he wants to capsize the values and structures of the Liberal market society, with its fiction of equal opportunity, which he believes enslaves humankind. . . .

A CONTEMPORARY MARXIST ANALYSIS OF EQUAL OPPORTUNITY

Given this summary of Marx's critique, it is not surprising that few Marxist theorists are enthusiastic—or write specifically—about affirmative action. Some speculation, therefore, is necessary. It may be, however, that contemporary Marxist theory is not totally hostile to public policies such as affirmative action. This possibility is analyzed by focusing on the views of one contemporary Marxist theorist.

In an article criticizing Liberalism's equal opportunity principle, Schaar makes several important criticisms relevant to affirmative action policy. First, he argues that the equal opportunity principle does not allow everyone to develop his or her talents, because every society rewards only those talents consistent with its values. He says, therefore, that the equal opportunity doctrine actually means

> equality of opportunity for all to develop those talents which are highly valued by a given people at a given time.
>
> When put in this way, it becomes clear that commitment to the formula [of equal opportunity] implies prior acceptance of an already established social-moral order. Thus, the doctrine is, indirectly, very conservative. It enlists support for the established pattern of values. It also encourages change and growth . . . but mainly along the lines of a tendency already apparent and approved in a given society (1974, 234–35).[8]

If one approves of the equal opportunity doctrine, he says, one must be willing to accept the dominant values of the society and accept the resulting meritocracy (1974, 235–36). He says that the equal opportunity principle lends moral legitimacy to a competitive and inegalitarian culture while it preserves the "fiction of moral equality" and generosity—when true generosity would abandon the competitive model (1974, 236–37).

Schaar's major complaint is that the equal opportunity principle debases "a genuinely democratic understanding of equality" (1974, 240). He complains that with the equal opportunity principle "individualism . . . is the reigning ethical principle. It is a precise symbolic e pression of the liberal-bourgeois model of society, for it extends the marketplace mentality to all the spheres of life" (1974, 240).

Schaar continues that the equal opportunity principle puts everyone on his or her own:

> Resting upon the attractive conviction that all should be allowed to improve their conditions as far as their abilities permit, the equal-opportunity principle insists that each individual do this by and for himself. Thus, it is the perfect embodiment of the Liberal conception of reform. It breaks up solidaristic opposition to existing conditions of inequality by holding out to the ablest and most ambitious members of the disadvantaged groups the enticing prospect of rising from their lowly state to a more prosperous condition. The rules of the game remain the same . . . the social-economic system is unaltered. All that happens is that individuals are given the chance to struggle up the social ladder, change their position on it, and step on the fingers of those beneath them.

This is a common Marxist point. MacPherson states that equal opportunity only leads to some mobility between classes but leaves class divisions and the related unfreedoms intact (1973, 86). Echoing Marx, MacPherson argues that mere distributive justice is not consistent with equal moral freedom (1973, 83). Schaar continues,

> A great many individuals do, in fact, avail themselves of the chance to change sides as offered by the principle of equality of opportunity. More than that, the desire to change sides is probably typical of the lower and middle classes, and is widely accepted as a legitimate ethical outlook. In other words, *much of the demand for equality,* and virtually all of the demand for the kind of equality expressed in the equal opportunity principle, *is really a demand for an equal right and opportunity to become unequal.* (1974, 240–41, my emphasis)

Schaar thinks this kind of thinking is antithetical to a genuinely democratic concept of equality, which is opposed to oligarchy even if it is an oligarchy of the talented (1974, 243). Despite these harsh criticisms, Schaar notes that the "equal opportunity principle is certainly not without value. Stripped of its antagonistic and ine-qualitarian overtones, the formula can be used to express the fundamental proposition that no member of the community should be denied the basic conditions necessary for the fullest participation in the common life" (1975, 244). He concludes that this concept must be interpreted carefully, to prevent it from becoming "just another defense of the equal right to become unequal" (1974, 244).

Schaar's analysis illustrates problems with the equal opportunity principle. It seems as though he would reject policies such as affirmative action as perpetuating the illusions of equality fostered by liberal equal opportunity ideas. Nevertheless, this last paragraph, where he suggests that the equal opportunity principle might have some value if stripped of its antagonistic implications, suggests that it may be possible to endorse affirmative action as one means toward increasing the inclusion of disadvantaged persons in the common life.

In any case, although Marxist principles of justice focus on production, not distribution, the focus on the conditions necessary for free production does shift Marxist theory significantly away from the liberal preoccupation with fair procedures, to greater concern with the conditions of people in society. Put more simply, with Marxist theory, there is greater emphasis on the ends than there is with Liberalism. This then leads to the fourth approach to the affirmative action issue; it explicitly focuses on the consequences of such policies.

Justice as the Greatest Good: Consequentialist Approaches to Affirmative Action

Many of the strongest arguments both for and against affirmative action are grounded upon consequentialist premises. The following analysis of consequentialist approaches to affirmative action begins with J. S. Mill's rule utilitarianism and illustrates the strengths of utilitarian theory as well as the problems of reconciling beneficence, justice, and autonomy principles in such theory. After this general discussion, specific consequentialist arguments against and for affirmative action are summarized.

J. S. MILL: RULE UTILITARIANISM AND AFFIRMATIVE ACTION

Mill attempts to reconcile tensions between his principle of utility (which is grounded in his greatest happiness, beneficence principle) and the principles of justice and autonomy, by arguing that justice and autonomy principles do not conflict with, but are actually grounded in, the principle of utility.

The major tenets of Mill's thought are well known. Values always come before principles (all action ought to be motivated toward promoting human well-being), and principles are grounded in a priori values such as human well-being and the idea of the greatest good (1957, 4). Through human conscience, which is a "subjective feeling" in the mind acquired through learning, human beings can apprehend the aim of morality: the Good is that which maximizes the aggregate happiness or well-being of humankind (1957, 34–39). According to Mill, the legitimacy of this greatest happiness value cannot be proven. Nevertheless, he argues, the fact that everyone acknowledges personal and general happiness as an end illustrates that utility provides as much a basis for morality as any other idea of morality (1957, 44, 45–51).[9]

Mill responds to those who dispute his contention that justice is grounded in utility with his rule utilitarianism—asserting that justice is the name for especially important general rules that promote social utility (or the greatest good). This is how he attempts to reconcile tensions between his principle of utility as the greatest good and various principles of justice and autonomy: he argues that justice and autonomy principles do not conflict with, but are actually grounded in, utility. Beyond this, justice principles are the most important rules of utility; they are "sacred" and may be overruled only in extreme cases (1957, 73). Mill writes, "Justice is a name for certain moral requirements which, regarded collectively, stand higher in the scale of social utility, and are therefore of more paramount obligation, than any others, though particular cases may occur in which some other social duty is so important as to overrule any one of the general maxims of justice" (1957, 78).

If justice principles are the most important rules for utilitarian theory, then it would appear that the rule utilitarian approach would involve determining which public policies best obey the rules. Presumably, in Liberal culture with all its assumptions, policies such as affirmative action would be evaluated by how congruent they are with rules such as the equal opportunity principle. But as critics of utilitarian theory suggest, there are problems with this rule utilitarian approach.

Various critics of Mill's rule utilitarianism raise several objections. First, even though Mill speaks of justice and rights as sacred rules, he appears to reserve the right to override any rules if so doing serves the overall end. The preceding paragraph provides one example, where Mill reserves the possibility of overruling an existing justice rule in the interest of moral requirements "higher in the scale of social utility," and gives the example of stealing if required for survival (1957, 78).

Second, some critics point out that, at least with respect to its consequences, Mill's principle of utility permits excessive inequality which can lead to a tyranny of the majority against minorities. (Theoretically, inequalities and tyranny are morally acceptable to utilitarianism, if a rational calculus indicates that these are expedient to the aggregate happiness.)

Third, some suggest that Mill does not really ground his principles of justice in utility as he claims, but imports them (without attribution) from elsewhere. MacIntyre argues that Mill must appeal to norms other than utility, because there is no content to his greatest happiness principle—so he must covertly import norms from elsewhere to give definition to his principle of utility (1966, 238). Rawls makes a similar point, arguing that Mill senses intuitively and then imports principles of justice (such as reciprocity) which are alien to his theory (1971, 502).

Mill does not adequately explain, if, as he claims, justice and autonomy principles are congruent and both grounded in utility, where the different and competing principles of justice (and rights) come from; and further, how can utility itself arbitrate conflicts over which principles of rights or justice ought to be given priority in public policy decisions (or put differently, when can they be overridden by utility). The problem of deciding among justice principles suggests that some principle of justice must be imported, beyond utility itself, to decide how to choose among different concepts of justice.

Fourth, others point out that often, if not usually, it is difficult to calculate the consequences of all the various possible rules. This is especially difficult given all the diverse social contexts in which such rules must be implemented. This makes it difficult to know for certain which among the various possible rules really would promote the greatest good.

The preceding discussion of objections to Mill's utilitarian theory does not falsify utilitarian theory but instead shows the difficulty of grounding the principle of justice in utilitarian theory. Although these criticisms illustrate the difficulties in applying a utilitarian calculus to the problem of affirmative action, the consequentialist approach continues to be taken by many analysts in the affirmative action debate. It seems to me, however, that for an evaluation of affirmative action based on consequentialist theory alone, certain conditions must be met. (1) A critic must despair of finding some central principle of rights or justice to arbitrate the conflict among contending principles of justice and their correspondingly different views of affirmative action. (2) A critic must come to the conclusion that it is possible to predict the outcome of policies such as affirmative action with enough accuracy to determine whether they promote the greatest good. Given the previous discussions of the three deontological approaches to affirmative action, and the difficulties of each approach in resolving the affirmative action dilemma, it is not surprising that much of the argumentation about affirmative action is in terms of its overall social impact.

CONTEMPORARY CONSEQUENTIALIST ANALYSES AND
AFFIRMATIVE ACTION

The following reviews the most common consequentialist arguments for and against affirmative action. Many of these arguments sound similar to those grounded in the premises of Liberalism, because these consequentialist arguments are taking place in a Liberal culture, which assumes that equal opportunity and merit hiring in a capitalist, market society is efficient and promotes utility. Thus consequentialist arguments in a Liberal culture tend to center on whether affirmative action helps the efficient working of the capitalist "free" market.

It is not possible to divide the arguments into distinct consequentialist traditions (such as utilitarian approaches *for* affirmative action and conservative, civic republican arguments *against* affirmative action) because it is not possible to identify specific consequentialist traditions that would or would not endorse affirmative action. This is partly because, given the dominant idea within a Liberal culture that relatively free economic markets are most efficient, many if not most consequentialist analyses focus on the impact of affirmative action on market efficiency and productivity. Thus, there tends to be an important focus of shared concern when it comes to consequentialist analyses of affirmative action. This shared focus underlies the central idea and unifies most concepts of the Good which might be used to judge affirmative action.

Another reason it is difficult to identify distinct consequentialist traditions clearly supporting or opposing affirmative action is that there may be variations in the overall concepts of the Good within the different consequentialist traditions themselves, and these variations then make possible a wide range of evaluations of affirmative action. For example, because the civic republican tradition can be properly classified as conservative consequentialism (because social stability and preserving social institutions are central ends), it may seem that civic republican ethics would tend to oppose affirmative action. But theorists from this tradition would not come to a uniform evaluation of affirmative action because, depending on the analysis of the facts, affirmative action can be seen as promoting or eroding the good, orderly, society. Certainly, for example, if some civic republicans view some forms of democratic socialism as essential to preserving Western democracy against the undemocratic effects of income inequality (Sullivan 1982, 208–24), it is conceivable that affirmative action could be affirmed as one strategy toward preserving such democratic institutions.

Finally, there is another dynamic, which makes the consequentialist landscape muddier still. Many of those who argue about affirmative action's impact on society are not true consequentialists but fall back on such arguments, either because they have not found in deontological principles compelling rationales for or against affirmative action, or because they are merely supplementing their deontologically grounded arguments with some of their perceptions about the social impact of affirmative action.

Whatever their overall normative orientation, opponents of affirmative action raise five major fact-based objections to affirmative action. First, affirmative action is impractical because it is difficult to choose who should benefit (N. Glazer 1975, 197), to predict the consequences, and to evaluate the success or failure of such programs (Gross 1978, 5, 28, 93; Newton 1977, 171–72). Second, affirmative action is not necessary because the trajectory of U.S. history shows that previously excluded persons are being increasingly included (Glazer 1975, 6–7, 8–19; Gross 1978, 117)—so discrimination is not serious enough to require policies such as affirmative action which have serious negative consequences. (These negative consequences include the following third and fourth objections.) Third, affirmative action leads to increased color consciousness and racial hostility between groups (Glazer 1975, 200; C. Cohen 1975). Fourth, affirmative action leads to a decline in productivity and efficiency either because unqualified or less qualified persons get positions they would not have otherwise received or because the high costs of litigation or the programs themselves divert resources that businesses need to remain efficient, productive, and competitive. And fifth, affirmative action and its race and gender classifications harm those they intend to help by stigmatizing them, destroying self-confidence while leading everyone to believe that they cannot compete on their own merits (C. Cohen 1975; Heslep 1976, 46). (According to Fullinwider, rule utilitarians could argue against affirmative action on the grounds that policies using racial classifications never promote overall utility; 1980, 241.)

On the other hand, proponents argue that affirmative action is warranted because it eliminates present discriminatory practices and integrates society as it increases opportunities for minorities. This promotes the greatest good in many ways. For example, economic benefits reduce income inequalities and social expenditures on welfare. Reducing income inequalities and increasing opportunities also reduce social strife and the stigmas of inferiority and racial conflict and provide positive role models for traditionally excluded persons. Affirmative action overcomes discrimination, which harms economic efficiency by depriving society of the natural talents of persons who otherwise would be prevented by discrimination from developing and making contributions with their talents (Fullinwider 1980, 242–47, 68–78, 84–91). (While advancing a different case, Nickel 1975 also provides a good summary of this argument.)

It has also been suggested that the inclusion of minorities can benefit institutions by providing the diversity of perspectives essential to the quest for truth and social progress (Wasserstrom 1977). Fullinwider asserts that these types of utilitarian arguments are the best grounds for affirmative action: whites are more willing to accept utilitarian arguments than arguments implying that whites are somehow less deserving of a position because of rights or justice principles (1980, 247).

Many of the arguments between consequentialist proponents and opponents of affirmative action involve simple disagreements about facts. Such disagreements, like those over the extent of discrimination and the impact of affirmative action policies, underscore the difficulty involved in applying a utilitarian calculus in an evaluation of affirmative action. Beyond this, the deeper theoretical problem has not been resolved by contemporary consequentialist approaches to affirmative action: how to decide which among the competing principles of rights and justice are really grounded in (or congruent with) utility, and related to this problem is the question of how much inequality is really permissible from the moral point of view.

Summary: The Problem of Justice and Affirmative Action

There are four major moral approaches to affirmative action. Depending on one's view of the social facts, each approach could lead to a positive or negative moral evaluation of affirmative action policies. Among those whose views are grounded in Liberalism, libertarians and conservatives tend to disapprove of affirmative action. They do so largely because they stress their principle of freedom (autonomy) over any principle of justice or any particular social end, and they tend to see affirmative action as violating such freedom. And they do so because they tend to think either that affirmative action harms market society or that discrimination is in decline, making state intervention based on compensatory justice ideas decreasingly needed. On the other hand, liberals tend to support affirmative action. They do so largely because, unlike libertarians and conservatives, they insist that disadvantaged individuals should take precedence over those individuals who already have free access and free choice in market society—public policy should enhance the chances of disadvantaged persons to compete in the market society, and affirmative action is a means to that end. Further, in their analysis of the facts, liberals tend to think that past and present discrimination continues to affect negatively the social prerequisites of equal opportunity, particularly for disadvantaged persons.

Marxists, with a different view of freedom, and with their communitarian sentiments, might seem likely to approve of policies such as affirmative action. However, since liberal equal opportunity is clearly not what they want, it remains a matter of speculation as to whether they would support affirmative action. Those who do would probably be derided as "revisionists" by those who do not, which illustrates one of the internal problems of Marxist theory: its vagueness with regard to particulars makes it difficult to apply its theory to specific policy issues.

For utilitarians and other consequentialists, the issue is especially up for grabs. Depending on the specific content that different consequentialists give to their values and ends, combined with different possible calculations of the consequences of the various policy alternatives, all sorts of positive or negative evaluations of affirmative action are possible. Some consequentialists strongly argue for affirmative action, while others strongly argue against it. Meanwhile, the problem of how to arbitrate conflicts between competing principles of justice, rights, and beneficence remains unresolved.

The present purpose has been to develop an understanding of the key moral issues underlying the affirmative action controversy. This background helps make part 2 more intelligible; the preceding ethical analysis of the *normative* arguments serves as background for part 2's comprehensive *descriptive* ethical analysis of the attitudes of ordinary working people toward affirmative action. Chapter 7 concludes the research, first reexamining the theoretical issues outlined in chapter 3, then returning to reflect on the normative ethical issues in light of the descriptive analysis of the perceptions and ethical attitudes of those who have experienced firsthand an aggressive affirmative action policy.

Part II

THE EMPIRICAL RESEARCH

INTRODUCTION

PART 2 of this volume explores empirically the attitudes of employees of the California State Department of Parks and Recreation toward affirmative action and the rationales offered for it.

Chapter 3 discusses the theoretical questions and puzzles that have driven the research, linking these questions to the normative ethical analysis of chapter 2. It then describes the two-phase methodology of the research, which uses both qualitative and quantitative methods to assess respondent attitudes. Chapter 4 describes impressions gained during participant obervation and from interviews about attitudes and perceptions related to affirmative action. Chapter 5 and 6 discuss the survey research data. Chapter 5 asks: Do the respondents approve of affirmative action? And if so, to what extent do they approve, and which type of affirmative action do they endorse? This leads into chapter 6, which asks: Why do the subjects approve or disapprove of affirmative action? That is, what are the reasons, including moral arguments grounded in differing principles of distributive justice that inform respondent approval or disapproval of affirmative action? The survey research examines especially differences in attitudes among four respondent groups: white men, white women, nonwhite men, and nonwhite women.

Chapter 7 provides a brief review of the empirical findings in light of the theoretical questions raised and concludes with a discussion of the normative implications of this research for the ethical evaluation of affirmative action in general and for organizations with affirmative action programs, in particular.

3

RESEARCH THEORY AND METHODOLOGY

THE EMPIRICAL PART of this research explores the attitudes of employees in the California State Department of Parks and Recreation toward affirmative action. Since 1975 the Parks Department has been under strong pressure by the California State Personnel Board (which has ultimate authority over the state's affirmative action efforts) to improve its hiring rates for all women and nonwhite men. A sanctions agreement between the department and the Personnel Board articulated the types of actions the department would undertake to improve its rates of hiring women and nonwhite men. Given the longevity of the sanctions agreement and the resulting affirmative action program, virtually all departmental employees are acquainted with the program.

Three methods were used to assess the departmental employee attitudes toward affirmative action: participant observation, interviews, and survey research. Before describing the rationale for using these methods and the specific implementation of these methods, I will discuss the major expectations and questions the research was designed to illuminate and the major theoretical assumptions that underlie the overall approach.

Expectations and Puzzles: Questions for Resolution

Not only did the research design attempt to address initial theoretical expectations, it also was designed to be "open to new theoretical possibilities" (Emerson 1983, 94) in the examination of attitudes toward affirmative action. Of course, all research is guided by expectations and puzzles to test and explore. My basic expectations and the central questions for the empirical part of this research can be divided into four major areas.

First, and most generally, I wanted to determinine if there are differences in the way four major groups—white men, white women, minority men, and minority women—think about the morality of affirmative action. Do these different groups bring the same moral premises and perspectives to this issue? Do these groups decide about this issue by applying some variation of the four ethical approaches to distributive justice summarized in chapter 2? I also wanted to determine if there were differences related to characteristics such as age, class, job type (management versus rank and file and maintenance versus clerical versus professional), religious sentiments, and geography. And I wanted to see if there were significant differences among nonwhites.

In the second major area, I expected that white men, who presumably are hurt or threatened by affirmative action, would tend to oppose it, while white and nonwhite women and minority men, who stand to benefit from affirmative action, would tend to support it. On the other hand, however, on this point, following Karl Marx and other interest theorists, I realize that sometimes people endorse moral values supporting economic structures that work against their own objective economic interests. I therefore wanted to check my initial expectations about who would approve and disapprove of affirmative action; first, by trying to assess the extent to which the feelings and moral sentiments people have about affirmative action go against their own interests; and second, by exploring the characteristics of the moral ideals that people endorse, especially when such ideals work against their interests.

In the third major area of inquiry, following Emile Durkheim, I expected that, overall, religious and ethical values would reflect and reinforce prevailing cultural norms; so I expected that most people would endorse the basic premises, including the moral and religious legitimations, of a Liberal, market society. On the other hand, following Max Weber, it is possible for moral and religious values to be decisive factors in the complex matrix of variables that lead to social change. So I wanted to look at the extent to which moral and religious moral values legitimize affirmative action policy. More broadly, I wanted to look at the extent to which attitudes toward affirmative action reinforce or challenge the modes of economic distribution that accompany a Liberal market society. Specifically, do different ethnic, gender, or class groups ground their attitudes toward affirmative action in norms that support or contradict a Liberal market society's distributive norms?

The fourth major area of inquiry has been informed by recent research and discussion about the pervasiveness of individualism in U.S. culture and how such individualism impedes individual expression of ethical concern for common goals and the good of the community (e.g., Bellah and others, 1985). Some of this discussion has posed puzzles particularly relevant for my research. For example, feminists have asserted that women tend to approach the moral life less individualistically than men—by grounding moral sentiments more on an ethic emphasizing human interdependence, relationship, interpersonal responsibility, compassion, and care—than on principles of rights and justice which are derived by individuals thinking rationally (Gilligan 1982, 1983). Gilligan asserts that theories of moral development such as Kohlberg's (which see individual, rational reflection on moral principles as the highest stage of moral development) contain the individualistic premise that the aim of moral development is to make people *independent* of civil society, whereas women more than men tend to recognize human interdependence (1983, 39). According to Gilligan, rational, principled approaches to ethics inevitably emphasize individual autonomy and neglect an ethics of care and responsibility (1983, 40).

Gilligan and other feminists want to promote a moral way of knowing grounded primarily in women's experience, which appropriates affect, based in relationship, into an ethic of caring. Gilligan asserts that when an ethic of care is developed, grounded in an understanding of relationship, such an ethic is not

> bound by the same cognitive restraints that apply to the understanding of justice and rights. No longer would only moral philosophers or analytic thinkers reach moral maturity but also people who have come through the experience of relationship to understand the dynamics of interdependence. Thus, the ethic of care restores the concept of love to the moral domain, uniting cognition and affect by tying reflection to the experience of relationship. (1983, 45)

So Gilligan first suggests that there is an alternative moral way of knowing, which draws on both affect and cognition for moral insight. She hopes, second, to promote simultaneously just such an integration of the rational and the affective as sources for moral insight and practice.

Gilligan's two thrusts, then, suggest two questions for this research: (1) Do women approach the affirmative action issue with a "different voice," appropriating affective and nonlogical modes of moral evaluation? If a different voice is discernible, what are its differentiating characteristics? If there is no different voice, what sorts of traditional, rational, and moral analysis characterize the moral perspectives of women and others? (2) If women tend to look at moral questions less individualistically than men, do *nonwhite* men do so also, and perhaps nonwhite women most of all?[1] This seems logical given the extent to which nonwhite people in the United States have been victims by virtue of their membership in vilified groups. This also seems plausible given differences among different cultures abroad: perhaps nonwhite immigrants do not easily appropriate the individualism of the U.S. culture. So perhaps nonwhite people tend to endorse group-conscious public policies because such people do not hold individualistic premises, which automatically suspect any policy that relies on group classifications.

This fourth major area of inquiry can be summarized in terms of two major research questions: (1) Are nonwhite men, nonwhite women, and white women more likely than white men to approve of group-sensitive approaches to moral questions in general, and affirmative action in particular? Further, do white men really tend to dislike group-sensitive approaches, as is often assumed? (2) If these same groups do endorse group-sensitive approaches to affirmative action, does this reflect a genuine moral concern for building community (that is, does this reflect or show sympathy for truly communitarian ideals), or does this reflect another form of individual self-interest, where individuals recognize and desire personal benefits from group-sensitive policies such as affirmative action?

Both qualitative and quantitative sociological methods have been used in order to obtain the greatest possible breadth of information about questions such as these. What, then, are the reasons for utilizing these two methods, and what are the specific steps taken in implementing these two methodologies?

Rationale for the Methodology

Various empirical methods are available for analyzing social settings and questions such as the ones just discussed. These diverse methods generally are divided into qualitative and quantitative modes of inquiry. Qualitative (or field) research assesses the quality or characteristics of social phenomena (Lofland 1971, 4). Its two primary methods are participant observation, "which involves the assembling of field notes," and intensive interviewing (Lofland 1971, vii).

One type of participant observation is called grounded theory research. The grounded theory approach involves a participant observer who tries to look with few or no preconceptions at a social setting or phenomenon. Grounded theory proponents see observation and the development of theory as a simultaneous process, through which theory (understood as explanation or prediction) about a social setting or phenomenon is developed (Charmaz 1983, 109; Glazer and Strauss 1967, 31, n22). Grounded theorists seek to minimize a priori theoretical constructs, because they believe such constructs may perpetuate ideas that need discarding or can lead the researcher to ignore other important dynamics (Charmaz 1983, 110–11). Grounded theory proponents see the development of theory, and the testing of such theory through quantitative statistical research, as different but complementary aspects of social science research (Charmaz 1983, 111).

A second major type of qualitative research is based on interviews. When the goal is to develop an understanding of what is important to the interviewees, the interview should be as unstructured as possible (Lofland 1971, 76). Theory and hypotheses, and ideas from interviews, can be combined to construct an interview guide as "a list of things to be sure to ask about" during the interview (Lofland 1971, 84). This guide can also remind researchers about the issues that prior research and theoretical assumptions have indicated are important, but it should be flexible enough to allow new perspectives and theory to emerge. There are two major weaknesses with qualitative research. First, it tends to tolerate greater subjectivity than quantitative research, and this subjectivity casts doubt on the accuracy of its findings. Second, qualitative research usually involves small numbers of subjects, making it difficult to generalize about the perspectives expressed or the conclusions reached. Quantitative studies can compensate for these weaknesses and complement qualitative studies.

Quantitative research usually involves surveys and scientifically selected samples and attempts to quantify the characteristics of some social phenomenon. This is done through statistical analysis, which tests the theories and hypotheses that the researcher brings to the phenomenon in question. Inferences are carefully made from samples of people to the general population, or to some specific population. "Quantitative studies serve primarily to firm up and modify knowledge first gained in a fundamentally qualitative fashion" (Lofland 1971, 6). So quantitative research has the advantage of being able to test hypotheses generated by field research, using quantitative techniques to compare a variety of subgroup differences with relative ease in order to generalize from a probability sample to the population (Blackstrom and Hursh-Cesar 1981, 16). The major weakness of quantitative research is in an area where field research is strong—the ability to probe in depth (Blackstrom and Hursh-Cesar 1981, 16).

While practitioners of the two major approaches to social science research sometimes seem at odds, both attempt to explore fully a social setting or phenomenon. In the present research, both approaches were employed in an attempt to understand the attitudes toward affirmative action held by people who have experienced it firsthand. Throughout the process of collecting and analyzing both the qualitative and quantitative data, I found the data of each method required another look at the data from the other method. I also had to look again at my developing theoretical perspectives, modifying these perceptions again and again. Through this dialectical process I have tried to achieve what Emerson calls a "double fitting of fact to theory and theory to fact" (Emerson 1983, 94). In summary, then, my empirical analyses, through both qualitative and quantitative techniques, uses both inductive and deductive approaches. I will now describe the specific steps taken in both aspects of this research.

Qualitative Research

Method One: Participant Observation

My employment with the California State Department of Parks and Recreation provided the opportunity for participant observation. For fifteen years, I was a state park ocean lifeguard—a position with duties similar to that of a park ranger, with the additional responsibility for ocean rescue. I was involved in curriculum development and training for the department's affirmative action programs and with the Equal Opportunity Employment Committee (a statewide advisory committee responsible for advising and assisting the department in the creation, implementation, and evaluation of its affirmative action policies) between 1984 and 1988. The observations made while participating in these activities provided the first source of data on the views held by individuals from the various social groups.

My employment with the department gave me access to the chief of the Human Rights Office and to the director of the department, both of whom consented to the research. I entered into a research agreement with the department, which granted access for the interviews and the survey, in return for a report interpreting the results.

Method Two: Fifty Interviews with Parks Department Employees

Once granted access, I obtained a computerized list of all department employees. I separated employees first by ethnicity (in detail) and gender, and then into the four main social groups: white men, white women, nonwhite men, and nonwhite women. I subdivided these groups further in two ways: first, into management and rank-and-file groups; and, second, into three different types of job classifications: (1) clerical/administrative (including a few professionals like computer programmers, historians, and archaeologists), (2) maintenance services, and (3) visitor services (a classification that includes park rangers and lifeguards—positions with peace officer powers). These further subdivisions permitted me to analyze the extent to which persons in different job classifications differ in their feelings about affirmative action. Theoretically and from my experiences within the department, I judged that there could be differences among these types of employees.

Next I chose locations in each of the five regions of the state for interviews. Within these regions, to make scheduling of the different groups easy, larger districts were chosen for the interviews. The director of the department and the chief of the Human Rights Office then contacted the field managers in these districts, requesting their help in facilitating the research. Field managers then, as a rule, wrote memoranda to their subordinates, urging them to participate in the interviews if asked, and authorizing them to do so on state time. Usually, I would make the initial contacts with potential interviewees myself, although on a couple of occasions managers wished to make the initial contacts, so I submitted the names of the people I wished to interview, and the interviews were scheduled for me.

While making the initial contacts, I explained the purposes of the research, that all responses would be confidential, and that interviewees would not be affected negatively in any way if they chose not to participate. I began each interview by having the interviewees read and sign an "informed consent agreement" that reiterated the same ideas, and by giving them an opportunity to ask questions.

Once I had decided which districts to visit, I took the computer readouts for these districts and systematically chose every third name in each category. When an individual was unavailable during my visit, I tried to contact the next third name within that category. I ended up interviewing seventeen managers, twelve from targeted groups (all women and minority men) and five white males, and thirty-three rank-and-file employees, averaging five or six clerical workers, maintenance people, and visitor services personnel from each of the four research groups. I also interviewed four persons who were not randomly selected, but whom I knew to be activists either for or against the department's affirmative action policies (three in management and one rank-and-file employee). I felt it was important to interview a few especially politicized individuals, in case their views were not typical, because their views might have been left out by random sampling.

Before conducting any official interviews, I designed the initial interview guide, with questions derived from discussions among social philosophers and from attitudes I had heard in the workplace. I then conducted exploratory mock interviews with several friends in the department, and afterward I discussed the interview questions with them. I used their comments to revise the interview guide for the first interviews.

During these first interviews, I referred to the interview guide, although I often did not have to go through it systematically, because many people would spontaneously address many of the issues in the guide. After the first fifteen interviews and some preliminary analysis, I made some minor changes in the guide in order to follow better the themes that were emerging. The purpose of this revision was to follow leads and to stay close to the data, and to avoid making the views of the interviewees fit into the initial conceptual categories that I established at the outset of the interviews.

Each interview began with a three-part story about a black woman who sued an employer alleging discrimination. This woman used statistics regarding minority hiring as evidence for her case. In the case study, a settlement was reached, she was given a job, and the employer agreed to set hiring goals as a means to increase the representation of black women in the employer's work force. At several points during the story, the interviewees were asked for their views about the fairness of what happened.

By starting with a general case study, I aimed to generate spontaneous reactions to a typical example of affirmative action, without imposing my own conceptual categories on the respondents (Blackstrom and Hursh-Cesar 1981, 128). I probed interviewee responses to the case study to get them to free-associate their opinions about affirmative action. (Theoretically, spontaneously offered attitudes are seen as more credible than responses to questions put by a researcher [Becker 1970, 30]. This approach also helps to depersonalize responses on this highly charged issue.)

After exploring the case study with the respondent, I moved to the more structured part of the interview. The interview concluded by asking the interviewees to respond to the ideas related to the four basic ethical approaches to the affirmative action issue—approaches that parallel the four major approaches to affirmative action outlined in chapter 2. (See appendix A for the final version of the interview guide.)

After the interviews were completed, I transcribed them, paraphrasing when the statements were lengthy or off the subject, but otherwise quoting verbatim. During the transcribing process, and afterward while reading the transcripts, I coded the responses into various perspectives. I then went back through the transcripts again, first making a one- or two-page summary sheet of each respondent's perspective (including the most relevant quotations) and then making a one paragraph summary of each person's views. This made it easier to compare responses and to find the quotations that best illustrated certain perspectives. I used these interviews, along with debates among social philosophers about affirmative action and my theoretical questions, to set the agenda for the survey.

Quantitative Research: The Survey

The survey has three parts. (The complete list of survey questions is contained in appendix B). The first and largest part involved seventy-two questions which addressed about fifteen issues. Respondents were allowed four possible responses: strongly agree, agree, disagree, and strongly disagree.[2] Second, there were five open-response questions. (Again, here I was trying to get responses not restricted by prior conceptual categories.) Seven demographic questions asked about age, political philosophy, social class, religion, religious commitment, place of primary residence, and disability. Finally, each questionnaire had a preattached, coded, identification label, with ethnic, gender, and job information.

There are about 2,300 employees in the Parks Department. Again using a department computer listing, I separated these employees into four groups: white men, white women, nonwhite men, and nonwhite women, and then separated them further into management and rank-and-file categories, producing a total of eight subgroups. I then determined how many people would be in each of these eight categories if only one quarter of those within each category were chosen. (This was done to insure that I would get enough responses in each category to have a fair representation of the total subgroup if questionnaires were sent to only one quarter of the employees.) In several of these eight subgroupings there were not enough people to expect a high enough return. (In the entire department, there were only 67 white female managers, 12 nonwhite female managers, 156 female rank-and-file workers, and 43 male nonwhite managers.) So I decided to oversample and send questionnaires to every person in each of these categories: white female managers, nonwhite male managers, and all nonwhite females, whether management or rank and file. (Since I was not interested in departmentwide percentages, but in the attitudes of the different groups, there was no need to readjust the figures at a later time to compensate for the oversampling.)

The questionnaires were sent with a letter explaining the purposes of the study, the voluntary nature of the survey, and the assurance of confidentiality. A stamped envelope was supplied, addressed to "Affirmative Action Research" at an address that made it clear it was not being mailed to the department.

The overall return rate was 45 percent, with white men responding at the highest rate (53 percent), followed by white women (47 percent), nonwhite men (44 percent), and nonwhite women (33 percent). The return rates for subgroups such as blacks, Asians, Hispanics, and native Americans were high enough to permit generalizations about these groups, and sometimes even between men and women within these groups.[3] Table 1 shows the percentages of the responding racial and gender subgroups. Except in the categories that were oversampled, the numbers sent reflect one quarter of the department's employees in these categories.

I coded the questionnaires upon their return. For the open re-

TABLE 1
Race and Gender of Questionnaire Respondents

	Women		Men		Total	
	N	% of Response	N	% of Response	N	% of Response
White	97[a]	47	158[b]	53	255	50
Nonwhite	50[c]	33	129[d]	44	179	39
Black	6	19	18	43	24	32
Asian	10	37	30	55	40	49
Hispanic	25	31	52	38	77	35
Native American	7	35	19	50	26	45
Filipino	2	25	8	50	10	42
Pacific Islander	—	—	2	67	2	67
Unknown[e]	—	—	—	—	10	

a. Questionnaires sent: rank and file, 141; management, 67.
b. Questionnaires sent: rank and file, 141; management, 85.
c. Questionnaires sent: rank and file, 156; management, 12.
d. Questionnaires sent: rank and file, 231; management, 60.
e. Identification label was removed.

sponse questions, I developed a coded list of up to ninety possible answers. The statistical analysis proceeded in four stages. First, the *tau-b* scores of each Likert item were compared with the other Likert items. I produced a correlation matrix and used it to examine the relationships among these questions. This provided clues as to which concerns or perspectives about affirmative action were interrelated.

Second, I looked at all the respondents at once, by examining relationships between the Likert items and the demographic variables. For these bivariate analyses, I used chi-square for nominal data (race, religion, geography, job type) and *tau-c* for ordinal and dichotomous variables (age, politics, class, sex, job level, religious participation).

Third, where I found relationships among more than one demographic variable and a Likert item, and where there was some theoretical interest in the relationships between the two correlations, I examined the reciprocal influences of the demographic variables. This was done by looking at the relationship between a given question variable and a demographic variable, while holding a second demographic variable constant (that is, while controlling for a second demographic variable). For this analysis, I used zero-order and first-order gamma. This type of analysis is particularly helpful when there is a relationship between a dependent variable (such as with the Likert items) and an independent variable (such as race), and you suspect that race is not the only factor influencing that relationship. By controlling for another variable (such as gender), one can see if that variable influences the strength of the original relationship between the independent and dependent variables.

Fourth and most important, I looked for differences between the four major research groups (white men, white women, nonwhite men, and nonwhite women) by examining the percentage responses to the question variables. These are the results upon which the discussion most often focuses. (Sampling error is ±3 percent; differences among groups are considered statistically significant when such differences are greater than or equal to 5 percent.) After looking for differences among the four groups, guided by clues from the three methods discussed above, I first examined differences within each of the four primary subject groups, and then again looked at these four subject groups when broken down further by the various demographic variables (the most important of which have proven to be race, gender, political ideology, class, job type, age, and religion).

While inferences from these data are integrated into the descriptive and normative analyses of affirmative action, no claim is being made that these data are perfectly representative beyond the work force of the California State Department of Parks and Recreation. It is well established, for example, that Californians are more liberal than others in the United States on civil rights issues. For example, in a recent poll, by 62 to 53 percent, more Californians than respondents from other states disagree that "we have gone too far in pushing rights in this country" (Skelton 1987, 28). And as far as the Parks Department is concerned, it might seem at first glance, given its mission to protect and interpret the resources within the parks, that many of those drawn to the department would tend to be more liberal than the population at large, especially within the ranger ranks. However, several factors mitigate this possibility. First, there is a large group of military veterans among the rangers, due to a large number of preference points (10 out of 100 possible) they receive for their military service during entry-level qualifications appraisals. Further, for over twenty years there has been an increasing emphasis on law enforcement in the department (rangers are now peace officers), so the traditional image of the ranger as a naturalist or "ecology freak" is decreasingly accurate. Arguably, the peace officer and military preference factors significantly balance the ideological composition of the depart-

TABLE 2
Ideological Self-Identification of Respondents
(in percent)

	Conservative	Moderate	Liberal	N
White				
Men	27	45	28	(158)
Women	21	44	35	(97)
Nonwhite				
Men	24	40	36	(129)
Women	17	56	27	(50)

ment's work force, which might otherwise be significantly more liberal than the population at large.

This analysis would seem to be supported by looking at how employees departmentwide identified themselves politically. The data in table 2 show that, at least among white men, no more respondents identify themselves as liberals than conservatives: roughly equal proportions identified themselves as conservative (27 percent) and liberal (28 percent) than as middle of the road (45 percent). As we might expect in the general population, 10–14 percent more white women, nonwhite men, and nonwhite women identified themselves as liberals than as conservatives, and even more said they were middle of the road politically.

Summary: Research Theory and Method

This chapter discussed the agenda for the research, the major theoretical expectations and puzzles that have guided the research, and the rationale for using both qualitative and quantitative research methods. Details of these methods were also described.

In the following chapters, we examine the qualitative interview data (chapter 4), and report the empirical results from the survey (chapters 5 and 6). These three chapters set the stage to discuss the importance of the results to the theory discussed earlier in this chapter before concluding with a discussion of the implications of the data for the normative ethical analysis of affirmative action (chapter 7).

4

IMPRESSIONS FROM THE WORKPLACE AND INTERVIEWS

THIS CHAPTER discusses the qualitative data generated by participant observation and interviews. The purpose is to convey general impressions gained from the interviews and observations in the workplace, not to catalogue or quantify all the sentiments expressed. The impressions gained through this phase of the research contributed to the types of questions asked in the survey phase, discussed in subsequent chapters.

The interviews followed an interview guide (appendix A). To elicit the spontaneous attitudes of respondents, I began the interview with a case study about discrimination; at several points, interviewees were asked to give their reactions to it. Respondents were encouraged to elaborate on their own attitudes toward affirmative action before the more structured part of the interview was undertaken. I concluded the interview by asking respondents to react to the most common arguments of social philosophers about affirmative action.

The Parks Department's Affirmative Action Program: Background

There is an ongoing struggle within the Parks Department over the nature of its affirmative action program. The struggle is over whether or not the program should attempt to ensure "pure equal opportunity" and the hiring of the "best qualified" or to give preference to target groups. Evidence of this struggle is found throughout the department, beginning with the various ways people define the nature and purpose of affirmative action. Some say affirmative action means equal opportunity, others emphasize that affirmative action is a remedial process that temporarily gives preference to women and nonwhite men in an attempt to increase their numbers in the work force.

Periodically, there are discussions within the department's affirmative action bureaucracy (the Human Rights Office, the Equal Opportunity Employment Committee, recruiters, counselors, and so on) over whether personnel procedures should aim for equal opportunity or practice preferential treatment. For example, drafts of revised hiring procedures have been circulated that suggest adding preference points to the scores of underrepresented candidates based on the extent to which the individual's ethnic group is underrepresented. This idea was rejected, not because the pure equal opportunity version of affirmative action prevailed, but because preference could be extended without explicitly adding preference points. Many felt that preference points would engender too much controversy and hostility; some felt that preferences in general detract from the true purpose of the department's affirmative action efforts, namely, promoting pure equal opportunity. But extending preference remains the idea behind the efforts to improve the representation of women and nonwhite men in the department's work force.

Other evidence illustrating the ongoing struggle over the soul of the department's affirmative action program can be seen in the resistance by some in the department's affirmative action bureaucracy to using any language in training and in documents that characterizes affirmative action as preferential treatment. Even though certain aspects of the department's affirmative action program are clearly preferential to women and nonwhite men, some within the affirmative action bureaucracy constantly maintain that the department's program is designed to ensure that in each case the best qualified are hired and promoted. Many in the department, however, view such assertions as disingenuous. Even some employees who originally supported the department's affirmative action programs now resent them. They were told the programs were meant to ensure equal opportunity, but they became disillusioned when they saw that the programs really promoted preferential treatment.

The lack of clarity about the nature of the department's program produces tensions all the way down the line. In one recent example, a hiring panel (made up of a white man, a Hispanic woman, and a Hispanic man) scored all three white male candidates above a Hispanic candidate (the scores ranged from 79 to 93 out of 100 possible points). The Hispanic male panel member wanted to hire the Hispanic candidate, but the Hispanic female was adamantly opposed and demanded that she be shown where it is written in department policy that one minimally qualified may be hired over the best qualified. Her perspective prevailed in the discussion, and the panel recommended hiring the white male candidate. The white male district superintendent, however, although conceding that the three white male candidates were better qualified, said that meeting the minimum qualifications was sufficient. He overruled the panel's recommendation and selected the Hispanic candidate because this would help meet the department's hiring goals for Hispanics. The point to note here is that even among members of this panel, which was formed to include nonwhites sympathetic to affirmative action, there was controversy and uncertainty over what affirmative action is really supposed to be.

The overruling of the panel's recommendation was greeted by great anger among white male staff members. These men complained that such policies destroy one's incentive to improve one's skills, and also erodes the incentive of affirmative action candidates, because skill is not the criterion for hiring or advancement. Such sentiments are common in the department.

Attitudes Toward Affirmative Action in the Parks Department

Hostility and Disillusionment

There is much hostility toward affirmative action in the Parks Department.[1] Some of the anger toward the department's affirmative action program is related to the struggle over the nature of the program. Some employees are angered by what they think is dishonesty in how the program is presented. They say they have been told that the program promotes equal opportunity and hiring the best qualified person regardless of gender or ethnicity; however, the more they experience it, the more they realize that the program provides very strong preferences, and they feel they have little if any chance for jobs and promotions. Some are angry because they oppose preferences on principle.

Others are angry and disillusioned by the dishonesty itself. For example, one white male employee endorsed goals and hiring the "just qualified" over the "best qualified" as a way to extend a "helping hand" to people who need it, but he complained that sometimes the department is not honest. He said the department tells its people to hire the "best qualified," but they really mean hire the "adequately" qualified in order to meet the department's affirmative action hiring goals. I know of several disillusioned individuals who stopped actively supporting the program when they concluded that the department was misrepresenting its program.

In some locations within the department, opposition to affirmative action is so strong that to avoid constant, uncomfortable verbal debates over affirmative action, one does not express support for affirmative action. Even supporters of affirmative action say nothing during affirmative action bashing sessions. At times, it seems that such policies are defended only during officially sponsored training sessions.

Some of the most outspoken critics of affirmative action believe their careers have been significantly, even irreparably, harmed by affirmative action. These people are sometimes so emotional in discussing affirmative action that their analysis of the situation becomes irrational and prone to exaggeration. For example, I heard more than once that affirmative action "quotas" preclude white men from being hired or promoted. I even heard this kind of sentiment in an entry-level ranger trainee class, where over half of the trainees were white men.[2] In another example, a young white man came nervously into the interview carrying several sheets of notes on all the reasons affirmative action was wrong. His hands shook slightly as he explained that he did not want to forget anything. Obviously, the issue was of intense personal concern for him.

At one training session, a manager expressed a common management complaint, that the effort to meet affirmative action goals detracts from the more central mission of the department: maintaining park facilities, serving visitors, and protecting resources. A maintenance manager stated that it seemed to him that his mission (maintaining parks) and the trainer's mission (promoting affirmative action) were incompatible. When the trainer did not immediately respond to this statement, another maintenance manager, visibly agitated and with his arms folded across his chest, said loudly: "You better answer that, Buster." The intensity of this response was especially out of place given the sedate context of the training session. This manager deeply resented affirmative action.

Hostility toward the department's affirmative action policy reached the extreme of people vowing not to cooperate with such efforts. One individual explicitly stated that if he were promoted and gained power, he would do everything he could to sabotage the program. While this kind of sentiment is not often heard, it raises the question: How many department employees are so hostile to affirmative action that they actively resist it?

Fear

Closely related to hostility is fear about the negative consequences of affirmative action on one's career. More specifically, some interviewees feared that if their attitudes about affirmative action were to become known by certain people in the department, their careers could be ruined.

For example, one black employee, while declining to be interviewed, complained that people were always challenging him about affirmative action. He thought that a great deal of the hostility in his workplace toward affirmative action was also directed against him. He said he just tried to do his job, to do his best, but his co-workers were watching him, waiting for him to make a mistake. He was very suspicious and worried about "paybacks" if he were to state his views: "I really don't want to deal with it, its not worth the risk, there are always repercussions. They [management] might call me in later and say 'Well, you said this. . . . ' " When I explained the procedures I was using to insure confidentiality, he said he would talk to his attorney and get back to me. He never did. Another black employee, a woman, expressed fear that, with all the pressure on supervisors to meet affirmative action goals, the program had become too much of a "numbers game." She said that she was afraid of a "backlash" in response to this pressure, and she wished the pressure would be eased.

Other employees, when considering applying for positions in the Human Rights Office (which has overall responsibility for the department's affirmative action policies), have been strongly advised by some field managers not to take such positions. They have been told that the Human Rights Office is "hated," and that those who work there are stigmatized, their future career options limited. The accuracy of these perceptions cannot be easily substantiated, partly because relatively few people have worked in the Human Rights Office. However, there may be some truth to this perception; most of the positions in the Human Rights Office are fairly high-level civil service positions, with little room for promotion. On the other hand, some have been promoted to positions outside the office.

In another example, I learned after conducting interviews in one location that a group of white men thought my research was not really for academic purposes but was part of a sting operation to discover who in the department was prejudiced. Some of these workers did not believe that the sampling was, in fact, random. One white man needed assurances that no personal characteristics would be mentioned in the research write-up that might make it possible for someone to identify him. He was afraid that if his views were to become known he would lose his chance for promotion.

The fears these examples illustrate may well have rational grounds. Virtually all hiring interviews in the department now include some questions designed to assess a candidate's knowledge of and level of support toward the department's affirmative action programs. Since the department is relatively small, it is not unusual for a person to know someone on the hiring panel. Therefore, it may be a rational decision to conceal one's true feelings about affirmative action.

Beyond these examples, I have often heard white men and women say that in the current climate, characterized by strong affirmative action goals, they would not encourage young white men to pursue careers in the department. One white woman, a strong supporter of affirmative action, said she would not advise her son to go into the Parks Department. It would be better for him to enter the private sector, she said, where there is not so much pressure to promote women and minorities.

To summarize: fears expressed in the workplace and during interviews seem to be of two types. First, there is fear about the consequences of letting one's true feelings about affirmative action become known. But since most respondents did not care about the assurances of confidentiality, and since many employees are outspoken about their negative attitudes toward affirmative action, those who fear having their views known are clearly in the minority. But the few who were fearful were *very* concerned about keeping their views to themselves. Several employees said that they did not trust the department to keep things confidential or to refrain from persecuting them for their views. For example, 14 of the nearly 500 surveys returned had the coded gender and ethnicity boxes cut off. A few added sarcastic comments about confidentiality, indicating that they did not believe that responses would remain confidential. Second, there is fear among (and for) white men that affirmative action will ruin their careers and that no amount of effort to improve their qualifications will help them.

Reactions to the Moral Issues

Indifference or Discomfort

Although apathy toward affirmative action is not prevalent, it was the overriding attitude of a small number of respondents. One rank-and-file Japanese woman indicated that she had no strong feelings about affirmative action and that she accepted it because it is the law. The entire interview indicated that she was not only unreflective about whether affirmative action is morally right or wrong, but also basically unreflective about moral values in general.

Another form of apathy reflects a purely individualistic egoism—among both those who might benefit from affirmative action and those basically opposed to it. For example, the black man discussed above, who was fearful of reprisals if he were to discuss affirmative action, said, "I'm already in the department; I'm not interested in [affirmative action]. It may be of interest to those who have not gotten in, but I'm not interested."

Over 5 percent of the respondents wrote in the survey's fill-in section comments like these: "Affirmative action is a question of law, not morals"; "What do morals have to do with affirmative action?"; "Affirmative action is not a moral issue"; and "Morality has nothing to do with affirmative action." Fill-in answers do not accurately assess the extent of such sentiments, but these responses do suggest a measure of intensity regarding the idea that moral concerns are relevant to affirmative action.

Such sentiments also came out in interviews. Some respondents suggested that affirmative action should be implemented because it is the law, or because it is department policy, and seemed to be indifferent to the moral arguments about it. Some who felt this way fit the stereotype of bureaucrats who cannot think for themselves and can only follow orders. For example, one Asian woman manager, who seemed to have no clear, principled, moral response to affirmative action, said, "I do feel strongly we should take the party line; . . . whatever the policies are, we should follow the guidelines." When asked, what if the guidelines are wrong? she replied, "I would probably leave." The only general ethical principle she could identify as important was "integrity."

Another example of this avoidance of moral issues by deferring to department policy can be seen in the following exchange with a white male manager (brackets indicate paraphrased material or clarification):

Q: [Do you think setting minority hiring goals is fair?]

A: I think it is if it is the policy of that agency. Maybe you're making policy by making that decision.

Q: [Was it fair to hire the black woman although a white man scored two points higher?]

A: On the surface it doesn't seem fair, but it has a lot to do with the policy you set for yourself first. If before you made your decision to hire 25 percent, and people were told about it, and perhaps there was in-service training and everybody knew what to expect, then on the surface it might seem unfair to take the lower scoring person, but . . . as long as you're within [official policy, then] nobody has any gripes, you knew it was coming.

Q: So fairness for you is. . . .

A: What you know up front.

According to this kind of bureaucratic mentality, anything is morally permissible as long as everyone knows what the policy is. This is one way to make irrelevant any discussion of the rightness or wrongness of affirmative action law and policy.

An Asian man, who also found it difficult to evaluate morally affirmative action, similarly concluded, "If it is the law, it's fair—what else is there?" While this response might seem to reflect a social contract view of justice—the right is that to which people agree—his overall axiom was obedience to the law and department policy. For example, when presented with the argument that affirmative action violates the rights of white men, he said, "You have to have sympathy for a person like that; however, there are certain things that you have to abide by, and until they can change that—it's—nothing is fair." This shift is interesting. Previously, he had said the law was fair because people agree on it. But here he admitted that the law may be unfair, even though people may agree on it (through the legislative process). Nevertheless he insisted that one must obey the law. This strict cleavage to law as the ultimate authority permittd him to side-step any serious discussion about the moral dilemmas posed by affirmative action and may have been related to his apparent discomfort with moral discourse in general.

But those who defer to department policy or civil rights law are not the only ones uncomfortable with addressing the moral issues surrounding the affirmative action controversy. For example, an affirmative action consultant who conducted training sessions for the department tried to get the people to stop thinking about affirmative action in moral terms such as fairness. Affirmative action, he said, may not be fair; the important thing is that it is an understandable, "reasonable," response to underrepresentation and past discrimination. Many supporters of affirmative action in the department seized on this term, replacing the idea that affirmative action is "fair" with the idea that it is "reasonable." I think they embraced the idea of reasonableness over fairness because they had been harassed by people complaining that affirmative action is unfair. An emphasis on reasonableness was a safe linguistic island to which they could retreat. Given the individualistic moral premises that dominate U.S. culture, these supporters did not have a moral language for responding to claims that affirmative action is unfair to individuals.[3]

An interview with a white woman manager who is a strong supporter of affirmative action illustrates the two points I am making here. First, many department employees are uncomfortable with discussing their overall ethical values; and second, even the strongest supporters of affirmative action would like to avoid taking a *moral* stand in defense of affirmative action. Early in her interview, this woman indicated that she was uncomfortable discussing moral values:

Q: What are the moral values that you feel are most important?

A: Don't shit close to the house. [She laughs, pauses a long time, and then gives off a distressed groan.] Moral values—everything I think of sounds so corny. I can rattle off a whole list of cliches. No, really, they sound really corny when I think about them.

She ended up saying that, for her, honesty is number one, followed by wanting to be happy and for her children to be happy. But her overall discomfort with moral discourse is also found in the following exchange about the morality of affirmative action.

Q: [Was the settlement of the discrimination lawsuit, which involved establishing hiring goals, and hiring a black woman who scored two points lower on the exam, fair?]

A: Ah—fair: as we all understand the word *fair?* I think it's fair for the black woman. I don't think its necessarily fair for the white males competing against them. So, what's fair for one doesn't necessarily make it fair for the other.

Q: Well, if you have two people with different views of what's fair, who is right? They both can't be right, can they, about what's fair? Or can they both be right?

A: I think they can both be right. I really do. I think [she refers to a white man who some think lost a job to a less qualified woman] is getting a raw deal. But I don't think [the hiring panel] should have made any selections any differently than they did. That was fair for them. So they're both right. . . .

Q: Are you saying that it's understandable that [the white male employee] thinks it's unfair, but really when you look at the big picture it [really is] fair? Or do you really think that both of these . . . views of fairness have equal validity?

A: I think they both have equal validity.

Q: If they both have equal validity, why is your conclusion right?

A: I'm not saying my conclusion is right.

Q: Well, your conclusion was that what happened was right. And I assume you mean morally right.

A: Because I believe in remedying past wrongs.

Q: So it seems to me that you have this larger picture of fairness, that is like an ultimate. . . .

A: Fair, right.

Q: And then you have, like, penultimate fairness. . . .

A: Subfairs [laughs] yes.

Q: And that, on balance, when you take them all into consideration. . . .

A: One's more fair than the other.

Q: And this big-picture view of fairness. . . .

A: Has more weight.

Q: Takes into view, overrides, the individual views of fairness?

A: That's right. [laughs]

This woman wanted to maintain that every moral view is equally valid. But when I pushed her a little, it became clear that she really did not think that arguments for and against the fairness of affirmative action were equally valid.

Part of the problem here is that this woman had some strong moral sentiments, such as the idea that past wrongs should be remedied, but she lacked an adequate moral language with which to discuss and defend her moral sensibilities. Without such a language, despite her strong support for affirmative action, she was forced to say that opponents of affirmative action had as strong a case against it as she did for it. She was not, however, the only person interviewed for whom the moral landscape is confused.[4]

Confusion and Inconsistency

Many respondents seemed to be at a loss when asked about their most important moral values. Quite often, long pauses suggested that a respondent rarely if ever reflected on his or her moral values. Some, when asked questions about whether some aspect of affirmative action policy is morally right, did not understand that the question had to do with *moral* values, and replied instead with irrelevant nonmoral statements of various kinds, including whether affirmative action benefits them. For example, one white male maintenance worker said that "retirement" was his most important moral value. It was not that he had no values; for example, he said he would like to see more equality in society. But he either did not know what the word *moral* means or had trouble articulating his values.

Some respondents could not even identify what moral values were important to them. Others came up with terms such as "honesty," "integrity," "hard work," "self-sufficiency," "excellence," "happiness," and "fairness" (understood as being unbiased). I had the impression that for some respondents these terms were cliches they used to have something to say; they did not know how to state what values were important to them.

The moral landscape surrounding the affirmative action controversy cannot help but be confused when many people's moral horizon is limited to such concepts as honesty and integrity and when few in the department discuss the heart of the matter: what principles of distributive justice ought to be applied, and whose interests ought to be promoted, when preferred jobs and salaries are distributed.

In summary, some respondents find the moral landscape very confusing. While they can ascertain whether affirmative action advances their interests, some cannot clearly identify any possible moral basis against or for affirmative action. This explains some of the ambivalence about affirmative action found in some respondents' attitudes.

Ambivalence

At least 10 percent of the respondents wrote statements in the fill-in section of the survey such as "Affirmative action is not completely right or wrong" and "I can't say whether or not it is morally right or wrong." Such answers in the fill-in section do not quantify ambivalence about affirmative action, but they do indicate ambivalence.

While some respondents confessed to being confused and ambivalent about affirmative action, the ambivalence of others is found in contradictory statements both for and against affirmative action. Some of this ambivalence was directly related to confusion about what affirmative action is supposed to be. Does it refer to pure equal opportunity: always hiring the best qualified, regardless of race or gender? Or is it about extending preferences to women and nonwhite men? Some respondents endorsed the nonpreferential aspects of the affirmative action program, while expressing hostility or ambivalence toward the preferential aspects of the program.

Some respondents said that what they really wanted was pure equal opportunity, but when asked about the preferential aspects of the department's affirmative action program, they endorsed preferential practices. Some white women were torn between pure equal opportunity, their men who may be harmed by affirmative action, and communitarian moral sentiments. The interviews indicate that more white women than white men expressed communitarian sentiments or looked at the overall effect of policies on the social whole. Nine of twelve (75 percent) of white women interviewees expressed strong concern for their group or the social whole, while only five of eighteen (28 percent) of white male interviewees expressed such sentiments.

While it is not easy to quantify ambivalence about affirmative action, my judgment is that only about 5 percent of department employees were so ambivalent that they could not bring themselves to evaluate affirmative action. So while many employees expressed ambivalence about affirmative action, most either opposed or supported it. The next section discusses the most commonly heard arguments for and against affirmative action.

Responses to the Philosophical Arguments About Affirmative Action

Virtually all of the arguments voiced by social philosophers about affirmative action were also expressed in the interviews. However, most respondents did not articulate a comprehensive and coherent ethical perspective. Their arguments can be divided into two broad areas of concern.

First, most arguments centered on whether affirmative action fulfills, promotes, or works against the equal opportunity distributive justice principle. Given the dominance of philosophical Liberalism in U.S. culture, it is not surprising that most arguments about affirmative action revolve around its impact on equal opportunity. The language of equal opportunity is pervasive in the culture, and there is an overwhelming cultural consensus in favor of this principle (see chapter 6). The second major argument is whether, overall, affirmative action benefits one's group, workplace, or society.

The following discussion is divided into arguments against affirmative action and arguments for it, stated in terms of the two positions: individualism (embodied in the equal opportunity principle) and communalism (embodied in the consequentialist principle).[5]

Arguments Against Affirmative Action

The strongest opponents of affirmative action were those whose opposition is grounded in principles that place a premium on the individual, such as the idea of equal opportunity.

THE EQUAL OPPORTUNITY PRINCIPLE

One of the most common objections to affirmative action suggests that it is just plain old discrimination (sometimes labeled reverse discrimination, or sometimes the complaint was that affirmative action is just a numbers game, or that all hiring and promotion should be color-blind). Such sentiments imply that past and present discrimination against women and nonwhite men is morally equivalent to the discrimination involved in affirmative action programs. Of course, such arguments ignore the very different purposes of the two types of discrimination: one seeks to exclude, the other seeks to include, individuals from traditionally vilified groups. These arguments also presuppose that concern for the individual ought to be the most important principle when evaluating policies.

This premium on the individual is seen even more clearly in another common objection to affirmative action. Most respondents objected strenuously to rationales for affirmative action grounded in notions of compensatory justice. This sentiment was especially strong among white men. A common objection to compensatory justifications for affirmative action was that affirmative action unfairly compensates women and nonwhite men by requiring that a few white men pay for discrimination for which they themselves are not responsible. This objection took different forms.

For example, for two white men, rejection of compensatory ideas was not grounded in purely individualistic premises. While they agreed that it is unfair to ask a few individuals to bear the cost of remedying discrimination, they suggested that, instead, the costs of overcoming discrimination and its effects should be socialized and assumed by society at large.

In another example, a high-level, white, male manager, who called himself a fanatic about hiring the best qualified and insuring equal opportunity, but who was nevertheless willing to give preference to a woman or nonwhite man in situations where the competitors' qualifications are equal, was "adamantly opposed" to compensatory rationales for affirmative action. He argued: "Two wrongs don't make a right. We've made a lot of mistakes in the past, . . . but I personally feel no sense of personal shame about what has happened in the past. . . . Maybe that's a cop-out. . . . [But] now is the time to correct it, not by going to the other extreme, because if we do, then we discriminate against some other group."[6]

While at first glance this man sounds libertarian in his analysis of the issue, he did not go as far as libertarian thought tends to do, viewing affirmative action as a violation of rights. When asked to respond to such a libertarian argument, he said: "I don't know about violating rights, you don't need to get carried away with phrases like that, but I don't feel like we have to correct, to overcorrect everything that is done in the past." And in spite of his strong, principled objection to deviating from the merit principle, he also brought consequentialist considerations into his evaluation of affirmative action. He thought that hiring goals could be beneficial to the institution and society if quality was not sacrificed. And he believed that hiring goals could promote social stability and, if not pushed too fast, could reduce tensions among people.

The white, male, evangelical or fundamentalist Christians who were interviewed were unanimous in rejecting compensatory rationales for affirmative action. All three of these men argued that affirmative action is deceptively billed as equal opportunity and that it is really racist. All three insisted that pure equal opportunity and merit hiring ought to be the standard. They rejected compensatory ideas because of the tendency toward overgeneralization (discussed in chapter 2). One complained that white males never get any breaks; the other two emphasized that they are not guilty of discriminating against anyone. All three insisted that people can get jobs if they want to (expressing strong faith in the American Dream) and complained that affirmative action works against individual initiative.[7] Finally, all three suggested that "God Himself" makes people different, so that differences in rewards based on talents are based on God's will and too much equality precludes excellence. As striking as the symmetry in the views of these three conservative Christians is the lack of ambiguity in their assertions: they were supremely confident in the rightness of their views.

Two Jewish respondents also had strong feelings against affirmative action and particularly against compensatory justice rationales for it. Both of these individuals complained that their careers had been irreparably harmed by affirmative action. Both strongly stressed that racial classifications (or any group classifications) themselves are dangerous and argued that protection of the individual is the most important value of a decent society. Both explicitly grounded this sentiment in the historical experience of the oppression of Jews. Both strongly rejected compensatory rationales for affirmative action, because given their experience as Jews, they did not feel they owed anyone anything. One told me that he was the first person in his family in generations to have a chance to be happy and that he should not have to sacrifice his chance for happiness to compensate people for discrimination for which he is not culpable.

Unlike the evangelicals, they recognized discrimination against women and nonwhites as a problem. One suggested alternatives: for example, strong enforcement of antidiscrimination laws and an emphasis on recruitment and education. After these things are done, he believed, there would be no reason to be concerned with how things are distributed. The other agreed that recruitment and even goals are acceptable *if* the best qualified are ultimately hired. He also stressed that education is the key to overcoming unequal opportunities. He differed from his colleague in his desire for a more egalitarian and environmentally conscious world. But he thought that affirmative action cannot contribute to a new social order, because it uses the racist methodology of the old order. He concluded that affirmative action may be well intentioned, but that it threatens to stamp out excellence and is definitely unjust to individuals.

One of the ideas expressed by these two Jewish employees was shared by some of the more hostile opponents of affirmative action, who argued that all ethnic groups have been discriminated against at one time or another in the United States and that it is wrong to single out nonwhite ethnic groups for favoritism, since white ethnics have overcome discrimination without help.

CONSEQUENCE-BASED ARGUMENTS AGAINST AFFIRMATIVE ACTION

There are two major consequentialist objections to affirmative action. The first suggests that affirmative action leads to inefficiencies in institutions, which harm these institutions and society itself. The second suggests that affirmative action is not needed. The first is probably the more common.

The overwhelming concern expressed in the interviews and observed in the workplace is that affirmative action harms the mission of the Parks Department. Some employees suggested that the huge amount of time, money, and effort spent on affirmative action makes it particularly hard for the department to fulfill its primary mission, especially in times of statewide budget cuts and increasing department responsibilities.

But by far the most commonly heard complaint about how affirmative action harms the department is that it reduces the quality of employees. Many complained that affirmative action has become a "numbers game," where qualifications are less important than meeting "quotas." Even some supporters of affirmative action thought there is too much pressure to meet hiring goals; they feared that this has led (or may lead) to the hiring of unqualified workers. Some added that affirmative action hinders individual initiative and creates a work environment where excellence is not rewarded. Still others complained that affirmative action has a negative impact on the morale of white and nonwhite employees alike, by limiting the opportunities of white men, on the one hand, while calling into question the competence of women and nonwhite men, on the other hand. Concern about the quality of employees seemed to be expressed most often by white men but was shared by many women and nonwhite men.

Others argued that affirmative action harms society at large, by negatively affecting the efficiency of its institutions, partly by placing unqualified people in positions of responsibility. A few people suggested that affirmative action harms the self-esteem of women and nonwhites, by implying that they are not good enough to get the job without preferences, and may thereby hinder such people from effectively contributing to society. Still others believed that affirmative action increases hostility among ethnic and gender groups.

The second fact-based objection, that affirmative action simply is not needed, is reached through two analyses. The first suggests that discrimination is in decline and that opportunity exists (even if perfect equal opportunity has not yet been achieved), and so affirmative action is not really needed. This perspective is often tied to the idea that the cure (affirmative action) is worse than the disease (discrimination). This line of thought seems to assume that the rationale for affirmative action is equal opportunity and not some other ends-based social goal. (Arguably, the assertion that affirmative action is not needed may implicitly depend on deontological premises, such as the notion that pure equal opportunity is always morally right.) The second analysis asserts that there are better ways than affirmative action to deal with discrimination.

These beliefs were expressed in several ways. For example, one person insisted that there is work out there for people who want to work. Others explicitly professed faith in the "American Dream" or asserted that opportunity already exists for all people.[8] Others believed that discrimination is no longer prevalent. Still others suggested that while the American Dream is intact, there is a dangerous "welfare" mentality that leads many people to fail. For example, a few respondents asserted that it is usually people's bad attitudes that cause them to fail, such as expecting to get something because of one's gender or ethnicity, instead of by one's qualifications.

The second major idea underlying the belief that affirmative action is no longer needed asserts that there are better ways than affirmative action to overcome discrimination, unequal opportunity, and the resulting inequalities. As mentioned earlier, one Jewish employee suggested strong enforcement of antidiscrimination laws. However, all respondents were asked if the enforcement of antidiscrimination laws were enough, and few thought it was. Many thought this idea was naive, and pointed out that since people today are aware that discrimination is illegal, they do not make statements implicating themselves, making it very difficult to prove discrimination.

Much more often, opponents of affirmative action suggested that improving education is the proper alternative to affirmative action. Some respondents seemed to think that education is the key to remedying all social ills related to discrimination. One white female ranger, for example, said that providing education is the "extent of responsibility" society owes minorities. Two white men and one black woman were less strident but still argued that the "focus" of the antidiscrimination fight ought to be on education. Even among supporters of affirmative action, many heavily stressed education. Some (two black women and one white man) even seemed to view it as a panacea for all the social ills related to discrimination. Almost all respondents, whether proponents or opponents of affirmative action, at one time or another emphasized education (or work-related training) as a key to dealing with discrimination.[9]

Arguments Sympathetic to Affirmative Action

As with arguments against affirmative action, many of the arguments in its favor center on the equal opportunity principle; other arguments focus on its consequences.

THE EQUAL OPPORTUNITY PRINCIPLE

Probably the rationale most commonly offered by those promoting affirmative action within the Parks Department is that affirmative action promotes equal opportunity. This is seen in the language used by supporters. For example, although most supporters do not think that the best qualified are being hired because of the pressure on supervisors to meet numerical hiring goals, they still use language expressing the idea that—after carefully recruiting women and nonwhites and after carefully scrutinizing the personnel procedures for bias—hiring panels should hire the best qualified.

Others argued that while the ultimate ideal is pure equal opportunity and merit hiring, affirmative action is a remedial process in response to the lack of equal opportunity. The implication, seldom stated explicitly, is that sometimes the ideal has to be temporarily set aside in order to promote long-term the ideal of equal opportunity.[10] But nevertheless, in spite of the compromising of the ideal, the rationale for affirmative action remains, ultimately, the ideal of pure equal opportunity.

Some respondents argued that affirmative action is true to equal opportunity by asserting that it is needed for women and nonwhite men to "get their foot in the door," or to be given a "fair chance" or "equal consideration" for jobs and promotions. Several respondents pointed out that, before affirmative action, many job classifications in the department were not open to women and nonwhites, and they argued that without affirmative action such persons would never have been considered seriously.[11] Several women asserted that white men still controlled the department and that without the pressure from affirmative action, these men would not give up their monopoly of power. Thus, those expressing sentiments in favor of affirmative action justified their views in terms of the principle of equal opportunity and believed that, at least in the long term, affirmative action promotes this principle.

Others, however, although expressing the prevailing assumption in favor of the principle of equal opportunity, made statements that seemed to qualify or make less absolute their support for the ideal of equal opportunity. For example, some endorsed the equal opportunity principle but then said that hiring a less qualified person (to meet hiring goals) would be acceptable if the qualifications were not too far apart—in other words, as long as the person could do the work. Others suggested that hiring the less qualified of the applicants was acceptable if the department then provided these persons with training so they could do the job. The interesting thing here is that while the people making these concessions expressed support for hiring the best qualified (a dominant Liberal idea), what was actually more important to them was that the employee could *do* the job. While these individuals professed allegiance to the equal opportunity principle, getting well-qualified workers was more important than ensuring that the best-qualified person always got the job. For those who qualified their support for the equal opportunity principle, the consequences of affirmative action on their workplace team was more important to them than protecting in an absolute way the principle of pure equal opportunity.[12]

Others qualified their endorsement of pure equal opportunity by supplementing the equal opportunity principle with another principle, which then was given priority. For example, one black female maintenance worker did not like preferences or the affirmative action "numbers game" and insisted that the American Dream is real: one can overcome discrimination with hard work. She also forcefully rejected preferences for nonwhites and women, as well as notions of compensatory justice.[13] But when it came down to whether she endorsed affirmative action hiring goals that helped a black woman, she said that they are fair because they benefited the woman, "giving her a job and trying to improve things" for her.

This woman seemed to approve of pure equal opportunity, but when given a concrete example of a black woman who benefited from affirmative action preferences, she endorsed hiring the woman, even though she scored lower on the hiring interview.[14] This suggests that among respondents who strongly endorsed the rhetoric of equal opportunity, some thought that perfect equal opportunity is not an inviolable principle—that there may be times when it is more important to help people in one's group. If concern for the group can sometimes override strong beliefs in individualistic notions of equal opportunity and hiring the best qualified, the question arises: How prevalent is a group-concern principle when people evaluate affirmative action?

My impression from the interviews is that all groups are heavily influenced by the equal opportunity rhetoric so pervasive in the Liberal culture. Nevertheless, it seems that women and non-white men, more than white men, articulate group-sensitive concerns that mitigate the influence of more individualistic equal opportunity ideals. In fact, some are suspicious of the idea of equal opportunity and hiring the best qualified based on merit. One Hispanic male ranger, for example, said, "Merit is a good principle . . . if you could somehow make an objective criteria for merit. . . . But the problem is that the people who have done the discrimination are defining merit."[15]

My impression is that, of the various groups interviewed, blacks are more suspicious of the principle of equal opportunity than other groups. For example, of seven blacks interviewed, none gave unqualified support to the equal opportunity principle. One explicitly rejected it, saying that the very idea of hiring the "best qualified" is stupid, because many people can do any job: "There is no such thing as any person who is best for a job. People may . . . approach jobs in different ways, but you can take any number of people and make [them] successful in any job." The "best qualified" criterion "automatically will stack up in favor of . . . white males," because blacks have been disenfranchised and therefore will never have as qualified a background and experience as whites.

Several blacks favored equal opportunity but then heavily qualified these sentiments. One maintenance worker from the inner city, after agreeing that equal opportunity was a good principle, qualified this by saying that the equal opportunity principle should be put in perspective, arguing that the idea of hiring the best qualified is stacked against blacks, because they do not get a decent education or good training. He also argued that nine out of ten applicants can do the job and added that he knew that discrimination was prevalent because he had often been encouraged over the telephone but discouraged when he applied for a job in person.

Another maintenance worker favoring equal opportunity argued that hiring the well qualified instead of the best qualified was acceptable because it benefited society and promoted integration. Another black man strongly endorsed hiring the best qualified candidate but said that blacks should compete against blacks, and whites against whites, for specific numbers of jobs determined by parity goals. Another black man, a fervent believer in equal opportunity, said that for now this principle must be compromised and that, while he understood how this seems unfair to the white male, one must "defer to the greater good." He emphasized that it was good that affirmative action has benefited blacks.

The point that united the five blacks who expressed reservations about the equal opportunity principle is solidarity with their black ethnic group, which seems to be at the base of their rejection of an exclusively individualistic approach to the evaluation of affirmative action. These respondents seem to discern that the equal opportunity principle may not always work in the interest of their group and that therefore the equal opportunity principle may require modification. However, only one black attacked the principle itself.

For more pragmatic reasons, others have reservations about hiring the best qualified. These people suggested that the whole idea of hiring the best qualified is naive. For example, one high-level, white manager—interestingly, a strong, politically active Republican—said that pure equal opportunity is a flawed concept, because he can train almost anybody to do most of the jobs for which he is responsible.

Another high-level, white, male manager, in a briefing of his managers about affirmative action, asserted that affirmative action is supposed to promote competition on an equal basis. But then he questioned one of the main tenets of the equal opportunity principle, the idea of hiring the best qualified. "I despise the term *most qualified*," he said, because the hiring process is always subjective, and three different hiring panels interviewing the same people would usually select different candidates. This manager wanted his employees to focus on a candidate's long-term potential.

Many people within the affirmative action bureaucracy ridicule the idea of hiring the best qualified and feel it is just a tool people use to legitimate hiring who they wanted in the first place. At the same time, most of these individuals do not seriously question the equal opportunity principle itself.

Finally, a minority of women and nonwhite men seem willing to compromise on the equal opportunity principle. These individuals explicitly endorsed preferential affirmative action on the grounds of compensatory justice. For example, among those interviewed, three of five Hispanics, two of seven blacks, six of twelve white women, two of three native Americans, and one of four Asians expressed sympathy for compensatory rationales for affirmative action.[16] Only one of eighteen white men, a maintenance worker, agreed that the compensatory argument for affirmative action made sense. However, he added that he started at the bottom and deserved what he had. While there were differences among those sympathetic to compensatory rationales for affirmative action, what united these people was their rejection of an approach that evaluates affirmative action by examining only its impact on individuals.

The strongest advocates of affirmative action were those who most self-consciously rejected the individualism of the equal opportunity principle. These strong advocates were also the most likely to endorse compensatory rationales for affirmative action. But others who expressed strong individualistic sentiments (such as individual initiative, competitiveness, and merit hiring) qualified these sentiments with strong expressions of concern for their group or for the society as a whole. Greater proportions of each ethnic and gender group were more concerned about the good of the group or the whole society than endorsed compensatory rationales for affirmative action: Of those interviewed, 15–33 percent of white men, 70 percent of blacks, 60 percent of Hispanics, 67 percent of native Americans, and 75 percent of white women gave at least qualified support for affirmative action—support grounded, at least in part, in group-sensitive sentiments.

This analysis, combined with the earlier analysis of arguments against affirmative action, suggests that there is a relationship between relative individualism in one's overall moral outlook and one's view about affirmative action: the more individualistic one's moral predisposition, the more likely one is to oppose affirmative action; the more concern one expresses for the group or the social whole, the more likely one is to approve of affirmative action.

One interesting example of sentiments grounded in group concern (sentiments that provide a strong rationale for affirmative action), is the idea that since all groups pay taxes, it is only fair that one's own group benefit from tax expenditures. I never encountered this argument among social philosophers, but it was voiced by one native American man and two black men. This argument reflects a group-based principle of distributive justice, which runs directly counter to the individualism of the equal opportunity principle. This argument is consistent with other group-based arguments voiced by nonwhites, arguments that bring the good of one's ethnic group into the public policy equation.

CONSEQUENCES-BASED ARGUMENTS FOR AFFIRMATIVE ACTION

Several respondents (three white men, one white woman, one black man) pointed out that social stability has been threatened by the exclusion of nonwhites from the mainstream of society and argued that affirmative action benefits society by promoting social stability and preventing revolution. Others suggested that affirmative action benefits society by promoting harmony among ethnic and gender groups or by developing the talents of individuals from groups whose talents were usually previously denied to society. Sometimes this argument was put in the form of affirmative action success stories—how a woman or nonwhite was doing a terrific job after getting a position she or he probably would not have received in the absence of affirmative action.

Another argument asserts that affirmative action integrates the work force and thereby provides better public service. For example, an ex–inner city black employee suggested that a black ranger would have greater success in dealing with black visitors than a white ranger, whom some black visitors may distrust.

Another argument, especially among managers, concerns demographic changes that are increasing the proportion of nonwhites in California.[17] The concern is that since groups such as Hispanics and blacks traditionally have not been exposed to or employed in nonurban parks, they may not fully appreciate their value. This argument continues that if the mission of the Parks Department is to succeed, the growing nonwhite constituency must be integrated into the deparment and visit the parks so that members of these groups will appreciate and support the department's mission. The overall moral argument is that affirmative action benefits both the department and society as a whole (assuming that preservation of parklands is important to society), by insuring continued public support for parks in times of great demographic change.

Summary

This chapter introduced the wide range of sentiments held by persons within the California State Parks Department about affirmative action policies. There is a struggle within the department over the definition and nature of the its affirmative action program. Some people are intensely hostile toward affirmative action in general and the department's policies in particular. Some employees fear retaliation if they speak candidly of their feelings about affirmative action, while others do not hesitate to express their views. A few are apathetic about affirmative action, although most are not.

Some people have very little idea about what moral values are important to them, let alone how to think about moral issues such as affirmative action. These people therefore do not know how to evaluate morally affirmative action policies. Many do not seem to understand what ethical issues are at stake in the controversy, and others are torn or ambivalent about competing ethical arguments about affirmative action, sometimes endorsing contradictory principles and ideas.

People's moral judgments regarding affirmative action depend on the relative priority they accord individual interests, on the one hand, and one's group or society's interest, on the other. There does seem to be a relationship between individualism in one's overall moral outlook and attitudes toward affirmative action: the more individualistic one's outlook, the more likely one is to oppose affirmative action. The more concern one expresses for the group or the social whole, the more likely one is to approve of affirmative action.[18] Those who strongly oppose affirmative action tend to do so with a principled individualism, asserting that the best qualified individual ought to always be hired. Less strong opponents seem to argue more about the consequences of affirmative action and tend to be more ambivalent about affirmative action—in part because they can see that it may also have positive consequences. Ambivalent supporters of affirmative action have an individualistic concept of equal opportunity, as do its opponents, but nevertheless end up supporting affirmative action, either by approving preferential affirmative action or by expressing moral concern for society or the group, which contradicts an exclusively individualistic approach.[19] The strongest proponents of affirmative action give their group or society as whole a clear and strong priority over the individual.[20]

Related to this individualism/group continuum, nonwhites and white women are much more likely than white men to express group-focused ideals and concerns. This suggests that the differences among these groups is probably a significant part of the reason why nonwhites and white women are more supportive than white men of affirmative action. But at the same time, such expressions remain sketchy and incomplete. For example, group-focused concern is expressed in phrases here or there; one man said, for example, that affirmative action is good because the survival of blacks is important and is promoted by affirmative action. But even among those who express such group-sensitive concerns, few articulate a coherent moral vision about what concepts of the Good ought to inform the ends that people pursue. The interviews suggest that some people have intuitions in the direction of more communitarian values but do not have a language adequate to express such sentiments.[21]

This summary reviews impressions of department employees' attitudes. These impressions were gained through several years of observing and analyzing the language of individuals in the workplace and through analyzing the interviews with fifty department employees. Chapters 5 and 6 report the results of the survey research. Impressions gained from the qualitative phase of the research reported in this chapter, as well as from questions raised by the social philosophers in the literature about affirmative action, provide a framework for analyzing the results of the survey. Chapter 7 then summarizes and comments on the results of both phases of the empirical research.

5

SURVEY RESPONSES:
APPROVAL AND DISAPPROVAL OF
AFFIRMATIVE ACTION

T HE AXIAL questions of this chapter are: Do respondents approve of affirmative action? And if so, to what extent do they approve, and which types of affirmative action policies and practices do they endorse? This provides a background to chapter 6, which asks: *Why* do the respondents approve or disapprove of affirmative action? That is, what are the reasons, including the moral arguments grounded in principles of distributive justice, that inform respondent approval or disapproval of affirmative action?

Responses to some of the survey questions are divided into four sections. The first examines respondents' sentiments toward the civil rights movement as well as their perceptions about prejudice in society and in their workplace. The second section examines how respondents define affirmative action and understand its purpose. The third section examines respondents' approval or disapproval of the morality of affirmative action. The last section examines respondents' approval or disapproval of specific affirmative action programs.

The examination of respondents' attitudes in each of these areas involved an analysis of each of the independent variables for which this study controlled. First, I examined the survey data for significant differences among the four main subject groups: white men, white women, nonwhite men and nonwhite women. Second, I looked for significant differences across nonwhite racial and gender subgroups: specifically to see if native Americans, Asians, Hispanics, and blacks differed and if there were differences related to gender among these subgroups. Third, the data were examined for significant differences among and within each of the four main

subject groups when these groups were subdivided by political ideology, age, job type, class, and religion.

Views on Prejudice

There was wide agreement among respondents from all subject
groups that *racial and gender prejudice is very common in the
United States* (see statement 1, table 3). However, nonwhite men
and women and white women felt this more strongly than white
men—they more often strongly agreed that prejudice is common.
Further, race enhanced differences between the sexes on this issue.[1]

When asked if racial or sexual prejudice in the Department of
Parks and Recreation was very common today, fewer respondents
agreed than agreed with the previous statement. The figures (in table 3) show that white men have different perceptions from the
other three groups about the extent of prejudice in society and especially in the Department of Parks and Recreation. (Only 5 percent of white men agreed strongly, compared with 15 percent of
white women, 17 percent of nonwhite men, and 21 percent of nonwhite women.) Within nonwhite subgroups, blacks agreed most
often and most strongly that prejudice is prevalent, followed by
Asians, Hispanics, and native Americans.

Women agreed more often and more strongly than men both
that prejudice is prevalent in society[2] and that prejudice is prevalent in the department.[3] However, this was not true for Asian men
and women: more Asian men than women agreed that prejudice is
common in society (93 percent) and in the department than Asian
women (70 percent and 60 percent, respectively).[4]

Analysis according to political identification shows that liberals
more than moderates and conservatives agreed that prejudice is
prevalent in society[5] and in the department.[6] For white men and
women, this relationship was moderately strong. The relationship
was weak among nonwhite men and women: being nonwhite
seems to level the impact of ideology when evaluating the extent
of prejudice. Ideology is a more important factor in perceptions
about prejudice among whites than nonwhites.

Views on Civil Rights

The survey also examined attitudes toward the civil rights movement in order to establish overall attitudes toward movements that

promote the interests of nonwhites and women. Respondents were asked if they think that *civil rights leaders are pushing too fast* and if they are pushing *in the wrong direction* (statements 3 and 4, table 3). More respondents agreed with the latter statement than with the former.

Generally, on these two questions, blacks disagreed more often and more strongly, followed by Asians, and then by Hispanics and native Americans. And continuing the pattern discussed earlier, more Asian women (50 percent) than Asian men (11 percent) agreed that civil rights leaders were pushing too fast. On both statements, black women unanimously disagreed, while 83 percent of black men disagreed.[7]

Older people agreed slightly more often than younger people that civil rights leaders were pushing too fast[8] and in the wrong direction.[9] Age difference was especially pronounced among white men and women. Among white men over fifty years of age, 50 percent agreed that civil rights leaders were pushing too fast, and 61 percent agreed they were pushing in the wrong direction. Only 25–30 percent of white men under fifty agreed with these two statements.[10]

Among white women over fifty years of age, 48 percent agreed that civil rights leaders were pushing too fast, and 50 percent thought these leaders were pushing in the wrong direction. Only 10–15 percent of white women under fifty agreed that civil rights leaders pushed too fast, and only about 20 percent agreed that these efforts were in the wrong direction. With nonwhite men, a different pattern emerges: 33 to 35 percent over fifty and under thirty years of age agreed that civil rights leaders were pushing too fast, while very few nonwhite men in their thirties and forties agreed. This pattern of agreement between the oldest and youngest nonwhite men continues in response to the "wrong direction" statement. No clear differences related to age could be seen among nonwhite women.

Slightly more lower-class than higher-class persons agreed that civil rights leaders were pushing in the wrong direction.[11] Nonwhite male managers agreed more than nonwhite male rank-and-file employees that civil rights leaders were pushing in the wrong direction (44 to 29 percent). White maintenance personnel, whether management or rank and file, revealed more anti–civil rights sentiment than those in other job classifications (60 to 70 percent were in agreement, versus agreement ranging between 20 and 35 percent for nonmaintenance personnel). Interestingly, white, male maintenance workers agreed with the anti–civil rights statements more than other white men in the department.

TABLE 3
Agreement with Survey Statements, by Race and Gender
(in percent)

	White		Nonwhite		
	Men	Women	Men	Women	(N)
PREJUDICE AND CIVIL RIGHTS					
1. Prejudice is common in society today.	76	85	88	90	(417)
2. Prejudice is common in the Parks Department.	37	57	66	77	(415)
3. Civil rights leaders are pushing too fast.	30	21	27	27	(417)
4. Civil rights leaders are pushing in the wrong direction.	41	27	32	25	(402)
AFFIRMATIVE ACTION					
5. Affirmative action is morally right.	62	85	82	89	(416)
6. Affirmative action law is wrong and should be changed.	53	26	28	20	(415)
7. Affirmative action is wrong and should not be obeyed.	7	3	9	2	(411)
8. Affirmative action should be implemented because it is the law (or policy), and ethical concerns are not very relevant.	18	16	24	25	(408)
RELIGION					
9. My religious beliefs strongly affect my views about affirmative action.	24	21	28	26	(403)
10. My religious beliefs lead me to disapprove of affirmative action.	8	6	4	7	(396)
11. My religious beliefs lead me to approve of affirmative action.	25	20	33	33	(391)
GOAL-TYPE AFFIRMATIVE ACTION					
12. I approve of parity hiring goals.	46	68	69	74	(425)
13. I approve of focused recruitment.	58	66	66	68	(423)
14. I approve of supplemental certification.	40	64	60	76	(334)

INDIVIDUAL INTERESTS AND THE COMMON GOOD

					(N)
15. With public policies, it is better to focus on groups than on individuals.	81	82	85	90	(410)
16. I place the social good over my own advancement.	46	55	44	51	(394)
17. I place doing well financially above overcoming economic inequality in society.	50	32	40	18	(400)

CONSERVATIVE AND LIBERTARIAN PERSPECTIVES

					(N)
18. Affirmative action violates the rights of white men.	75	57	46	46	(409)
19. Prosecution is a better response to discrimination than affirmative action.	53	37	48	47	(407)
20. White men have benefited from past discrimination.	71	77	83	83	(418)
21. Preferential treatment of victims of discrimination is appropriate compensation.	25	30	39	47	(403)
22. Affirmative action helps many who do not need help.	63	54	48	55	(400)

THE AMERICAN DREAM

					(N)
23. With effort, anybody can succeed.	75	63	74	65	(425)
24. White men should accept fewer opportunities so that others may have a chance to succeed.	15	21	20	22	(416)
25. Improving education is the best way to deal with discrimination.	89	87	80	81	(426)
26. More money should be spent on education.	85	84	92	94	(418)

LIBERAL PERSPECTIVES

					(N)
27. Equal opportunity is a very good moral principle.	97	94	92	96	(418)
28. It is usually possible to identify who is best qualified.	82	75	63	69	(419)
29. It is morally right always to hire the best qualified.	74	70	65	71	(405)
30. Affirmative action promotes equal opportunity.	25	41	51	61	(406)

TABLE 3, continued
Agreement with Survey Statements, by Race and Gender
(in percent)

RATIONALES FOR AFFIRMATIVE ACTION IN THE PARKS DEPARTMENT

					(N)
31. Affirmative action is needed to remedy the effects of discrimination.	47	73	73	86	(422)
32. Affirmative action is needed to ensure that women and non-white men get serious consideration.	34	63	71	86	(421)
33. The naturally talented deserve the best jobs.	68	52	62	47	(405)
34. The naturally talented deserve higher salaries.	65	41	52	47	(400)
35. Inequality should be reduced between talented people and less talented people who try equally hard.	15	30	40	41	(402)
36. Affirmative action should be broadened to include all disadvantaged persons.	27	26	50	43	(390)

CONSEQUENTIALIST PERSPECTIVES

					(N)
37. I can tell whether affirmative action is right or wrong without thinking about its effect on society.	29	18	42	36	(382)
38. On balance, affirmative action benefits society.	64	81	82	87	(403)
39. Affirmative action reduces tensions among different racial and gender groups.	38	56	64	59	(399)
40. Affirmative action reduces employee quality in the Parks Department.	69	48	40	26	(404)
41. Affirmative action harms the mission of the Parks Department.	57	37	33	19	(415)
42. Overall, the workplace is better because of affirmative action.	40	60	67	67	(395)

AFFIRMATIVE ACTION TRAINING IN THE PARKS DEPARTMENT

					(N)
43. The department adequately explains the reasons for its affirmative action program.	35	47	47	45	(418)
44. The department provides adequate affirmative action training.	38	40	30	29	(416)

AFFIRMATIVE ACTION POLICIES IN THE PARKS DEPARTMENT

					(N)
45. Its goals have become quotas, mandating the hiring of precise numbers of women and minorities.	71	65	73	80	(417)
46. I approve of its Women in Trades program.	77	80	78	85	(407)
47. I approve of its discrimination complaint process.	80	82	77	81	(395)
48. I approve of having EEO counselors available to advise employees of their rights.	90	93	91	96	(419)
49. I approve of its sexual harassment policy.	94	97	85	87	(417)
50. I approve of recruiting persons on welfare.	38	50	50	50	(422)
51. I approve of reasonable accommodation for the disabled.	94	98	92	98	(431)
52. Women and minorities tend not to be interested in State Parks jobs.	29	13	18	16	(420)
53. It is especially hard to dismiss affirmative action candidates.	76	58	58	57	(411)
54. Affirmative action harms transfer opportunities; women and minorities get the best locations.	41	46	30	32	(408)

GENERAL ETHICAL OUTLOOK

					(N)
55. A good family life is more important than making a lot of money.	94	93	94	98	(422)
56. Compassion and caring should be a basis for public policies.	76	63	77	74	(409)
57. Compassion and caring tend to lead to support for affirmative action.	68	72	55	70	(404)
58. Preferential treatment is unfair—other groups have overcome discrimination without it.	48	26	30	30	(409)
59. Money used on affirmative action should be spent elsewhere.	57	43	34	31	(403)

Note: For exact wording of survey statements, see appendix B.

Conservatives were more likely than moderates or liberals to agree that civil rights leaders were pushing too fast[12] and in the wrong direction.[13] Christians agreed with these statements more than non-Christians (by about 8 percent for white men, and 12–15 percent for white women, nonwhite men, and nonwhite women.[14] It also seems that evangelical Christians agreed with these anti–civil rights sentiments more than other Christians.[15]

Views on Affirmative Action

How moral issues are framed can be a decisive influence on attitudes about such issues. It is important, therefore, to analyze what comes into the minds of respondents when they think about affirmative action.

As I argued in part 1, affirmative action is best understood as a continuum of responses to discrimination. This continuum ranges from what I call protective affirmative action—which includes efforts to reduce and prevent discrimination in the workplace—to preferential affirmative action—which usually involves numerical hiring goals. One cannot always be sure which concept of affirmative action was in the minds of respondents as they answered survey questions. As shown in chapter 4, this was due largely to the ongoing struggle within the department over the nature and definition of the its affirmative action program, specifically over whether the department should implement a protective or preferential form of affirmative action.

A clearer picture of what people have in mind when they think about affirmative action can be gained from three sources of information: the institutional context that contributes to understandings about affirmative action, impressions gained from the interviews when interviewees were asked what they understood the meaning and purpose of affirmative action to be, and responses to a survey fill-in question posing the same question.

In 1975, the department established hiring goals to bring about labor force parity—a work force reflecting the racial and gender balance of the work force at large. However, most of the language used to explain and justify the program uses rhetoric of equal opportunity. It is not surprising, then, that in response to the survey's fill-in question, almost 40 percent of respondents defined affirmative action as equal opportunity and over a third mentioned the attempt to reach parity. This squares with the impressions from the interviews, where roughly equal proportions of interviewees had equal opportunity in mind as had goals in mind when they thought about affirmative action. Meanwhile, in the fill-in section of the survey, less than 5 percent referred to affirmative action as preferential treatment, while about 20 percent offered a negative definition.[16] Probably the best conclusion is that most people believed that the department's affirmative action program intends to promote equal opportunity but that goals are a central part of the program. Sometimes goals were seen as a strategy to promote equal opportunity, at other times as contradicting equal opportunity. Many people, however, did not strictly equate goals with affirmative action. And most people recognized that goal-type affirmative action programs do extend preferential treatment to women and nonwhites. This point is demonstrated further by responses to a survey proposition (statement 45, table 3) that suggests that *the department's goals have become quotas.* Majorities of all subject groups agreed. Nevertheless, people did not strictly equate affirmative action with goals or preferences, since more resondents approved of affirmative action in general than approved of goals in particular.

This somewhat fluid picture of what people had in mind provides a context for the next two sections, which analyze attitudes about the morality of affirmative action and specific affirmative action policies.

Views on the Morality of Affirmative Action

Affirmative Action as Morally Right

Respondents were presented with several statements concerning their overall evaluation of the morality of affirmative action. To the proposition, *In general, I think affirmative action is a morally right public policy,* majorities of all of the four main research groups agreed, including a surprising 62 percent of white men (statement 5, table 3). The following strongly agreed: 15 percent of white men, 16 percent of white women, 19 percent of nonwhite men, and 32 percent of nonwhite women. Interestingly, only 7 percent of white men, 5 percent of white women, 3 percent of nonwhite men, and 2 percent of nonwhite women disagreed strongly. At first glance, then, there seems to be significant moral approval of affirmative action as public policy, even among white men.

TABLE 4
Agreement that Affirmative Action Is Morally Right, by Ideology
(in percent)

	Conservative	Moderate	Liberal	(N)
White				
Men	64	58	70	(148)
Women	85	79	97	(90)
Nonwhite				
Men	71	79	88	(118)
Women	71	88	100	(45)

Note: Agreement includes both "agree" and "strongly agree."

Asians and blacks agreed most often (92 percent), followed by
Hispanics (78 percent). Native American men and women differed
widely: only 58 percent of these men agreed (11 percent strongly),
but 100 percent of these women agreed (29 percent strongly), total-
ing 69 percent of native American respondents. Eleven percent of
native American men strongly *disagreed*. Although the small
numbers of native American respondents urge caution in generalizations, nevertheless, on question after question, native American
men were more hostile to affirmative action than all other nonwhite subgroups, both in general and in response to questions
about specific affirmative action policies and their premises. Native American men answered very similarly to white men on most
questions. Meanwhile, native American women usually were more
sympathetic to affirmative action, including its implementation
and premises.

Women more than men agreed that affirmative action was morally right.[17] Asians are an exception: 97 percent of Asian men
agreed (15 percent strongly), 80 percent of Asian women (10 percent
strongly). Again, while the numbers are relatively small, this pattern continues on many of the survey's questions. While on some
questions Asian men and women answered similarly, when they
differed, which was often, Asian men tended to be more supportive
than Asian women of affirmative action.

Liberals were more likely than moderates and conservatives to
agree that affirmative action is morally right.[18] But as the data in
table 4 show, white male and female conservatives agreed that affirmative action is morally right more than moderates, but less
than liberals. It is surprising to find white conservatives endorsing

affirmative action more than moderates. This is possibly because conservatives, more than moderates or liberals, conceive of affirmative action more in terms of their ideal of pure equal opportunity than in terms of preferential affirmative action.

While there is little difference related to age among nonwhite women, there are some age-related differences within the other groups. Among white men, those in their thirties were least likely to agree that affirmative action is morally right (only 53 percent), while those in their forties were most likely to agree (72 percent). White men under thirty and over fifty fall in the middle (62 percent). Similarly, all white women in their forties agreed, while 80 percent of white women in other age groups agreed. No inference can be made about nonwhite women because of low numbers of respondents, but there appear to be big differences among older and younger nonwhite men. Nonwhite men in their forties and fifties agreed much more often, at 83–86 percent, than nonwhite men in their twenties and thirties, at 55 percent.

During the interviews, a few conservative, evangelical Christians strongly expressed disapproval of affirmative action. Overall, however, when asked if their religious beliefs influenced their views of affirmative action, most interviewees thought their beliefs did not. Those who did think their religious beliefs were influential usually could do little more than mention the golden rule as the religious principle that informed their views. With the exception of evangelical Christians and two persons educated in the Jesuit tradition, respondents seemed unaware of any of the major traditions in religious ethics. No one, including black respondents, ever mentioned Martin Luther King or his ideas, or spoke in terms of social justice.

Thus, the impression resulting from the interviews is that religion had a minimal effect on respondents' attitudes toward affirmative action. This impression was confirmed by responses to several survey statements about the influence of religious beliefs on attitudes toward affirmative action. These responses further indicate that those whose views were influenced by their religious beliefs were much more likely to approve than disapprove of affirmative action. I also found evidence of the relative lack of influence of religion on respondents' attitudes when looking at the entire range of survey questions for differences related to religious affiliation and levels of commitment. Overall, I discovered few such differences related to religion (statements 9–11, table 3).

There were, however, some differences among persons holding different types of jobs. For example, among white men in maintenance jobs, only 55 percent of rank and file (9 strongly) and 63 percent of management (none strongly) agreed that affirmative is in general morally right. Agreement was slightly greater among white men in visitor services jobs, at 60 percent for rank and file (14 percent strongly) and 67 percent for management (23 percent strongly). Agreement was highest for rank-and-file white, male professionals and administrators, at 71 percent (19 percent strongly). Nonwhite, male, rank-and-file maintenance and visitor services personnel were less supportive of affirmative action (79 and 77 percent, respectively) than nonwhite, administrative/professional men, of whom 96 per- cent agreed (30 percent strongly) that affirmative action is morally right.

To summarize, then, when presented with the general statement, *Affirmative action is morally right,* there was a high rate of agreement among each of the four main subject groups, although fewer white men agreed. However, while strong majorities agreed in general, the apparent consensus broke down in the answers to a series of clarifying questions designed to assess attitudes toward affirmative action in more detail.

Affirmative Action as Wrong

Respondents were presented with the statement, *Affirmative action law is wrong and should be changed.* When the proposition about affirmative action was posed in a this way, excluding the word *morally* and including the idea of changing the law, support for affirmative action dropped, especially among white men (statement 6, table 3). This represents a decline of almost 15 percent from the general proposition. With the affirmative action question framed in this new way, a majority of white men now expressed disapproval of affirmative action.[19]

The other three subject groups agreed with this revised framing of the question much less than white men, dropping 10 percent. This poses a puzzle: why is there a discrepancy in responses related to different forms of the question? But before addressing this puzzle, we need to ask: what differences are there among and within subgroups with regard to the statement that affirmative action law is wrong and should be changed?

Among nonwhite subgroups, patterns are similar to those found under statement 5, table 3, dealing with the overall morality of af-

TABLE 5
Agreement that Affirmative Action Is Wrong
and Should Be Changed, by Ideology
(in percent)

	Conservative	Moderate	Liberal	(N)
White				
Men	64	54	41	(146)
Women	35	24	18	(91)
Nonwhite				
Men	37	35	14	(115)
Women	25	23	8	(47)

Note: Agreement includes both "agree" and "strongly agree."

firmative action. Blacks remained the most supportive of affirmative action, followed by Asians and then Hispanics. These groups strongly disagreed that affirmative action law and policy is wrong and should be changed: all black women disagreed, 94 percent of black men (53 percent strongly), 75 percent of Asian men (32 percent strongly), 80 percent of Asian women (10 percent strongly), and about 70 percent of Hispanic men and women (25–21 percent strongly). However, only 44 percent of native American men disagreed (11 percent strongly), apparently differing from native American women, 86 percent of whom disagreed. As found in the previous question, the answers of native American men resemble the responses of white men more closely than the responses of other nonwhite subgroups.

More women than men disagreed that affirmative action law is wrong and should be changed.[20] There is also a moderately strong relationship between political ideology and this negative view of affirmative action law: more liberals than moderates and conservatives disagreed.[21] And when we control for political ideology, political ideology significantly enhances differences related to sex (table 5).[22]

There is a weak relationship between social class and this negative assessment of affirmative action. People who identified themselves as lower class agreed more than upper-class persons that affirmative action law is wrong and should be changed.[23] The only difference related to religious affiliation was found between evangelical Christians who agreed more often than other Christians that affirmative action is wrong and should be changed (62 percent to 34 percent).[24] Non-Christian white women were slightly more sympathetic than Christian white women to affirmative action and its premises.

Finally, differences were found related to age. Those in their forties seemed most sympathetic to affirmative action. Only 45 percent of white men in their forties agreed that affirmative action law is wrong and should be changed, compared to 61 percent of those age fifty and older, 55 percent of those in their thirties, and 63 percent of those under thirty. No white women in their forties agreed with this proposition, only 20 percent of those in their thirties agreed, 45 percent over fifty, and 71 percent of those under thirty. For nonwhite men, the only possible difference was that 45 percent of those under thirty agreed that affirmative action law is wrong, and this is 15–18 percent higher than the responses of their elders. For nonwhite women, again those in their forties were most sympathetic to affirmative action: only 11 percent of nonwhite women in their forties agreed that affirmative action law is wrong, compared with 21–23 percent for all other ages. Despite the low numbers of respondents in some of the categories above, the pattern seems to hold across many of the survey questions.

Among persons holding different types of jobs, there were some significant differences related to the statement that affirmative action law is wrong and should be changed, especially among white men. For example, among white men in maintenance jobs, 78 percent (28 percent strongly) of rank-and-file workers and 63 percent (13 percent strongly) of maintenance mangers thought that affirmative action law is wrong and should be changed. But fewer white men in visitor services jobs agreed, only 55 percent of rank and file (13 percent strongly) and 43 percent of management (10 percent strongly). Among rank-and-file professionals, still fewer white men (20 percent) agreed. This pattern, with administrative/professional white men most supportive of affirmative action, followed by visitor services and maintenance personnel, is similar to the responses under the previous cast of the question, and with several other types of questions about affirmative action and its premises.

As with white men, nonwhite men in maintenance jobs, whether management or rank and file (38 percent and 34 percent, respectively), agreed more often than those in other classifications that affirmative action law is wrong (only 21–25 percent of those in visitor services and professional/administrative jobs agreed). Thus, for nonwhite men, similar differences exist with regard to the previous proposition, Affirmative action is morally right, but with this cast of the question these differences are more pronounced. (Such comparisons could not be made with women, as they had not yet significantly penetrated maintenance and management jobs.)

On Disobeying Affirmative Action

The interviews revealed some sentiments in favor of sabotaging the department's affirmative action efforts. To assess the extent of such sentiment, the survey asked for reactions to the statement, *Affirmative action law is wrong and should not be obeyed.*

Few employees in any of the subgroups agreed with this extreme position. Men agreed more than women.[25] Blacks *disagreed* most, followed by Asian men and Hispanics. Those native Americans, white men, white women, and Asian women who disagreed did so much less strongly than members of other groups. While the employees who agreed that affirmative action law should not be obeyed were few, they still may be capable of doing significant damage to an affirmative action program. However, fewer male managers (2–4 percent) agreed than male rank-and-file employees (10 percent). This suggests that with men, those most able to sabotage the program are least likely to do so.

For white women, although the figures are not clearly significant, it appears that the opposite is true: more female managers (6 percent) than rank-and-file workers (2 percent) agreed that affirmative action policy should be disobeyed. (There were too few nonwhite female managers to draw inferences. More important, no nonwhite women agreed that affirmative action law should be disobeyed.)

White male Christians (2 percent) agreed less than white male non-Christians (12 percent) that affirmative action law should not be obeyed. Fewer white female Christians (2 percent) agreed than white female non-Christians (7 percent). However, the opposite seems to be true for nonwhite men, among whom more Christians (11 percent) than non-Christians (5 percent) endorsed sabotaging affirmative action programs.

The Relevance of Ethics

As chapter 4 explained, some employees do not think that affirmative action is a moral issue. Some asserted that because it is the law (or department policy), ethical concerns are not relevant. To assess the extent of such sentiments, the survey included the statement: *Affirmative Action policy should be implemented because it is the law (or departmental policy), and ethical concerns are not very relevant* (statement 8, table 3). Among the four main subject groups, less than 25 percent agreed with this statement. More Asian men than Asian women agreed, 24 percent and 10 percent, but men and women did not differ within other nonwhite ethnic subgroups. Older respondents, slightly more than younger respondents, agreed that ethical concerns are not relevant to the affirmative action issue.[26] This age difference is found among white men, nonwhite men, and nonwhite women, but not among white women.

What is more interesting than the small differences among the four subject groups, or the differences among persons of different ages, is that a small but significant number of respondents denied that ethical values are important to their attitudes about affirmative action and asserted simply that if affirmative action is the law or policy, then it should be supported. It would be interesting to know if most public policies based in law enjoy such apparently unqualified, uncritical support.

Views on Affirmative Action Practices

Hiring Goals and Labor Force Parity

Perhaps the most central practice of the Parks Department's affirmative action program involves its hiring goals, which promote parity representation of women and nonwhite men. To assess the extent to which respondents approved of this element of the department's program, respondents were asked to respond to the statement: *In general, I approve of using hiring goals to try to make the department's work force as ethnically and sexually diverse as is society.*

Responses to this statement indicate the extent of support for affirmative action, not understood as protective antidiscrimination measures, but understood to include the preferential treatment of women and nonwhite racial groups. In other words, here we find attitudes not primarily about the idea of pure equal opportunity or protective affirmative action, although this might be in the minds of some, but primarily and clearly about preferential affirmative action. It is clear that the overwhelming majority of people equate goals with preferences, because most respondents agreed that goals had become quotas in the department (statement 45, table 3). Since no concept conveys a stronger image of preference than *quotas*, clearly when responding to questions about quotas, people had in mind a preferential form of affirmative action.

For all four of the main subject groups, 14–16 percent fewer respondents supported goal-type affirmative action preferences than agreed that, in general, affirmative action is morally right (statement 12, table 3). Only 46 percent of white men agreed that hiring goals are good (10 percent strongly); however, 22 percent strongly disagreed. Nevertheless, large majorities of white women and nonwhite men approved of goals (17 percent and 27 percent strongly, respectively). Nonwhite women approved most of all (33 percent strongly). Women were more likely than men to approve of goals.[27] These data show that support for affirmative action, when understood to involve goals, was strong in all groups except white men, the majority of whom disapproved of goal-type affirmative action, many strongly.

With this question about attitudes toward goals, differences previously noted among nonwhite ethnic groups are not as pronounced as they are with regard to more general statements about the morality of affirmative action. Black men and women still agreed more emphatically than other groups (71 percent and 83 percent). But when the question was about goals, Asians and Hispanics were not clearly different. Native American men approved of goals more than white men, at 56 percent (22 percent strongly), but 33 percent of the 44 percent who disagreed did so strongly. Interestingly, while on virtually all other questions, native American men were at least as hostile as white men to affirmative action and its premises, here, with regard to goals, *unlike* white men, a majority of native American men supported this key element of affirmative action policy.

The more liberal the respondent, the more likely she or he was to endorse goals.[28] However, this was not true for each of the four main subject groups. Among white men, more liberals than moderates approved of affirmative action goals, and more moderates than conservatives approved of affirmative action goals. But among white women, nonwhite men, and nonwhite women, while liberals approved of affirmative action goals most often, moderates and conservatives did not differ (table 6). This again suggests that differences related to political ideology were less pronounced among white women, nonwhite men, and nonwhite women than they were among white men.

For differences related to age, the patterns noted previously continue. White men in their forties (57 percent, 20 percent strongly) approved of goals more than those in their thirties (44 percent,

TABLE 6
Agreement with Use of Hiring Goals
to Promote Work Force Parity, or by Ideology
(in percent)

	Conservative		Moderate		Liberal		
	Agree	Strongly Agree	Agree	Strongly Agree	Agree	Strongly Agree	(N)
White							
Men	34	2	44	5	59	18	(153)
Women	65	5	63	5	78	38	(92)
Nonwhite							
Men	64	18	59	16	80	43	(117)
Women	62	13	65	17	92	54	(47)

only 7 percent strongly), and much more than those over fifty and under thirty (about 35 percent of whom approved, and none strongly). White women in their forties also approved most often (89 percent, 28 percent strongly), followed by those in their thirties (74 percent, 20 percent strongly), while even fewer white women over fifty approved of goals (55 percent, and only 5 percent strongly). Among nonwhite men, those in their thirties (76 percent) and forties (72 percent) were most likely to approve of goals, compared to 66 percent of such men over fifty, while only 42 percent of nonwhite men in their twenties approved of goals. With nonwhite women, low numbers urge caution, but 86 percent of these respondents in their thirties approved of goals, compared with 78 percent of those over forty, and 59 percent of those under thirty.

Again, among white women, non-Christians approved of goals more than Christians (90 percent and 58 percent; 40 percent and 7 percent strongly). However, the opposite was true for white men and nonwhite men: among white men, Christians approved of goals more often than non-Christians (52 percent and 40 percent); while among nonwhite men, Christians approved of goals more than non-Christians (73 percent and 44 percent). No difference is evident among nonwhite women when divided into Christian and non-Christian subgroups.

By about 12 percent, more white male and white female managers than rank-and-file employees approved of goals, 72 percent and 67 percent. Among rank-and-file white men, fewer visitor services personnel approved of goals (37 percent) than maintenance workers (44 percent) or administrative/professional employees (50 percent).

Among rank-and-file nonwhite men, fewer maintenance workers approved of goals (23 percent) than visitor services or administrative/professional employees (36 percent and 41 percent).

Focused Recruitment and Supplemental Certification

Two of the most controversial means of promoting hiring goals in the department are focused recruitment and supplemental certification. Arguably, taken together, hiring goals, focused recruitment, and supplemental certification form the core of the department's affirmative action efforts.

Focused recruitment involves efforts to expand the applicant pool of minorities and women, without paying similar attention to expanding the pool of white male applicants, by recruiting in places with high concentrations of target group members. Supplemental certification gives hiring interviews to target-group members who may not have scored high enough on initial interview lists to receive a face-to-face interview (if and when there are no target group members reachable by normal criteria). Both focused recruitment and supplemental certification practices go beyond pure equal opportunity and extend explicit preference to nonwhites and women.

When presented with the statement, *In general, I like the DPR's focused recruitment of minorities and women,* respondents answered similarly to their responses about hiring goals (statement 13, table 3). It is not surprising that responses would be similar, because goals and focused recruitment are so closely linked—it is hard to think how such goals could be pursued without such recruitment.

Supplemental certification, however, is another matter. It is possible to promote goals without extending further preference through supplemental certification after the applicant pool has been expanded. Supplemental certification extends preference further and is therefore more controversial than either goals or focused recruitment. For example, in response to the statement, *In general, I approve of the DPR's use of supplemental certification,* among all four main subject groups, support for supplemental certification was far below that for affirmative action in general (statements 14 and 5, table 3). Among white men, white women, and nonwhite men, support for supplemental certification was also significantly below support for parity hiring goals.

More blacks and Asians approved of supplemental certification (71 percent) than Hispanics (62 percent), while only 45 percent of native Americans approved. Hispanic women approved of supplemental certification more than Hispanic men (71 percent and 60 percent). Native American women seemed to agree more than native American men (75 percent and 38 percent). Likewise, black women agreed more than black men (100 and 65 percent). Asian men and women approved similarly (71 percent). These figures suggest a continued pattern of strong black and Asian support, followed by solid Hispanic support for such strong affirmative action measures, while native American men disapproved of such measures.

Liberals were more likely to approve than moderates and conservatives of supplemental certification.[29] However, separate analysis of the responses of each of the four main subject groups reveals that this is only true among white men and women. Among white men, 48 percent of liberals approved of supplemental certification, compared to 44 percent of moderates and only 28 percent of conservatives. Among white women, more liberals approved (80 percent) than other groups, but again, among white women, more conservatives than moderates approved (60 percent to 53 percent).

Although no differences based on age were found among nonwhites, among whites and especially white men, age differences were present similar to those found on previous questions. More white men in their forties approved of supplemental certification (55 percent) than those over fifty and in their thirties (about 30 percent). Fewer white women over fifty approve of supplemental certification (55 percent), than those under fifty (65–75 percent).

No difference is evident among women when divided into Christians and non-Christians. (On other questions, non-Christian white women were slightly more sympathetic to affirmative action than white Christian women). Non-Christian white men approved of supplemental certification more than Christian white men (45 percent and 35 percent). This reverses the differences between white male Christians and non-Christians from their respective rates of approval of parity hiring goals—perhaps suggesting that white male Christians are more concerned with means than are their non-Christian counterparts. Nonwhite men were also divided by 10 percent, but in the opposite way: with Christians approving of supplemental certification more than non-Christians (63 percent and 53 percent).

Managers and rank-and-file employees differed in an opposite way than they did in responding to labor parity goals. While managers approved of parity hiring goals more than rank-and-file employees, among white men, white women, and nonwhite men, more rank-and-file workers than managers approved of supplemental certification: white male rank-and-fle employees (43 percent), white male managers (33 percent), white female rank-and-file employees (72 percent), white female managers (53 percent), nonwhite male rank-and-file employees (61 percent), and nonwhite male managers (50 percent). So while more managers approved of goals than rank-and-file employees, fewer managers than rank-and-file workers approved of supplemental certification as a means to these goals.

Summary

The most striking finding shown in this chapter is that while there was significant agreement among all groups that affirmative action is morally right, this consensus quickly broke down when affirmative action was discussed with greater specificity. When explicitly preferential types of affirmative action policies were mentioned, support dropped, and dropped most among white men.

Nonwhite women were most supportive of affirmative action, both agreeing that it is morally right and approving of it in practice. White women and nonwhite men were usually fairly close in the extent of their approval of the general idea and specific practices of affirmative action and were slightly less enthusiastic than nonwhite women. (On some points, nonwhite men were slightly less enthusiastic about affirmative action than white women.) For all three target groups (nonwhite men, nonwhite women, and white women), there was about 15 percent greater agreement that, overall, affirmative action is morally right than there was approval of the practices of the department's affirmative action program.

Only 10 percent of nonwhite women and about 15 percent of white women and nonwhite men consistently opposed both the idea and specific practices of affirmative action. As the estimates derived from several questions show, all four groups divide into three categories: strong supporters, strong opponents, and ambivalent supporters, who endorse the overall morality of affirmative action but who dislike many of the central elements of the department's affirmative action program (table 7).

A good part of the ambivalence in the swing groups is related to how affirmative action is defined. Given the data summarized in this chapter and the impressions from the interviews, it seems

TABLE 7
Support for and Opposition to the Overall Morality
of Affirmative Action
(in percent)

	Consistent Support	Swing Group[a]	Consistent Opposition
White			
Men	45	17	38
Women	70	15	15
Nonwhite			
Men	70	12	18
Women	75	15	10

a. Supports affirmative action in general but rejects most preferential affirmative action practices.

likely that many in the swing groups do not think that the preferences involved in goals and other measures, such as focused recruitment and supplemental certification, fulfill the "ideal" of affirmative action (understood as equal opportunity).

Also of interest are differences among nonwhite ethnic subgroups. Blacks were the most consistent and strong in their approval of affirmative action, followed closely by Asians. Hispanics were usually somewhat less enthusiastic than blacks and Asians. Black and Hispanic women were even more supportive of affirmative action than their male counterparts, but this was not true for Asian men and women. Native American men were usually as hostile or more hostile to affirmative action than white men, and while we cannot be certain about native American women respondents due to small numbers, it seems that on most questions these women were much more supportive of affirmative action than their male counterparts.

There are also some interesting relationships between political ideology and attitudes toward the morality of affirmative action. Political ideology was an especially decisive factor in the attitudes of white men, a moderately important factor for white women, and only slightly related to the attitudes of nonwhite men and women. As expected, liberals were more likely than moderates and conservatives to approve of the idea and practice of affirmative action (although for nonwhites and white women, conservatives were not always less supportive than moderates). Being nonwhite, and to a lesser extent being a white woman, tended to level out differences related to political ideology, whereas being white strongly increased differences related to political ideology. (It seems likely that nonwhites who identified themselves as conservative may have had more individualistic moral virtues in mind than issues related to the public realm, since it seems that conservative self-identification did not significantly put a dent in support for affirmative action among nonwhite people.)

In general, religion was not a very important factor in the attitudes of most respondents toward affirmative action. But when it was, it was more likely to influence attitudes toward approval than disapproval. The differences noted among Christian respondents were between evangelicals and nonevangelicals. (There were no differences found between Protestants and Catholics, nor any relationship between religious commitment—participation—and attitudes toward affirmative action.) Moreover, when persons with different religious affiliations did differ, they were much more likely to be white than nonwhite. In a way similar to the dynamic with political identity, being nonwhite tended to unify the views of those with different religious perspectives, but being white strengthened those differences in attitudes.

The other notable pattern is that for white women, and even more for white men, those in their forties tended to be most supportive of affirmative action, and those fifty and older tended to be the least supportive. Age differences did not seem as prevalent with nonwhite respondents, although it seems that young nonwhites tended to be less supportive of affirmative action than their elders.

The next chapter will keep these patterns in mind as it examines *why* the respondents felt as they did about the idea and practice of affirmative action.

6

SURVEY RESPONSES:
MORAL ARGUMENTS ABOUT
AFFIRMATIVE ACTION

THE PURPOSE of this chapter is to examine the survey data in order to analyze the affinity of the various groups toward the moral arguments underlying affirmative action.

Individual Interests and the Common Good

Chapter 1 discussed how one of the key moral dilemmas posed by policies such as affirmative action boils down to the relative priority that ought to be placed on individual interests, on the one hand, and society's interests or the overall common good, on the other. The analysis of the interview data in chapter 4 suggests that those who place a priority on the overall social good or the good of the group over the individual tend to be more supportive of affirmative action. The survey research, therefore, set out to assess the extent to which persons from the different subject groups tend to approach ethical issues in an individualistic rather than a group-focused way.

When respondents were presented with the statement, *In general, when making public policy, it is best to look more at how policy affects groups than on how such policy affects any single individual,* large majorities of the four main groups agreed (statement 15, table 3). White men and nonwhite women differ significantly on this question, the only other difference is related to ethnicity: fewer native American men than any other group agreed with this proposition (63 percent). No other significant subgroup differences exist. This is especially interesting because, on almost all other questions, there were differences related to political ideology and at least small differences related to gender.

TABLE 8
More Concern with the Common Good
over Personal Advancement, by Ideology
(in percent)

	Conservative	Moderate	Liberal	(N)
White				
Men	31	52	49	(141)
Women	53	56	55	(84)
Nonwhite				
Men	33	47	47	(114)
Women	43	40	73	(43)

Note: Agreement includes both "agree" and "strongly agree."

These responses seem at first glance to represent a striking rejection of a rigidly individualistic way of evaluating public policies. However, the reality is more complex. For example, another proposition (statement 16, table 3) stated, *I am more concerned with the overall social good than with my own personal advancement.* Here, when personal interests were included, individualism was a stronger factor than it seemed at first: about half of all respondents placed a higher priority on the social good than on their own personal advancement. The only clear difference among the four main groups is between nonwhite men. Fewer blacks agreed than any other subgroup, and blacks were the only ethnic subgroup to differ significantly from the other nonwhite groups. Only 27 percent of black men agreed, compared to 50 percent of black women. While not clearly statistically different, native American men (53 percent) agreed more than white men (46 percent), Asian men (48 percent), and Hispanic men (40 percent).

There are also differences related to political ideology. The data in table 8 show that among all men, fewer conservatives than moderates and liberals agreed that the social good should come before personal advancement. Liberal nonwhite women, more than their moderate and conservative counterparts, placed a greater priority on the social good. Interestingly, there are no discernible differences among white women related to political ideology, but when conservative white women are compared to all conservative men, these women were much more concerned about the common good.

Employees with different types of jobs also differed; rank-and-file employees agreed with this proposition more than managers.[1]

TABLE 9
Agreement that Doing Well Financially Is More Important
than Overcoming Financial Inequality in Society, by Ideology
(in percent)

	Conservative	Moderate	Liberal	(N)
White				
Men	56	46	49	(145)
Women	42	38	21	(89)
Nonwhite				
Men	58	36	30	(108)
Women	43	32	31	(45)

Note: Agreement includes both "agree" and "strongly agree."

While the four main groups did not differ greatly on the question
of placing the social good over personal advancement, when individual and social interests are defined in economic terms, there are
greater differences among these groups. For example, in response to
the statement, *Doing well financially is more important to me than
overcoming financial inequalities in society* (statement 17, table 3),
the figures suggest, and statistical analysis demonstrates, a significant
gender gap.[2] What is particularly interesting is that clear majorities
of all groups except white and Asian men thought that overcoming
economic inequality is more important than personal economic advancement—and even 50 percent of white men agreed (only 42 percent of Asian men concurred). This is hardly strong evidence of an
individualistic, self-interested approach to public policy questions.

    There are other interesting patterns related to this survey state-
ment. More conservatives than moderates and liberals placed personal financial gain over overcoming societywide economic inequality.[3]
But as the data in table 9 show, the only subgroup with *majorities*
who disagreed with this proposition is conservative men. More conservative women agreed with this proposition than their moderate
and liberal counterparts, but even among all conservative women,
only a minority rated personal financial gain over economic equality.

    Among whites, the gender gap on this question is found whether
respondents identified themselves as conservatives, moderates, or
liberals. But among nonwhites, the gender gap is found only among
conservatives. This suggests that all white women are more likely
than all white men to approach public policies with an eye to the
common good, but among nonwhites, this may be true only among
conservatives. This brings some empirical support to the impression
gained in the interviews: that white men are more likely than white

women and nonwhite men to approach public policies such as affirmative action in an individualistic way, and that this may be the base of some of the division between white men and others on the affirmative action issue. At the same time, the data suggest that the differences related to the relative priority placed on the individual and the social whole may be smaller than the interviews suggest.

The analysis of responses to the statements designed to reveal the extent of individualism in the ethical world view of the respondents suggests that individualism is not the axial premise behind the attitudes of most of the respondents. This conclusion should be kept in mind as reactions to statements about the specific moral rationales for affirmative action are examined.

Conservative and Libertarian Analyses of Affirmative Action

In the United States, libertarians and conservatives tend to agree on domestic policy: that people have a right to what they possess as long as they did not personally acquire these possessions coercively, and that taxation beyond the minimum necessary to provide the bases of social solidarity (and free markets) is unfair. The premium is on the individual, and individuals ought not be adversely impacted by attempts to promote any particular vision of the common good—when they are adversely impacted in this way, their autonomy is violated as they are treated as means, not as ends in themselves.[4]

Sometimes during interviews people voiced similar sentiments: that affirmative action violates rights. Sometimes such people said the rights of white men were being violated by reverse discrimination—the implication being that, just as the individual was not being respected when discrimination occurred in the past, now the same thing is happening to white men. The survey attempted to quantify this sentiment.

Affirmative Action as a Violation of Rights

For example, one survey statement suggested, *Affirmative action violates the rights of individuals who happen to be male and white* (statement 18, table 3). Most white men agreed with this statement (39 percent strongly). This is puzzling, because at least 15–20 percent of these white men who believed that affirmative action violated their rights also responded in such a way as to be classified as strong supporters of affirmative action. But how can 15–20 percent say that affirmative action violates rights and still come across as strong supporters of affirmative action? In agreeing that affirmative action violates rights, it seems that most white male respondents must think affirmative action is unfair to individuals. It seems unlikely that white men who support preferential affirmative action practices would accept libertarian analyses claiming that affirmative action violates the basic human right to honestly acquired holdings.

A majority of white women also agreed that affirmative action violates rights. But minorities of nonwhite men and women agreed. Here again, more respondents *agreed* that affirmative action violates rights than *disapproved* of affirmative action. This suggests that although a significant number of those who endorsed affirmative action had sympathy for conservative or libertarian arguments, many, even among those who conceded that affirmative action violates rights, did not find libertarian and conservative reasoning decisive. Ambivalence such as this was also found in the interview data described in chapter 4.

Nearly as many native American women (67 percent) as native American men (74 percent, 42 percent strongly) agreed that affirmative action violates rights. Asian men and women appear to differ widely: only 35 percent of Asian men agreed, compared to 67 percent of Asian women. About 46 percent of Hispanic men and women agreed, and black men (38 percent) and black women (10 percent) also appear to differ, while remaining the strongest in rejecting the idea that affirmative action violates rights.

Political ideology is moderately related to responses to this question. Conservatives more than moderates and much more than liberals agreed that affirmative action violates rights.[5] And as the data in table 10 show, among white men, even a majority of liberals agreed that affirmative action violates rights; and among white women, only among liberals did a majority *disagree* that affirmative action violates the rights of white men. Also, for nonwhite men and women, again, only among liberals did a majority disagree that affirmative action violates rights.

Substitution of Compensation and Prosecution for Affirmative Action

Both libertarian and conservative theories place a premium on the individual and often suggest that, rather than permit affirmative action to violate individual rights, the proper response to discrimination is to compensate the specific individual who was in-

TABLE 10
Agreement that Affirmative Action
Violates the Rights of White Men, by Ideology
(in percent)

	Conservative		Moderate		Liberal		
	Agree	*Strongly Agree*	*Agree*	*Strongly Agree*	*Agree*	*Strongly Agree*	*(N)*
White							
Men	93	59	73	36	60	24	(149)
Women	78	28	74	26	23	10	(86)
Nonwhite							
Men	52	22	52	26	26	12	(115)
Women	43	43	58	15	27	11	(44)

jured, while prosecuting the perpetrator, ultimately making the perpetrator bear the burden of the compensation.

This idea was put to the respondents in the statement, *Instead of stressing affirmative action, we should just prohibit discrimination and prosecute those who discriminate* (statement 19, table 3). The most interesting thing about responses to this statement is that many who agreed were also strong supporters of affirmative action. It is not surprising that 53 percent of white men would agree with this statement, since only 40–45 percent of whites were strong supporters of affirmative action, and those who did not approve could be expected to endorse some alternative to it. But it is surprising that 47–48 percent of nonwhite women and men also agreed that affirmative action is not the best way to solve the discrimination problem. This does not seem consistent with the overwhelming support nonwhite women and men give to most of the premises and practices of affirmative action. Even white women agreed in greater proportions than one would expect given their overall strong support of affirmative action.

Significant differences are found related to political ideology: conservatives preferred strict enforcement to affirmative action more often than moderates and liberals.[6] However, as the data in table 11 show, differences related to ideology are, again, most pronounced among white men. Weak differences related to social class are also found among the four groups.[7] However, this is only true for white men and women: lower-class white men and women preferred strict prosecution over affirmative action more than those who identified themselves as being from a higher class.

TABLE 11
Agreement that Strict Antidiscrimination Enforcement
Is Better than Affirmative Action, by Ideology
(in percent)

	Conservative		Moderate		Liberal		
	Agree	Strongly Agree	Agree	Strongly Agree	Agree	Strongly Agree	(N)
White							
Men	70	38	54	22	36	14	(149)
Women	39	11	41	15	30	9	(90)
Nonwhite							
Men	52	30	48	22	43	15	(109)
Women	57	14	54	15	25	25	(45)

As the discussion in chapter 4 suggests, many interviewees argued that it is naive to think that strict antidiscrimination enforcement is preferable to affirmative action. Some suggested that discrimination is often systemic and not personal, and that those who discriminate decreasingly use hate language to advertise such discrimination. This recognition of the nonindividual and subtle nature of contemporary discrimination makes the high rates of agreement with this proposition, at around 50 percent for all groups except white women, all the more striking. Do respondents who agreed with this proposition really think that emphasizing prosecution is a better way than affirmative action to address the problem of discrimination? Or are they misreading the statement somewhat, and simply expressing the sentiment that they endorse rigorous antidiscrimination enforcement?

The latter interpretation is more plausible. On quite a few points, a swing group of respondents in each subject group endorsed propositions that seem contradictory or mutually exclusive. One of the significant things such contradictions suggest is that there may not be clear majorities who agree, in an absolute and principled way, with any of the stated rationales for affirmative action and its premises.

As discussed in chapter 2, a key rationale offered for affirmative action suggests that affirmative action is required by the principle of compensatory justice. The next section examines the attitudes of the groups toward rationales for affirmative action grounded in notions of compensatory justice.

Compensatory Justice and Affirmative Action

Compensatory justice is concerned with righting wrongs. How *right* and *wrong* are defined depends on various principles of autonomy or justice. Concepts of compensatory justice usually include three conditions that must be met before compensation is approved as a morally appropriate remedy. First, an injury must be inflicted that is judged to be morally wrong. Second, the victim and perpetrator must be identifiable, and the compensation to the victim must be provided by the perpetrator—or by society at large. Third, the compensation must be proportionate to the injury.

Preferential affirmative action is often argued about in terms of compensatory justice. Nozick's (1974) rectification principle represents one type of compensatory justice concept. His rectification principle requires that the perpetrator and only the perpetrator bear the burden of the compensation, and that only specific victims be compensated. There are nonlibertarians, however, who, with different overall theories of distributive justice, argue for or against affirmative action based on the idea of compensatory justice, but who think compensation may be appropriate even when the strict conditions required by Nozick may be impossible to fulfill.[8]

I have chosen to discuss responses to compensatory justice principles in this subsection, concerning conservative analyses of affirmative action, for two reasons. First, conservative analyses often assert that affirmative action does not fulfill the requirements of compensatory justice; second, analyses of the interviews suggested that most people agree with the conservative argument that compensatory justice arguments do not provide an adequate moral justification for preferential affirmative action. So the current task is to see if the impressions from the interviews are supported by the survey data.

Since there are different ideas of how compensatory justice should be understood and under what conditions it ought to be implemented, the survey did not attempt to assess the extent of agreement with different versions of compensatory justice. In a survey it would be difficult to assess affinity with the full scope of ideas involved in each compensatory justice argument. Instead, the survey included a series of general statements to assess whether respondents thought it is morally right to use affirmative action to compensate women and nonwhites for wrongs they may have suffered.

As background, it is important to discover if respondents think white men have actually benefited from discrimination. (If white men have not benefited, then there is no reason to provide compensation.) While some conservatives deny that white men have significantly benefited from past discrimination, large majorities of the four major groups agreed with the survey statement, *White males have benefited from past discrimination* (statement 20, table 3).[9]

Since most respondents agreed that white men have benefited from past discrimination, it seems logical that something more than strong antidiscrimination enforcement is needed to address the moral problem of the ill-gotten gains resulting from past discrimination. (The term *ill-gotten* does not necessarily imply personal culpability.) But most conservatives and libertarians nevertheless seem to offer only one direct response to discrimination—strong antidiscrimination enforcement—even though this response cannot easily deal with the present effects and injustices grounded in past discrimination. Libertarians and most conservatives reject the idea that it is morally permissible to compensate victims of past discrimination, unless the perpetrators can be identified and made to bear the burden of compensation to specific victims.

Reactions to the statement, *White males should agree that preferential treatment of victims of discrimination is appropriate compensation* (statement 21, table 3) indicates that conservatives and libertarians are not the only ones who are uncomfortable with applying compensatory notions to affirmative action. Of course, conservatives and libertarians were expected to disagree with this proposition. But of all the propositions providing rationales for affirmative action, fewer respondents agreed with this rationale than any other.[10] Among ethnic subgroups, only among blacks did a majority (65 percent) endorse this rationale, compared to minorities of Asians (41 percent), Hispanics (44 percent), and native Americans (20 percent, 11 percent male, 50 percent female). Liberals consistently endorsed compensatory rationales for affirmative action more than moderates and conservatives.[11]

In summary, the high level of disagreement with this statement, along with the interview data, suggest that concepts of compensatory justice provide the least popular rationale for affirmative action. It also suggests that, even among nonwhites, points of view that see preferential treatment and compensatory ideas as unnecessarily unfair to individuals have considerable sympathy.

While this discussion shows how little support there is for compensatory rationales for affirmative action, the discussion so far does not explain why there is so little support for such a rationale. Chapter 2 illustrated how the problem of overgeneralization is a significant obstacle faced by those who promote compensatory justice rationales for affirmative action. (The overgeneralization problem refers to two dynamics: either affirmative action is underinclusive, and does not help those who have been most injured by discrimination; or it is overinclusive, and tends to help those women and nonwhites who, in spite of their gender or ethnicity, are fairly competitive.)

But the interview data described in chapter 4 suggest that the biggest problem most people have with justifying affirmative action in terms of compensatory justice is that affirmative action forces individuals who are completely innocent of any wrongdoing to bear the burden of the compensation, and this violates the central requirement of compensatory justice—that the perpetrator bear the burden of the compensation. The implication that white men today owe a debt for past discrimination is a big reason many respondents from all ethnic and gender groups felt uncomfortable thinking about affirmative action as compensation: few wanted some innocent white man to suffer because of discrimination for which he is not personally responsible. Part of this sentiment is discernible not only in the interviews, but also in responses to the survey question discussed above about affirmative action violating the rights of white men. (Here, also, we see evidence of the strong individualism throughout U.S. culture.)

Returning to sentiments that affirmative action is over- or underinclusive, which were also voiced in the interviews: how strong is such sentiment? To assess whether or not respondents are concerned about overinclusion, they were given the statement, *Affirmative action helps many who do not need help* (statement 22, table 3). Here, with the exception of nonwhite men, majorities agreed. To assess whether respondents were concerned about underinclusion, they were asked whether *affirmative action should be broadened to include disadvantaged people of whatever race or gender* (statement 36, table 3). Only a quarter of white men and women, and slightly less than half of nonwhite men and women agreed. This response is discussed in more detail under Marxist analysis.

Many ethnic subgroups agreed that overinclusion is a problem: for example, 57–58 percent of native Americans and Hispanics agreed that affirmative action helps many who do not need help (males and females did not differ). However, only 45 percent of

TABLE 12
Agreement that Affirmative Action Helps Many
Who Do Not Need Help, by Ideology
(in percent)

	Conservative	Moderate	Liberal	(N)
White				
Men	78	62	51	(139)
Women	69	59	39	(91)
Nonwhite				
Men	62	47	41	(110)
Women	50	69	27	(45)

Note: Agreement includes both "agree" and "strongly agree."

Asian respondents agreed (again, Asian men appear to be more sympathetic than Asian women to affirmative action rationales—here only 39 percent of Asian men agreed that affirmative action helps those who do not need help, compared to 60 percent of Asian women). And very few blacks agreed that overinclusion is a problem (27 percent, 31 percent male, 17 percent female). The majority of blacks apparently did not wish to concede any arguments against affirmative action.

Conservatives were more likely than moderates or liberals to agree that affirmative action is overinclusive.[12] As table 12 shows, this is true for all four groups.

The above analysis demonstrates overwhelming respondent agreement that affirmative action violates rights. This analysis also shows that a narrow majority of most subgroups agreed that affirmative action helps those who do not need help (a perception reinforced by the interview data). So the overgeneralization problem, along with the strong insistence by most interviewees that personal culpability be required for compensatory justice rationales to apply, account for the resistance to compensatory justice arguments for affirmative action. As shown in chapter 2, these are the key reasons that many social philosophers, both conservative and liberal, reject affirmative action, or at least compensatory arguments for it.

The American Dream and Affirmative Action

Conservative and libertarian arguments against affirmative action generally rely on certain assumptions about facts. Libertarians

believe that there is sufficient opportunity in market society to ensure that basic liberties—the prerequisites to participation (competition) in market society—are available to all. Conservatives tend
to agree with this, and as discussed in chapter 2, some also suggest
that discrimination is in decline in the United States, so given the
trajectory of U.S. history, drastic measures such as affirmative action, which adversely affect individual rights, are not needed. Put
more simply, libertarians and conservatives tend to assume that,
on balance, the American Dream is real, and despite vestiges of
discrimination, basic opportunities to compete in market society
remain intact.

The survey data show that most respondents share this faith in
the American Dream—even though majorities in each group also
believed that discrimination was common in their workplace and
in society, and even though (as discussed later in more detail) majorities in each group except white men thought affirmative action
was needed to ensure that women and nonwhites received serious
consideration for jobs.

Strong majorities agreed with the faith expressed in the statement, *Despite barriers to success such as discrimination, almost
anybody can succeed if she or he tries hard enough* (statement 23,
table 3). Men were slightly more optimistic than women.[13] Among
nonwhites, strong majorities of most subgroups agreed with this
statement reflecting the American Dream ideology. For example,
70 percent of all blacks (76 percent of men, 50 percent of women)
and 70 percent of all whites endorsed this version of the American
Dream. This is close to the responses of Hispanics, 77 percent of
whom agreed (78 percent of men, 73 percent of women).

Levels of agreement dropped off with Asian respondents, 55 percent of whom agreed with this statement (52 percent of men, 67
percent of women), again revealing the difference between Asian
men and women, the women being less sympathetic to affirmative
action than men). Native American men and women again appear
to differ widely: 90 percent of these men thought anyone could succeed with effort (this represents the highest rate of agreement of any
subgroup), but only 43 percent of native American women agreed.

Among white men and nonwhite women, conservatives agreed
more than moderates and liberals that anybody can do well with
effort, but among white women and nonwhite men, this pattern is
not apparent. The differences among white men and nonwhite
women varied enough to suggest that political ideology is related
to this statement when one examines all respondents.[14] For white

men, agreement ranged from 83 percent for conservatives to 66 percent for liberals. For nonwhite women, agreement ranged from 88 percent to 56 percent. Some differences are related to religious identity. Except for white men, Christians agreed slightly more than non-Christians that anybody can succeed, and evangelical Christians agreed more than nonevangelical Christians (91 percent and 67 percent).[15]

Related to this overall optimism about the American Dream was an optimism common to most contemporary economic thought, whether libertarian, conservative, liberal, or Marxist: that it is possible for economic growth to continue over the long term and thereby to expand opportunities for all people. For libertarians and conservatives, this axiom is used to assert that basic liberties in market society are assured, because opportunities for advancement are not limited by limits on the number of jobs or by natural resource scarcity. For liberals, this axiom is used to suggest that there are no intrinsic economic or resource constraints preventing the expansion of opportunities, although public policies (possibly including affirmative action) may be needed to ensure that competition for such opportunities remain open. This optimistic view, that the size of the pie can continue to expand over time, permits many liberals to believe that preferential affirmative action can be used to make sure that opportunities are increasingly accessible to previously excluded groups without requiring a corresponding decline in white male success rates.

It seems that most of the respondents shared this optimistic assessment about the potential for expanding opportunities. When presented with the statement, *White males should be willing to be satisfied with fewer job opportunities so that others may have a chance to succeed* (statement 24, table 3), very few (15 percent of white men, 20–22 percent of all others) agreed such sacrifice is necessary. Among ethnic subgroups, greater proportions of Asians and blacks agreed (28 percent and 25 percent) than Hispanics (17 percent) and native Americans (12 percent). Again, there seems to be a large gender gap among native Americans: only 5 percent of these men, but 29 percent of women, agreed. The only other subgroup difference on this question is related to political ideology, where, with the exception of nonwhite men (as table 13 shows), more liberals than conservatives agreed that white men must accept fewer job opportunities.[16]

The strong consensus even among supporters of affirmative action that white males need not be satisfied with fewer job opportu-

TABLE 13
**Agreement that White Men Should Be Satisfied
with Fewer Job Opportunities, by Ideology**
(in percent)

	Conservative	Moderate	Liberal	(N)
White				
Men	10	15	20	(149)
Women	11	10	42	(93)
Nonwhite				
Men	19	18	23	(116)
Women	29	12	42	(44)

Note: Agreement includes both "agree" and "strongly agree."

nities shows that most respondents were optimistic that there are solutions to the equal opportunity riddle that do not require significant sacrifices by white men. There is in the U.S. psyche a very strong belief in ever expanding opportunity. Nobody's horizon of opportunity need be narrowed to expand the opportunities of others. The implicit faith is that expanding markets will ensure that new opportunities for women and nonwhites need not come at the expense of white men. Related to this faith are respondents' attitudes toward education. As the interviews revealed, some saw education as the solution to virtually all social ills, including discrimination. Large majorities agreed with two statements about education: *Improving education is the best way to overcome discrimination* and *More public money should be given to improve education* (statements 25 and 26, table 3). For many respondents, education can overcome aberrations from the American Dream. For others, affirmative action is not the proper approach because the focus should be on preserving the viability of the American Dream through education.

Since many supporters of affirmative action believed that aggregate opportunities will expand, the question arises as to whether or not they would remain strong in their support if they were forced by social circumstance to change their optimistic analysis of the facts. What if those who supported affirmative action were to believe that economic and natural resources will become increasingly scarce. Is it possible that a significant number of supporters of affirmative action would not support affirmative action in times of scarcity and decreasing opportunities? If attitudes about affirmative action, pro or con, are grounded in an assumption about the long-term prospects for market expansion, and if the prevailing view of the facts were to change, different ethical analyses about the morality of policies such as affirmative action could become decisive. Probable views toward affirmative action in a context of scarcity are discussed in the next chapter.

Liberal Analyses of Affirmative Action

The Equal Opportunity Principle

The axial liberal principle of distributive justice is that of equal opportunity: jobs and rewards should be distributed according to merit or talents, under conditions characterized by fair competition, where no one is discriminated against for nonrelevant characteristics such as ethnicity or gender.

There is a very strong consensus among respondents from each of the four groups in favor of this equal opportunity principle. When asked if *Equal opportunity, hiring based on merit, is a very good moral principle* (statement 27, table 3), almost all respondents agreed. This is one of the few questions on the survey where there are no significant differences among the main groups or subgroups and this is virtually the only question where there are no differences related to political ideology: both conservatives and liberals supported the idea of equal opportunity.

Clearly, then, for all groups, the equal opportunity principle is an ideal. But when we look at responses to other survey statements, it becomes increasingly clear that for most respondents this ideal is not an absolute moral right or an inviolable principle of distributive justice. These data suggest that for most respondents the equal opportunity principle is one (albeit popular) principle among many that most people think should be considered when public and institutional policy is formed.

Hiring the Best Qualified

One indication that equal opportunity—hiring based on merit— is not an absolute principle for many respondents is that during the interviews and participant observation, many suggested that it was not easy, or even possible, to determine who is best qualified. The survey addressed this issue with the statement (28, table 3), *It is usually possible to identify the best qualified applicant.* Here, fewer respondents agreed than concurred with the previous

TABLE 14
Agreement that It Is Usually Possible
to Identify the Best Qualified Applicant, by Ideology
(in percent)

	Conservative	Moderate	Liberal	(N)
White				
Men	93	83	71	(151)
Women	85	81	63	(93)
Nonwhite				
Men	72	65	54	(116)
Women	83	52	100	(43)

Note: Agreement includes both "agree" and "strongly agree."

statement, that equal opportunity is a good moral principle. Among ethnic subgroups, the most notable difference is found among black men. For both men and women, majorities of all ethnic subgroups except black men (only 38 percent) agreed that usually the best qualified candidate can be identified (however, 67 percent of black women agreed). In other nonwhite subgroups, the sexes did not differ clearly: 76 percent of native American respondents, 74 percent of Asians, and 61 percent of Hispanics agreed. This question also again points to a difference related to religion. All evangelical Christians agreed (N = 20), compared to 68 percent of other Christians.[17]

As table 14 shows, except for nonwhite women, differences related to political ideology reemerged with this statement: Conservatives were more confident than moderates or liberals that it is possible to identify the best qualified.[18] For those who disagreed, clearly some other (or supplemental) principle must be used to make the hiring decision. And since 18–36 percent of the main groups disagreed that it is usually possible to hire the best qualified, it seems unlikely that these respondents would embrace the equal opportunity principle as an absolute right. So for some, the equal opportunity principle was not an absolute moral imperative.

This can be seen even more clearly in responses to the more direct statement (29, in table 3), *It is morally right always to hire the best qualified applicant.* Responses suggest that for at least 21–35 percent of the main groups, hiring the best qualified was not a moral absolute.

As with the previous proposition about the possibility of discerning the best qualified candidate, black men differ significantly

TABLE 15
Agreement that It Is Morally Right Always
to Hire the Best Qualified Applicant, by Ideology
(in percent)

	Conservative	Moderate	Liberal	(N)
White				
Men	83	73	66	(148)
Women	70	82	54	(85)
Nonwhite				
Men	79	67	50	(113)
Women	72	72	73	(43)

Note: Agreement includes both "agree" and "strongly agree."

from other ethnic subgroups. Majorities of all ethnic subgroups, but only 19 percent of black men, agreed that it is morally right always to hire the best qualified (84 percent of black women agreed). Moreover, as table 15 shows, there are weak relationships between the idea of always hiring the best qualified and political ideology: conservatives more than moderates or liberals tended to agree.[19]

The responses to the two previous statements (about the possibility of hiring the best qualified applicant, and the moral imperative to do so) show that at least one quarter of the respondents did not view equal opportunity as a moral absolute. Black men in particular seemed very suspicious of the equal opportunity principle, despite their initial approval of the language surrounding it. An examination of perceptions about whether affirmative action ultimately promotes equal opportunity further demonstrates that the consensus regarding the equal opportunity principle is less strong than it seemed when I first observed the strong approval of the idea of equal opportunity.[20]

Affirmative Action and Equal Opportunity

Since the idea of distribution based on merit and equal opportunity is the dominant notion of distributive justice in a Liberal culture, much of the controversy over affirmative action policy centers on whether affirmative action promotes or hinders hiring based on merit.

When presented with the statement (30, in table 3), *Affirmative action promotes equal opportunity, hiring based on merit*, only 25 percent of white men agreed (3 percent strongly), compared to 41

TABLE 16
Agreement that Affirmative Action
Promotes Equal Opportunity, by Ideology
(in percent)

	Conservative		Moderate		Liberal		
	Agree	Strongly Agree	Agree	Strongly Agree	Agree	Strongly Agree	(N)
White							
Men	5	33	25	25	39	20	(147)
Women	29	24	33	31	56	3	(88)
Nonwhite							
Men	54	18	36	21	63	20	(112)
Women	50	17	48	8	85	8	(44)

percent of white women (8 percent strongly), 51 percent of non-white men (8 percent strongly), and 61 percent of nonwhite women (20 percent strongly).[21] Among ethnic subgroups, more blacks agreed that affirmative action promotes equal opportunity (70 percent), than Hispanics (55 percent), Asians (50 percent), and native Americans (33 percent). Among Asians and Hispanics, men and women answered similarly, but among blacks, men and women differed (60 percent and 100 percent), and among native Americans, men and women also differed (28 percent and 50 percent). Native American men again answered like the white men.

Liberals agreed more than conservatives and moderates that affirmative action promotes equal opportunity.[22] However, as table 16 shows, among nonwhite men, conservatives agreed more than moderates; among nonwhite women, conservatives and moderates responded similarly.

By comparing these responses to statements about whether respondents approved of specific, preferential affirmative action practices, one can see that more respondents actually *endorsed* specific, preferential affirmative action policies than believed that affirmative action actually promotes equal opportunity. This raises a question: If adherence to the equal opportunity principle is *the* key to how respondents evaluate affirmative action practices, then one might expect that all who did not think affirmative action promotes equal opportunity would be against affirmative action. This is not the case, suggesting that those who did not think affirmative action promotes equal opportunity, but who nevertheless supported affirmative action, have some other rationale for their attitudes.

For example, only 24 percent of white men agreed that affirmative action promotes equal opportunity. However, as chapter 5 demonstrated, significantly more (40–45 percent) support even *preferential* affirmative action practices—practices that, at least in the short term, seem to violate the equal opportunity principle. So at least 15–20 percent of white men must have had some rationale for supporting affirmative action other than the idea that it promotes equal opportunity.

Meanwhile, only 41 percent of white women agreed that affirmative action promotes equal opportunity, although 70 percent strongly supported affirmative action; 51 percent of nonwhite men agreed that affirmative action promotes equal opportunity, while about 70 percent were strong supporters; 61 percent of nonwhite women agreed, 75 percent strongly. Therefore, for white women, almost 30 percent must have had some rationale for affirmative action other than the idea that it promotes equal opportunity, and this must be true for almost 20 percent of nonwhite men and at least 15 percent of nonwhite women.

Apparently, then, many who rejected affirmative action do so, at least in part, because they feel it violates the merit principle. At the same time, a significant number of respondents thought that affirmative action was consistent with and promoted the merit principle. And another group, while thinking of the merit principle as an ideal, did not take it as a moral absolute: this group depended on some other idea for their evaluation of affirmative action.

If equal opportunity was not the key rationale for some supporters of affirmative action, what was? The rest of this chapter addresses this question.

Affirmative Action Rationales within the Department of Parks and Recreation

Respondents were asked to respond to two statements that reflect the rationales for affirmative action most commonly heard in the Parks Department. The first is a standard rationale given by those in affirmative action bureaucracies, and by some philosophers, for affirmative action policy: *Affirmative action is needed as a remedial effort to overcome the effects of discrimination* (statement 31, table 3). Usually, such language implies the hope that affirmative action efforts should not last forever, but only until the effects of discrimination are overcome (including the underrepresentation of target groups in the work force).

The idea that affirmative action is needed to remedy the effects of discrimination is not very popular. However, responses to this question may help account for some of the discrepancy, where more respondents supported affirmative action than thought that it was justified as a means to equal opportunity. Compared with 62 percent of white men who agreed with the proposition that affirmative action is morally right, agreement among white men here drops almost 15 percent. So the idea that affirmative action is needed as a remedy to discrimination was not convincing to a majority of white men. This rationale was more convincing to white women and nonwhite men and most convincing to nonwhite women. Women agreed with this proposition significantly more than men.[23]

Among nonwhite subgroups, the patterns are similar to previous responses. For example, more black men and women agreed (89 percent and 83 percent) that affirmative action is a needed remedy, and many agreed strongly (50 percent and 67 percent). Asian men and women both agreed similarly (80 percent). Hispanic men and women differed slightly: 77 percent of men and 84 percent of women agreed. Native American women all agreed, but only 33 percent of native American men agreed. Interestingly, 14 percent fewer native Americans than white men agreed. Again, most of the common subgroup patterns are repeated: very strong black and Asian agreement with this rationale for affirmative action, strong Hispanic agreement (less so among men), strong white and native American female agreement, and much less agreement among white and native American men.

The more liberal the respondents, the more likely they were to agree with the idea that affirmative action is needed as a remedy to discrimination.[24] Table 17 shows this for each of the four main groups. The data also show that few conservative white men agreed that affirmative action is needed, but strong majorities of conservative women and conservative nonwhite men agreed.

Some age differences similar to those described in chapter 5 are evident in responses to the idea that affirmative action is needed to remedy discrimination. Whites in their forties seemed most sympathetic toward this rationale: 59 percent of white men agreed, but only 40 percent of white men in their thirties and only 31 percent of white men over fifty. Again, more white women in their forties agreed with this rationale (89 percent) than white women in their thirties (76 percent) or over fifty (65 percent). Only 29 percent of white women under thirty agreed. This pattern of age-related

TABLE 17
Agreement that Affirmative Action Is Needed to
Overcome the Effects of Discrimination, by Ideology
(in percent)

	Conservative	Moderate	Liberal	(N)
White				
Men	35	41	65	(146)
Women	65	66	88	(92)
Nonwhite				
Men	76	63	88	(120)
Women	63	85	100	(48)

Note: Agreement includes both "agree" and "strongly agree."

differences does not hold among nonwhite men, among whom 65 percent in their forties agreed, compared with 77 percent and 79 percent of those in their thirties or over fifty, and only 50 percent under thirty. Nonwhite women did not seem to differ by age group, except that those under thirty agreed less (71 percent) than their elders (whose agreement ranged from 89 percent to 95 percent).

Another difference is among those holding different types of jobs. For white men and women, more managers agreed that affirmative action is a needed remedy (52 percent and 78 percent) than rank-and-file personnel (44 percent and 70 percent). Further, among white men, only 25 percent of rank-and-file maintenance employees agreed, almost 25 percent below other white male employee groups.

A second common rationale for affirmative action offered in the department and in interviews was that affirmative action is needed to ensure that people are given a fair chance to compete for jobs. Respondents were asked if they agreed with the statement (32, table 3), *Without affirmative action, women and minorities would not get serious consideration for many department jobs.* Even fewer white men and women agreed with this than agreed with the previous statement—that affirmative action is needed as a remedy. But large majorities of nonwhite men and women agreed, at about the same rates as for the idea that affirmative action is needed as a remedy. There is a moderately strong correlation related to gender: women agreed more than men with the idea that affirmative action is needed to ensure that women and nonwhites get serious consideration for jobs.[25]

It is hard to imagine a more important dispute about fact. During participant observation, I heard a white male supervisor, who often insisted that the best qualified be hired and who believed that affirmative action hinders this, say that he did not hire a Puerto Rican applicant (whom he admitted was the best qualified) because he did not think the applicant would "fit in." Yet this white male supervisor considers himself unprejudiced and does not believe affirmative action is necessary to ensure that minorities and women receive serious consideration for jobs. This illustrates how there could be such wide disagreement as to whether affirmative action is needed to guarantee serious consideration.

Responses to the above survey statement show that two-thirds of white men denied that affirmative action is needed to guarantee equal consideration for jobs (and 24 percent strongly denied this), while large majorities of white women and nonwhite men and women thought that it was needed. Interestingly, 5 percent more white women and nonwhite men, and 9 percent more nonwhite women, agreed with this statement than with the statement that prejudice is common in the department. More members of target groups thought they would not always get an equal chance at department jobs than thought that prejudice is prevalent. White men did not answer these two questions differently.

Among nonwhite subgroups, greater proportions of black men agreed with this rationale for affirmative action (89 percent, 61 *percent strongly*) than Asian men (79 percent, 28 percent strongly) or Hispanic men (79 percent, 33 percent strongly). Meanwhile, as with white men, few native American men (37 percent, 16 percent strongly) thought that affirmative action is needed for nonwhites to be seriously considered for jobs. And 37 percent of the 63 percent of native American men who disagreed did so strongly, even more than white men (24 percent). Here is another point on which native American men were even more hostile than white men to affirmative action. This was also one of the few times when more Asian women than men agreed with a statement sympathetic to affirmative action. Roughly equal proportions of black, Asian, Hispanic, and native American women agreed (84–90 percent).

These responses provide another example of the overall pattern of very strong black and Asian support, strong Hispanic support, strong white female support, and probably strong native American female support, for affirmative action and its premises. The majority of white men (62 percent) and native American men (57 percent) did not support most of the ideas behind and practices of affirmative action. With the exception of affirmative action goals, which a majority of native American men endorsed, only on the

TABLE 18
**Agreement that Affirmative Action Is Needed to Ensure that
Women and Nonwhites Get Serious Consideration for Jobs, by Ideology**
(in percent)

	Conservative	Moderate	Liberal	(N)
White				
Men	21	27	39	(149)
Women	65	49	81	(91)
Nonwhite				
Men	72	60	80	(119)
Women	75	81	100	(47)

Note: Agreement includes both "agree" and "strongly agree."

general statement that affirmative action is morally right did white
and native American men appear to be sympathetic to affirmative
action and its premises.

As with earlier questions, variations in perceptions of fact are
related to political ideology: liberals are more likely than moderates and conservatives to agree that affirmative action is needed to
guarantee that all are given serious consideration for jobs.[26] As
table 18 shows, an exception to this dynamic is found among white
women and nonwhite men: liberals and conservatives agreed more
than moderates (compare tables 4 and 6).

Finally, older people agreed slightly more than younger people
that without affirmative action target group members would not
receive serious consideration for jobs.[27] However, this age difference does not occur among nonwhite women.

Marxist Attitudes and Affirmative Action

During the interviews, when asked to reflect on concepts of distributive justice related to Marxist theory, a surprising number of
respondents indicated that such concepts made sense to them. The
survey asked a series of general questions to measure the extent of
sympathy with Marxist-type thinking about distributive justice.
Two statements asked for reactions to one of the ideas related to
Liberalism's equal opportunity principle of distributive justice: the
idea that the most talented persons ought to get preferred jobs and
higher salaries. Responses to these statements provide background
to make easier comparisons with statements expressing Marxist

principles of distributive justice—principles which suggest that distribution ought to be based instead more on effort and need.

Natural Talents and Just Deserts

Respondents were asked to respond to two statements related to natural talents and to ideas about what constitutes just rewards: *Naturally talented people are entitled to better jobs than those who are less talented,* and *Naturally talented people are entitled to higher salaries than those who are less talented* (statements 33 and 34, table 3). These statements reframed the Liberal equal opportunity principle in order to highlight how merit is strongly linked to natural talents—which are, presumably, unearned.

When the statements were framed in this way, there was much less agreement with the liberal merit principle of distribution than with responses to statements discussed previously, when the statement's language more closely reflected the ways in which the merit principle is usually discussed: as equal opportunity and hiring the best qualified. Over 20 percent fewer women respondents agreed with the idea that jobs should be awarded based on natural talents than with the idea that the best qualified should always be hired. Fewer men also agreed with awarding rewards based on natural talents than with the idea of hiring the best qualified. Fewer women than men agreed with this proposition.[28]

Even fewer respondents agreed that naturally talented people deserve higher salaries than agreed that naturally talented people deserve the better jobs. Only among white men do a clear majority agree (no significant change from the percentage who agreed that naturally talented people deserve the best jobs). Agreement among nonwhite men is down 10 percent from the idea that naturally talented people deserve the best jobs. Among nonwhite women there is no change, and agreement is down 11 percent among white women.

There is a weak relationship between political ideology and views toward these two propositions about natural talents. Conservatives were more likely than moderates or liberals to endorse these propositions (except among nonwhite women, on the statement about the gifted deserving the best jobs).[29]

Among nonwhite ethnic subgroups, with these two propositions about natural talents, previous patterns related to affirmative action or its premises were not present. For example, when asked if naturally gifted individuals deserve higher salaries, almost as many native American men (63 percent) as white men agreed, although only 16 percent of native American women agreed. A majority of Asian men (57 percent) and half of Asian women also agreed. However, among Hispanic men and black men, only 47 percent and 38 percent, respectively, agreed, compared to 55 percent of Hispanic women and 60 percent of black women. So among male subgroups, a majority of whites, Asians, and native Americans agreed that naturally gifted people deserve higher salaries, while majorities of all Hispanics and blacks disagreed. Since blacks, Hispanics and native Americans belong to lower income groups than Asians and whites, attitudes toward distribution and natural talents (with the exception of the attitudes of native American men) seem to correlate with relative financial status as a group: generally those from higher income groups approved of giving higher salaries to those with greater natural talents.

Another finding worth noting is that when the survey statements were framed in this way (speaking of rewarding the naturally talented instead of the best qualified), support for the liberal idea of rewards based on merit engendered considerably less sympathy. When defining *merit* in terms of natural talents, a majority of Hispanic men were suspicious of awarding salaries according to natural talents, and they joined a majority of black men who were suspicious of salary distributions according to natural talents. From the beginning, black men were suspicious of the idea of always hiring the best qualified.

To summarize, at least when it comes to salaries, majorities of black and Hispanic men, along with majorities of each female subgroup (except Asian women who were equally divided), seem to think that something is amiss with Liberal distributive norms. So while at first glance the idea of equal opportunity based on merit and its application to the idea of hiring the best qualified seemed to gain a ringing endorsement from most respondents, something bothered many respondents when the implications of such principles were spelled out. (Few, however, made the connection on their own between the idea of equal opportunity based on merit and the idea that, by such a principle, the preferred jobs and higher salaries would be distributed largely on the basis of unearned natural talents.)

Given the responses to these statements, one could argue that there is less clear-cut endorsement of the Liberal merit principle than might at first appear. Faced with a proposition implying that merit may be related to unearned natural talents, only among white, Asian, and native American men do a majority still endorse the merit principle. The response of Asian men is interesting here: 57 percent of Asian men still supported the merit idea even when the question was framed in this way. My impression from the qualitative data is that Asian men tended to favor affirmative action because it promotes a merit-based society, not because it promotes some social end.

If a significant number of respondents were uncomfortable with basing the distribution of society's jobs and rewards primarily on natural talents, this provides more evidence that many respondents did not view the liberal merit principle as the inviolable principle of distribution. Chapter 7 will return to this point. The next section discusses whether those respondents who did not unambiguously embrace Liberal concepts of distributive justice were more sympathetic toward Marxist-type principles of distribution.

Distribution Based on Effort and Need

The previous section shows that some respondents were uncomfortable with the idea of distribution based on natural talents. However, relatively few were willing to endorse the idea of reducing inequalities in salaries by distributing income more according to effort, while majorities of all groups disagreed with the statement (35, table 3), *We need public policies to reduce inequality of income between talented and less talented people who try equally hard.* Twice as many white women than white men agreed, while even more nonwhite men and nonwhite women agreed.

Interestingly, among nonwhite, ethnic subgroups, equal proportions of native American men, black men, and Asian men agreed (37 percent) while 46 percent of Hispanic men agreed. Fewer black women agreed (20 percent) than Hispanic (30 percent), native American (50 percent), or Asian women (67 percent).

There is no significant difference related to political ideology and the idea that income distribution ought to be based more on effort. This is surprising and suggests that in U.S. political culture there is actually more that unites people than divides them: whether respondents called themselves liberals or conservatives, strong majorities unite in rejecting this non-Liberal principle of distribution. Moreover, among those who wished to reduce income inequalities and make rewards fit more closely with effort, this sentiment was not significantly related to differences in political ideology. If liberals were really as left-wing as conservatives often suggest, then one would expect that liberals would be more likely to embrace left-wing ideas such as distribution according to effort. (There is also a very weak relationship related to social class, with more lower-class individuals agreeing that effort should have a greater role in distribution than it currently has.)[30]

Respondents were also asked about affirmative action in such a way as to explore a second Marxist-type principle of distributive justice: whether rewards ought to be distributed according to need. One statement (36, table 3) suggested, *Affirmative action broadened to include all disadvantaged people would be a morally acceptable way to reduce inequality of income.* Broadening affirmative action to all disadvantaged people is one way to solve part of the problem of overgeneralization. While this would make affirmative action preferences available to white men, fewer white men and women endorsed this idea than nonwhite women and men. More nonwhites were willing to extend the helping hand of affirmative action to all who are in need, including whites, than were whites themselves.

The only other subgroup difference worth noting on this point is that there is a very weak relationship between ideology and the idea of broadening affirmative action to all disadvantaged people: liberals were slightly more likely than conservatives or moderates to approve of extending affirmative action to all disadvantaged persons.[31] But as table 19 shows, this ideologically related difference is not found among nonwhites, once again suggesting that whites are more divided by ideology than nonwhites.

This chapter has shown the strong affinity that respondents have for the equal opportunity principle. However, this analysis also has concluded that the merit principle was not embraced by a majority of respondents as *the* inviolable principle of distributive justice. In other words, for a majority of respondents, equal opportunity was not the only moral lens by which to judge affirmative action. A significant minority of respondents had some affinity for Marxist-type principles of distributive justice (when such principles are discussed in the context of the equal opportunity/affirmative action issue). The next section looks at responses related to arguments about affirmative action grounded in consequentialist ethical premises.

Consequentialist Analyses of Affirmative Action

Teleology and Deontology

To provide some background for specific questions about the impact of affirmative action in society, the survey determined

TABLE 19
Agreement that Affirmative Action Should Be Broadened
to Include All Disadvantaged People, by Ideology
(in percent)

	Conservative	Moderate	Liberal	(N)
White				
Men	21	23	40	(143)
Women	11	32	30	(84)
Nonwhite				
Men	46	52	45	(110)
Women	50	42	46	(41)

Note: Agreement includes both "agree" and "strongly agree."

whether respondents' approaches to affirmative action tended to be more deontological (focused on the intrinsic rightness or wrongness of such policy) or teleological (focused on results). In response to the statement (37, table 3), *I can tell whether affirmative action is right or wrong without thinking about the effect of affirmative action on society,* strong majorities of all subject groups disagreed, believing that assessing consequences is critical to the evaluation of affirmative action. Men were more likely than women to approach affirmative action relying on deontological principles.[32] (It is reasonable to ask if this form of the question accurately elicits teleological sentiment. But the analysis of the interview data in chapter 4 strongly supports the interpretation that consequences, for a majority, were decisive when evaluating affirmative action.)

As table 20 shows, except for nonwhite women, among the remaining three subject groups, liberals were slightly more likely than moderates and conservatives to take more of a teleological approach.[33] So most respondents think it is important to evaluate the impact of affirmative action on their society and the workplace. How do they perceive these impacts?

One pattern applies to all the survey statements having to do with the consequences of affirmative action in society and on the workplace: differences related to age. Among white and nonwhite men, and white women, those in their forties provide the most positive assessment of the impact of affirmative action, followed by those in their thirties, while greater proportions of those over fifty and under thirty thought that affirmative action has, on balance, negative consequences. There is no clear age-related pattern among nonwhite women.

TABLE 20
Agreement with Use of a Deontological Approach
to Affirmative Action, by Ideology
(in percent)

	Conservative	Moderate	Liberal	(N)
White				
Men	36	30	18	(137)
Women	16	27	6	(88)
Nonwhite				
Men	56	46	29	(106)
Women	17	35	44	(38)

Note: Agreement includes both "agree" and "strongly agree."

Affirmative Action and Society

Respondents were asked if they agreed with the statement, *On balance, affirmative action benefits society* (statement 37, table 3). The rates of agreement by group are almost the same as those for the statement that affirmative action is morally right.

Among nonwhite subgroups, blacks and Hispanics answered similarly about affirmative action benefiting society: almost 100 percent of black and Hispanic women agreed, compared to 87 percent of black and Hispanic men. Among Asians, 79 percent of men and 60 percent of women agreed, compared to 86 percent of native American women and 59 percent of native American men. Liberals agreed more often than moderates and conservatives (table 21).[34]

The similarity between the rates of agreement to the two statements—affirmative action is morally right, and affirmative action benefits society—may be coincidental. But given the previous analysis, which suggests that the evaluation of affirmative action is not based primarily on deontological principles—and given my impressions from the interviews and from observations in the workplace—I suspect that many respondents who agreed that affirmative action is morally right do so because they think that, overall, affirmative action benefits society. My impressions from both phases of the research are that the majority of respondents did not decide based on abstract moral rules, be they libertarian, conservative, liberal, or Marxist. Instead, they tended to evaluate affirmative action based on two factors: (1) how does it affect me? and (2) how does it affect society? A big part of how individuals think affirmative action af-

TABLE 21
Agreement that Affirmative Action Benefits Society, by Ideology
(in percent)

	Conservative	Moderate	Liberal	(N)
White				
Men	53	66	70	(144)
Women	68	83	91	(87)
Nonwhite				
Men	82	74	90	(112)
Women	63	88	100	(45)

Note: Agreement includes both "agree" and "strongly agree."

fects their own interests depends on how they think it affects their workplace (and, of course, their careers).

Many respondents were more positive in their assessment on how affirmative action benefits society than in their perceptions about how it impacts their careers. As discussed in chapter 5, there was significantly less support for the key elements of the Parks Department's affirmative action program (such as focused recruitment and hiring goals) than for the idea that, in general, affirmative action is morally right.

Further, there was always less support for affirmative action policies than for the ideas used to legitimate it. Furthermore, the more specific statements were usually supported less. For example, although many agreed that affirmative action benefits society, fewer respondents agreed with the statement (39, table 3), *In the long term, affirmative action will reduce tensions between racial groups and between gender groups.* Agreement among white men dropped 26 percent from agreement that affirmative action benefits society. Among white women, agreement dropped 25 percent. Among nonwhite men, agreement dropped 18 percent. And among nonwhite women it dropped 28 percent. So while for many the idea that affirmative action benefits society was important to their evaluation of affirmative action, relatively slim majorities of nonwhite respondents, and only a little over a third of white men, saw declining racial and gender tensions as one of those benefits. As with most rationales sympathetic to affirmative action, liberals more than conservatives and moderates agreed that affirmative action promotes racial and gender harmony.[35]

There seems to be a similar drop in agreement between the ideas that, on balance, affirmative action benefits society and that affirmative action benefits the workplace. The difference here again shows that there was less agreement with justifications for affirmative action the more specific such justifications became. While the data do not show a causal link between views about the consequences of affirmative action and attitudes toward affirmative action, the qualitative and quantitative data suggest that the reluctance to approve of the specifics of affirmative action were directly related to the perceived negative impact of affirmative action on the respondents' workplace and, for some, their careers.

Affirmative Action and the Workplace

The survey included a statement often heard during the interviews, *Affirmative action reduces the quality of the department's employees* (statement 40, table 3). A majority of white men agreed, as did 65 percent of native American men, although only 17 percent of native American women agreed. Majorities of all other groups disagreed that affirmative action harms employee quality. Only 45 percent of Hispanic men agreed, while even fewer Hispanic women (35 percent), Asian women and men (27 percent and 30 percent), of black men (18 percent), and no black women agreed.

There is an even stronger relationship between political ideology and this statement than there was with propositions about affirmative action benefiting society overall. As shown in table 22, conservatives are the most likely ideological group to agree that affirmative action reduces employee quality.[36] Men more than women thought that affirmative action reduced employee quality.[37]

While the figures just summarized show that many people, especially white and native American men, thought affirmative action reduced employee quality, fewer respondents (about 10 percent fewer) agreed with the statement (41, table 3), *Affirmative action harms the mission of the DPR*. The most common patterns among nonwhite subgroups were repeated with this statement. Here, even more native American men agreed (70 percent) than white men (57 percent), although only 17 percent of native American women agreed. Among all other nonwhite subgroups, the majority disagreed that affirmative action harmed the department's mission. Only 35 percent of Hispanic men and 21 percent of Hispanic women agreed. Even fewer Asian men (18 percent) agreed. Thirty percent of Asian women, only 12 percent of black men, and no black women, agreed.

It appears that political ideology, as with other questions about the consequences of affirmative action, is strongly related to re-

TABLE 22
Agreement that Affirmative Action Reduces Employee Quality,
by Ideology
(in percent)

	Conservative	Moderate	Liberal	(N)
White				
Men	89	64	56	(146)
Women	56	61	27	(86)
Nonwhite				
Men	48	45	30	(112)
Women	57	31	0	(45)

Note: Agreement includes both "agree" and "strongly agree."

spondent sentiment: conservatives were more likely than liberals to agree that affirmative action harms the mission of the department (table 23).[38] However, among white women and nonwhite men, there was no difference between moderates and conservatives, and conservative white men were *much* more likely than moderates and liberals to agree that affirmative action harmed the mission of the department.

Among white men, 61 percent of rank-and-file employees and 50 percent of managers, agreed that affirmative action harmed the department's mission. Responses by white women managers and rank-and-file employees regarding the department's mission were the opposite of those of white men: 43 percent of managers and 33 percent of rank-and-file workers agreed that affirmative action harmed the department's mission. Among nonwhite men, more managers than rank-and-file workers thought that affirmative action hurt employeed quality (46 percent and 39 percent).

In response to the statement (42, table 3), *Overall, the workplace is better because of affirmative action,* answers were similar to responses about the impact of affirmative action on the department's mission and similar with regard to political ideology.[39]

Affirmative Action and Consequentialism

There was much more agreement that affirmative action helped society than with the proposition that affirmative action improved the workplace. Similarly, fewer disagreed that affirmative action harmed the department's mission than agreed that it benefited society. For example, 24 percent fewer white men thought that affirmative action improved the workplace than thought it benefited

TABLE 23
Agreement that Affirmative Action Harms the Mission of the California State Department of Parks and Recreation, by Ideology
(in percent)

	Conservative	Moderate	Liberal	(N)
White				
Men	76	59	36	(152)
Women	39	42	27	(89)
Nonwhite				
Men	36	40	20	(113)
Women	43	22	0	(46)

Note: Agreement includes both "agree" and "strongly agree."

society (40 percent and 64 percent). Among white women, 22 percent fewer held this view (60 percent and 82 percent). Among nonwhite men, 15 percent fewer thought affirmative action improved the workplace than thought it benefited society (67 percent and 82 percent), while among nonwhite women 20 percent more thought affirmative action improved society than thought it improved the workplace (87 percent and 67 percent).

Apparently—in a way similar to the dynamic discussed earlier (where fewer respondents supported the specific aspects of the affirmative action policy than thought, in general, that it was morally right)—fewer respondents saw affirmative action as having positive consequences when its impact is felt closer to home. As with other public policies, many people agreed that there was a problem that needs to be addressed (in this case, discrimination and inequality), but preferred not to have to bear the burden themselves. And here, while significant numbers of respondents thought that society needed and benefited from affirmative action, many denied that affirmative action had a positive effect in their own workplace.

Summary: Affirmative Action and Distributive Justice

The purpose of this chapter has been to illuminate the question, Why do people feel about affirmative action as they do, and what sorts of moral reasoning influence their views? Table 24 summarizes the extent of employee approval and disapproval of the various rationales for affirmative action.

TABLE 24
Support for and Opposition to Specific Affirmative Action
Rationales and Practices
(in percent)

	Consistent Support	Swing Group[a]	Consistent Opposition
White			
Men	40–42	20–22	38
Women	70	15	15
Nonwhite			
Men	70	10	15
Women	75	15	10

a. Supports some but not all of affirmative action rationales and practices.

The most critical finding has to do with the individualism of Liberal culture and respondents' attitudes toward the equal opportunity principle, which is the central principle of distributive justice in a Liberal culture. Not surprisingly, given Liberalism's individualistic bent and dominance in the United States, most respondents placed a premium on the individual and on the equal opportunity principle. Large majorities of all groups endorsed the equal opportunity principle, agreed that affirmative action violated the rights of white men, and thought that individual initiative was the key to success. And for many, the impact of affirmative action on equal opportunity was an important part of how they evaluated affirmative action.

However, respondents did not take purely individualistic premises, such as the idea of equal opportunity, as *the* axial social organizing principle by which to evaluate public policies such as affirmative action. Although very large majorities said that equal opportunity was a good moral principle, majorities did not simply evaluate affirmative action by calculating whether or not it promoted equal opportunity. Narrow majorities of nonwhites thought that affirmative action promoted equal opportunity, while large majorities of white men, women, and native American men disagreed.

Moreover, more white women and all nonwhites approved of affirmative action than thought it promoted equal opportunity over time. Thus, some other principle of distributive justice must account for some of the support that affirmative action enjoys. However, in an important dispute, over two-thirds of these respondents thought that without affirmative action, women and nonwhites would not be seriously considered for jobs—but two-thirds of white men disagreed. So while not all the debates about affirmative action are in terms of equal opportunity, certainly disputes about the impact of affirmative action on equal opportunity are important for many of the respondents.

At the same time, many supporters of affirmative action had an affinity with consequentialist arguments for affirmative action. These arguments also provided additional justification for affirmative action for those who did not think the equal opportunity principle provides sufficient grounds for affirmative action. The central consequentialist arguments in favor of affirmative action suggest that affirmative action benefited either society or women and nonwhites. Such consequentialist arguments account for a significant part of respondent sentiment in favor of affirmative action.

When comparing attitudes toward the rationales for affirmative action (given in this chapter) with overall levels of support for such policies (in chapter 5), similar patterns are found among nonwhite ethnic subgroups. Blacks were the most supportive of the various rationales for affirmative action, followed by Asians and Hispanics. Black men were the most suspicious of the equal opportunity principle, and native American men were the most hostile, especially to compensatory justice rationales. Native American men also were more individualistic in overall outlook than members of other nonwhite subgroups. Black, Hispanic, and native American women were more supportive of the various rationales for affirmative action than their male counterparts. Asian men approved of affirmative action more than Asian women, but were less likely than Asian women to agree with many of the moral arguments in favor of it.

Political ideology was significantly related to attitudes about most of the rationales offered for affirmative action. Patterns discovered in chapter 5 are found again: differences in attitudes among white men were strongly related to political ideology on almost all issues. With target group members, however, the reality is more complex, and again, being a woman or nonwhite man reduced differences related to ideology. There are also several notable surprises. On many questions, conservative white women were more supportive of affirmative action than their moderate counterparts, including on questions dealing with whether to focus on groups or individuals when evaluating public policies, or whether the impact of affirmative action was positive or negative. Among nonwhites, however, conservatives and moderates tended to answer similarly about the various rationales for affirmative action, while liberals usually were more supportive. This demonstrates again that being nonwhite, and to a lesser extent being a white woman, tended to level out differences related to political ideology.

The task of the next chapter is threefold: first, in the light of these data, to reflect on the theoretical issues and puzzles that have guided the research; second, to return to the main normative ethical arguments about affirmative action, first discussed in chapter 2, to see if these data illuminate these arguments and provide some insight as to which are most compelling; and third, to reflect on what insights these data provide for those within organizations who are responsible for implementing affirmative action programs.

7

CONCLUSIONS AND IMPLICATIONS

THIS RESEARCH was driven by both descriptive and normative ethical concerns. It began by suggesting that the affirmative action issue provides an interesting window through which to view the struggle within the Liberal culture over competing principles of distributive justice. It then provided a normative ethical analysis of four major, competing approaches to distributive justice and affirmative action (chapter 2). Chapter 3 established a framework for the descriptive phase of the research, linking it to the normative ethical analysis of chapter 2 by addressing four theoretical questions about respondent attitudes. First, how far do the attitudes of ordinary people parallel the major types of ethical approaches advanced by social philosophers (explained in chapter 2)? Second, do individuals from traditionally oppressed groups approach distributive justice in general, and affirmative action in particular, differently from white men? Third, which among several demographic variables are most strongly related to attitudes about affirmative action and the various rationales offered for it, and why?

These three questions require as background an understanding of the four major approaches to affirmative action first explained in chapter 2. The fourth question of theoretical interest mentioned in chapter 3, about the overall impact of the affirmative action controversy on Liberal culture in general and on Liberal culture's norms of distributive justice in particular, will be discussed later in this chapter.

Beyond the descriptive interests, the other central aims of this research have been to develop descriptive data that illuminate the normative ethical debates about affirmative action and to make some recommendations for individuals in organizations who are responsible for affirmative action programs.

This research is unique in its twin methodology combining both qualitative and quantitative methods. The qualitative methods (participant observation and interviews) made it possible to probe attitudes in depth and helped uncover the nature of respondent concerns about affirmative action, enhancing the interpretation of the survey results. The quantitative survey research complemented the qualitative phase of the research by assessing the prevalence of attitudes expressed in the workplace and during interviews, and by making it possible to assess respondents' attitudes to specific theories.

This chapter brings together these descriptive and normative aims. Section 1 reflects the descriptive purpose, focusing on the significance of the descriptive ethical analysis to the theoretical questions. Section 2 examines how the empirical findings illuminate the typical arguments made about affirmative action. My aim is not to advance a comprehensive normative ethical judgment of affirmative action (which would be a different line of inquiry) but rather to contribute to the ongoing dialogue over the moral permissibility of such policy by suggesting which arguments against and for affirmative action are supported by the data. The third and final section discusses the implications of this research for organizations with affirmative action programs.

This research is most easily generalizable to organizations with relatively aggressive affirmative action programs, organizations that have established and are trying to meet specific hiring goals. While my respondents probably expressed slightly more liberal views than those in the nation at large, the research, with its twin methods, uncovered attitudes prevalent in the nation at large. More important, the research illuminates attitudes that likely would be found in institutions with aggressive affirmative action programs. This is particularly important to note, since it is the aggressive programs that are the most controversial. Thus, although one should always be cautious about generalizing, similar dynamics will probably also be found within other organizations with affirmative action programs.

Descriptive Ethical Analysis

This section reviews the major conclusions grounded in the descriptive ethical analysis of respondents' attitudes toward affirmative action, summarizes some patterns in the data that provide evidence for these conclusions, and discusses how these conclusions and patterns illuminate the descriptive theoretical interests guiding the empirical phase of this research.

The findings yield four specific conclusions. First, there was a strong consensus among respondents in favor of Liberalism's axial principle of distributive justice, the equal opportunity principle. While there are different versions of this principle (libertarian, conservative, and liberal), respondents overwhelmingly endorsed it. Second, there was at the same time great reluctance to conceive of distributive justice exclusively in terms of the equal opportunity principle. Both strong endorsement of and ambivalence about the equal opportunity principle coexist in the attitudes of many of the respondents. Third, this ambivalence was expressed in diverse ways: in apathy or indifference, in resignation toward current distributive norms and outcomes, in a reluctance to discuss ethical concerns, in confusion about ethical values, and in inconsistent attitudes about equal opportunity and preferential affirmative action practices. Fourth, this ambivalence reflects tensions among competing values in U.S. culture. Although Liberalism with its equal opportunity principle of distributive justice clearly dominates and frames most of the ethical debates over affirmative action, alternative ethical perspectives expressed in the Liberal culture counter this principle of justice.

I demonstrate these conclusions below by reviewing of some of the more important patterns uncovered during the descriptive ethical analysis of respondents' attitudes toward affirmative action.

Patterns of Belief and Ambivalence

Gender, ethnicity, and political ideology were the variables most consistently related to differing attitudes toward affirmative action. Among the four main research groups, white men were the most ambivalent about affirmative action: majorities of these men approved of it in the abstract but disapproved of the most important preferential elements of affirmative action programs (such as goals and focused recruitment). For the majority of white male respondents, no rationale offered for affirmative action was compelling.

Strong majorities of women and nonwhite men supported the idea, the practice, and most rationales offered for affirmative action. Nonwhite women were the most supportive of affirmative action, both in theory and (slightly less) in practice. There is a clear gender gap among the four main groups: white women and nonwhite women were more supportive than their male counterparts of the idea, the practice, and most rationales offered for affirmative action. The gender gap is much larger among whites than among nonwhites.

Aside from gender and ethnicity, the variable related most consistently to attitudes about affirmative action is political ideology. On most questions, liberals were more likely than moderates or conservatives to endorse the idea, the practice, and most rationales for affirmative action. Political ideology was an especially decisive factor in the attitudes of white men, was only moderately related to the views of white women, and was only slightly related to the attitudes of nonwhites. Being nonwhite, therefore, and to a lesser extent being white and female, tended to level out differences in attitudes related to political ideology that otherwise might be present; however, among white men, differences related to political ideology were much greater.

Among nonwhite ethnic and gender groups, blacks were the most supportive of affirmative action and most of the rationales offered for it, followed by Asians and Hispanics. Native American women strongly supported affirmative action, but native American men were ambivalent in a way similar to white men: majorities narrowly agreed that affirmative action was morally right, and they approved of goals (on this point, unlike white men), but they expressed ambivalence or hostility toward the other central practices of the program and endorsed none of the typical rationales offered for it. Black and Hispanic women were also more supportive of affirmative action than their male counterparts, even though black men appeared to be much more suspicious than black women of Liberalism's equal opportunity principle and the idea of hiring based on merit. However, among Asian men and women, the picture is less clear: on some points, Asian men were more supportive, on others, Asian women were. Asian men supported affirmative action practices more than Asian women, even though they were less likely than Asian women to agree with most of the rationales for affirmative action.

In addition to patterns related to gender, ethnicity, and political ideology, I found some patterns in attitudes toward concepts of distributive justice. These attitudes all fall broadly within the major approaches to affirmative action taken by social philosophers.

Views opposing affirmative action can be divided into three broad types, each emphasizing a different principle of justice. First, some opposed affirmative action because they believed it violated the absolute rights of individuals. This view depended on assumptions roughly analogous to the idea of natural liberty in libertarian theory (the idea that careers ought to be open to natural talents at the point of hiring, without concern for natural and social privileges that affect one's competitiveness, unless such competitiveness was wrongfully gained). Here the idea is that an individual has an absolute, inviolable right to equal treatment at the point of hiring. As first pointed out in chapter 2, such a version of individual rights ensures that those individuals who already have free access and free choice in market society take precedence over disadvantaged individuals. Not surprisingly, then, the view that affirmative action violates individual rights was most popular among white men. (This seemed to be especially true among conservative, Christian, white men, although more data would be needed to confirm this possibility.) Even among white men, however, those who expressd such an absolute, principled view of rights were in the minority.

Second, some did not go so far as libertarians in thinking that equal opportunity (as equal legal access to market society) was an inviolable human right and *the* morally right principle of distributive justice but who nevertheless rejected affirmative action because they thought it compromised too much on the equal opportunity principle. This conclusion was grounded in premises closer to natural liberty than Liberal equality (but without libertarian absolutism about the inviolability of market competition), combined with the perception that affirmative action extended excessive preference to women and nonwhite men.

Third, some believed that the social costs of affirmative action are too great, namely, declining efficiency and productivity, workplace morale, and racial harmony. This third objection was much more prevalent than the argument based on inviolable rights and somewhat more prevalent than the argument that affirmative action compromises too much on the principle of equal opportunity. Such consequentialist objections were also often expressed by those who also strongly objected to affirmative action on the grounds of some deontological principle. (This helps illustrate the limits of this threefold typology of the central arguments against affirmative action: the first two are not mutually exclusive of the third, making it difficult to assess precisely which arguments are most important. If I were to replicate this study, I would ask respondents to rank which are the most important among the various arguments for and against affirmative action.)

One point upon which most opponents and proponents of affirmative action agreed was that compensatory justice rationales for affirmative action are not compelling. Even though many of the rationales for affirmative action articulated by social philosophers (and by some respondents) justified the programs in terms of compensating persons for past wrongs, this rationale had little support. Even among the strongest proponents of affirmative action, only a few thought that affirmative action was justified on this basis. (As discussed earlier, the major complaint about this rationale was that affirmative action usually does not make the perpetrators of discrimination bear the compensatory burden.)

Much more important to those who supported affirmative action were two simple arguments grounded in the idea of liberal equality (with its version of the equal opportunity principle). (With Liberal equality, the libertarian version of equal opportunity—understood as a situation where there are no legal barriers to careers open to talents—is supplemented with the insistence that equal opportunity also requires that those with equal natural talents have *actual* equal opportunity, namely, the same life chances to develop and compete with these talents. This involves a shift wherein competitively disadvantaged persons now take precedence over those who already have free access and free choice in market society.)

These pro–affirmative action arguments boil down to two ideas. First, women and nonwhite men need affirmative action to get a fair chance for jobs. Second, equal opportunity is one good principle among others, but is not an absolute right; some short-term compromise of pure equal opportunity is needed to promote actual equal opportunity overall and over the long term. (To ensure actual equal life chances to develop one's natural gifts, of course, requires a certain level of social equality in cultural and educational opportunities. Usually, however, even those who believed that affirmative action was needed to promote equal opportunity over the long term were ignorant of the social building blocks necessary for real equal opportunity. Those who did make these connections tended to be better educated.)

Thus, while compensatory notions did not have much support, there was wider support for attempts to overcome current competitive disadvantages. But respondents were greatly divided over the factual question as to whether affirmative action was needed to ensure fair consideration for jobs: large majorities of white men thought it was not, but most others thought it was.

The other major affirmative action argument expressed by respondents focused on consequences, asserting that in many ways affirmative action benefits society and organizations. Such conseqentialist arguments often supplement one of the two arguments grounded in Liberal equality.

Respondents did not spontaneously express concern, as do Rawls (1971) and Schaar (1974), about a problem left unresolved by versions of equal opportunity under the umbrella of natural liberty and Liberal equality: that equal opportunity allows virtually unlimited material inequality resulting from unearned natural talents, which produces, in turn, not democracy, but meritocracy.[1] Respondents' lack of recognition about this problem illustrates the dominance of Liberalism's equal opportunity ideal; most respondents *assume* that it is morally right to distribute preferred jobs and rewards according to natural talents.

While no one spontaneously expressed concern about the meritocratic result of awarding positions largely according to natural talents, a surprising number were alarmed when Schaar's argument—that equal opportunity leads to inequality and meritocracy—was explained (as simply as possible). Some then expressed socialist sentiments, although if they used the word *socialist*, they usually added an *apologia*, aware they were entering the heretical zone. A few endorsed "socialized medicine," or mentioned that they liked socialist countries such as Sweden or New Zealand, or that they had Woodstockish values, like sharing everything. That people couched egalitarian sentiments in such language implies that they felt strong social pressures to limit their flirtation with such ideas. But quite a few respondents expressed substantive principles of equality but did not have a language or context for expressing or even understanding the importance of their moral sentiments. Substantive egalitarians were clearly on the defensive and were not finding much cultural reinforcement for their beliefs.

Curiously, only once did an interview respondent mention social scarcity (the limited number of jobs) as a central problem linked to the equal opportunity principle. A white woman, an active proponent of affirmative action, noted, "There is only so much room at the top." The lack of such recognition by others, combined with the affinity of many respondents for the fiction of unlimited opportunity (the American Dream), suggests that some attitudes were grounded in an optimism about the possibility of sustained economic growth or a reluctance to face up to both resource and social scarcity.

The other major point to remember in this overview is that while there are strong threads of individualism in the assumptions of almost all respondents (seen, for example, in their embrace of the American Dream and the equal opportunity principle), women and nonwhite men are more likely than white men to judge affirmative action based on its consequences for their own group or society as a whole. This tendency was particularly obvious in responses of those most hostile toward affirmative action: white men and native American men.

This summary of the basic attitudes of respondents shows that, indeed, most of the ideas expressed in the workplace do fit somewhere within the four major approaches to distributive justice and affirmative action. However, the respondents did not make the same fine distinctions as do social philosophers, and oftentimes respondents expressed contradictory sentiments. The descriptive analysis in chapters 4 through 6 described many points of inconsistency and ambivalence.

Reasons for Ambivalence and Inconsistency

There are so many possible explanations for the ambivalence and inconsistency in respondent attitudes that it seems almost presumptuous to offer an explanation. Nevertheless, a few reasons can be suggested. In one concrete example, two white women agonized over how affirmative action would hold back their husbands or sons but also saw it benefiting themselves or their daughters. Less concretely, but probably more important, is that the complexity of the issues surrounding the affirmative action controversy could explain some of the ambivalence and confusion. Chapter 2 noted that attitudes about affirmative action can be influenced by a wide range of assumptions. It is difficult enough for social philosophers, trained in ethical analysis, to eliminate all inconsistency from their views. This is all the more difficult for the average worker.

This difficulty was compounded by what is perhaps the major reason that I encountered so much confusion and ambivalence in my research: within the Liberal culture there are a number of competing ethical perspectives, and these different perspectives are reflected in the attitudes of ordinary people, even though these perspectives may rest on different assumptions and not fit coherently together.

For example, many respondents believed that the American Dream was real and thought that people bring failure upon themselves. In several ways they then contradicted this opinion, expressing resignation about their own place in the division of labor, suggesting that luck and privilege have a lot to do with success, or asserting that prejudice and discrimination were still prevalent in society and in their workplace.

The survey data reveal an overwhelming consensus in favor of the equal opportunity principle, but such agreement does not adequately measure the difference between true endorsement of the principles and mere acquiescence to it, especially when the principle is so prevalent that it confronts most people as a fact—a given.[2] Further analysis demonstrates that the apparent consensus in favor of pure equal opportunity broke down (and broke down the most among women and nonwhite men) when people responded to more specific statements related to the equal opportunity principle or to preferential affirmative action. Reactions to these statements show that fewer respondents thought that jobs and salaries ought to be distributed according to natural talents than endorsed in the abstract the equal opportunity principle. It came out in the interviews that those who were suspicious of distributions based on natural talents also felt strongly that something was amiss in the Liberal culture's distributive outcomes. So while most respondents did not explicitly and directly object to inequalities of wealth, they were nevertheless concerned with more than formal (procedural) justice. It is reasonable to conclude that some ambivalence was located in the simultaneous affinity with both procedural and substantive principles of justice.

Another example of ambivalence related to the equal opportunity principle is that sometimes a specific individual expressed support for both of the two basic versions of equal opportunity under Liberalism.

Finally, ambivalence toward the equal opportunity principle was found, in both the qualitative and quantitative data, in evidence of communitarian moral sentiments. For example, many thought that public policy ought to consider the welfare of groups and the overall social good, not just the welfare of individuals. It is probably not coincidental that the number of respondents who endorsed the overall morality of affirmative action closely matches the number of those who thought it benefited society.

The point is that many of the contradictory sentiments expressed by the respondents reflected, and can be traced to, contending ethical approaches to affirmative action in the Liberal culture. Some respondents thought that affirmative action violated rights, that the best qualified should always be hired, but nevertheless agreed that, without explicitly preferential policies such as affirmative action, some individuals would not get a fair chance and that ultimately equal opportunity would deteriorate. Still others approved of equal opportunity, but when push came to shove, what was really decisive was their perception about whether affirmative action positively or negatively affected their own group or society at large. Meanwhile, a few expressed a desire for greater equality of wealth and saw affirmative action as congruent with such a view of distributive justice.

To summarize: many respondents strongly endorsed the equal opportunity principle in the abstract, while being ambivalent about ideas related to it. Liberalism (with its individualism) has been very successful in framing the terms of the debate about justice in general, and issues such as affirmative action in particular, so that the overwhelming majority of all debate over affirmative action is in terms of the principle of equal opportunity. But despite this dominance, there are competing ethical perspectives in the United States, such as those found in some forms of civic republicanism, and in socialist thought, that work against people taking Liberalism's equal opportunity principle as sufficient grounds for distributive justice.[3] It is also clear, however, that such competing perspectives are on the defensive. This was clear from the interviews, where those who expressed communitarian values that place a high value on economic equality did so apologetically or tentatively. This was especially true for those respondents who could accurately be labeled *socialist sympathizers.*

The preceding analysis provides some empirical support for Kann's assertion that Liberalism (by which he means the Liberalism of Locke and his contemporary soul mate Nozick) is the dominant political ideology in the United States. He continues that republican ideology, which has "valued public virtue, substantive justice, and the commonweal," and was a strong part of the ideology of the founders of the United States, continues to provide countervailing values in contemporary America "in opposition to Locke's individualism, proceduralism, and acquisitiveness" (1982, 31–32). Kann argues that Lockean Liberalism has increasingly dominated U.S. political life. Nevertheless, Liberalism did "not eliminate the countercurrents of thought that make up American ambivalence. Rather it dominates and shapes public discussion to the extent that the countercurrents appear as nothing other than deeply submerged undercurrents, without channels into the mainstream" (1982, 32). Kann further suggests that such countervalues have become "automatically suspected as evil" (1982, 33). This marginalization of countervalues under the dominance of Lockean Liberalism, Kann believes, has continued to "make it difficult to detect the degree to which Americans temper their Lockean liberalism with democratic norms of community, justice, and public control over the economy" (1982, 33). I think it also makes it difficult to detect the American ambivalence itself.

Kann's analysis squares with my findings in two ways. First, his analysis fits with my perception that there is a significant amount of ambivalence toward the equal opportunity principle, in spite of the consensus endorsement of this idea in the abstract; and this ambivalence is related to concerns for outcomes and for substantive justice, which reflect significant countervailing values to those expressed in the equal opportunity principle. Second, his analysis squares with my conclusion—that, at least in part, the reason that countervailing values (such as those grounded in republican thought) are sometimes difficult to discern is due to the overall success that Liberalism has had in framing the terms of moral discourse in the United States.[4]

If it is true that the ambivalence and confusion in respondents' attitudes partly reflect the contending and unresolved tensions among the various ethical perspectives within U.S. political culture, this still does not address why there are differences among racial and gender groups. Many of these differences may be related to contending values grounded in the cultural heritages of the various racial and gender subgroups. It is not surprising, for example, that the dominant group in the culture (white men), along with the dominant political philosophy (Liberalism), are reciprocally supportive. Similarly, it is not surprising that those who were excluded from mainstream culture by virtue of their race or gender expressed more group-based sentiments than white men, who have never been excluded because of their race or gender.

As the interviews show, there was a difference in group-sensitive thinking. Thus, in addition to the countervailing pressures due to the competition among conservative, liberal, and communitarian ethical perspectives (such as those grounded in the egalitarian forms of republican thought and in Marxist values), the attitudes of those whose background included a non-Western cultural heritage may have been further complicated (and confused) by values grounded in their own cultural backgrounds. This may account for some of the differences among white men and the other racial and gender subgroups, especially native American men.

A brief case study examining the ambivalent and sometimes contradictory responses among native American men can illustrate how there may be many different countervailing pressures upon individuals in U.S. culture—particularly when they are also influenced by the non-Liberal traditions of their own group.

Comparing native American and white men is particularly interesting, because these groups are generally the most hostile to affirmative action. They both narrowly agreed that affirmative action is morally right, endorsed the equal opportunity principle and the hiring of the best qualified, agreed that the naturally talented deserved the best jobs and salaries, and disagreed that affirmative action promoted harmony and is needed to ensure a fair chance for jobs. However, native American men were less likely than white men to think that affirmative action was needed as a remedy for discrimination, more likely to focus on individuals instead of groups in forming public policies, more likely to think that affirmative action harmed the mission of the Parks Department, and more likely to think that civil rights leaders were pushing in the wrong direction.

On other questions, however, native American men were more sympathetic to ideas favoring affirmative action. For example, they were more likely to support greater economic equality in society, hiring goals, and distribution according to effort (not just natural talents). While all groups have members who expressed contradictory ideas (again suggesting that there are several ethical perspectives competing for allegiance in U.S. culture), native American men seemed more torn than most. This may reflect the diverse cultural streams to which they are exposed.

Those with especially diverse cultural backgrounds, with ideas grounded both inside and outside of mainstream philosophical Liberalism, may tend to exhibit greater moral confusion than whites, whose ethical heritage is more uniform. Native American men who are assimilated enough into the dominant culture to be employed by a government agency may have many culturally grounded ethical perspectives competing for their allegiance. Four examples are immediately apparent. First, these men may be influenced by their native American heritage: by the individualism of the warrior or hunter-hero (an individualism that ultimately serves the community); by anti-individualistic notions based on native American religion, which emphasize the interdependence and sacredness of all life; and by intertribal rivalries, which have often prevented native American solidarity and community.[5] Second, men in general, including native Americans (but not blacks), were more supportive than women of individualistic approaches to policy and of the equal opportunity principle, so there may be a difference related to gender. Third, native American men have been increasingly assimilated into the Liberal culture, which places a premium on the individual and is characterized by ongoing struggles over who shall take precedence and over the proper relationship between the individual and the general interest. Fourth, these native American men were influenced by the workplace subculture, in which affirmative action was often derided by those who claimed that unqualified people were getting hired.

This analysis has not attempted to uncover all of the reasons people express diverse and sometimes contradictory attitudes toward affirmative action, but has offered a few examples of how different ideas can compete for one's allegiance. This can make the affirmative action issue, and the underlying issues of distributive justice it raises, very difficult to resolve.

Conclusions from the Descriptive Ethical Analysis

The preceding analysis sustains the four conclusions I outlined at the beginning of this section: there was a remarkable degree of consensus about Liberalism's equal opportunity principle of distributive justice; there was also great ambivalence about this principle; ambivalence was expressed in various ways; and this ambivalence reflects sometimes contradictory attitudes grounded in the major contending ethical perspectives in U.S. culture. The combined interview and survey data show that many individuals simultaneously endorse (or acquiesce to) the equal opportunity principle, while also expressing ambivalence about it. For many in all the subject groups, these two sentiments coexisted, but among white women, nonwhite women, and nonwhite men, there was greater reluctance than among white men to take equal opportunity as *the* norm of distributive justice.[6]

With these findings established, it is possible to return to and discuss the central theoretical questions that guided this research. First, the attitudes of ordinary people clearly do reflect the major types of ethical approaches advanced by social philosophers. At the same time, most respondents are not as consistent in their views. Part of their ambivalence must be related to the appropriation of sometimes incompatible lines of thought. The result has been that many respondents end up with confused attitudes toward distributive justice and affirmative action. Sometimes their strong opinions about affirmative action do not square with their attitudes toward certain premises upon which affirmative action is based, or the specific practices it commonly involves.

Second, traditionally oppressed people tend to approach distributive justice in general, and affirmative action in particular, differently from white men. These people are more likely than white men to evaluate principles of distributive justice, or policies such as affirmative action, by emphasizing the impact on their group or upon the overall social good. While traditionally oppressed people still endorse equal opportunity and its individualism, they are more likely to embrace an individualism in which disadvantaged persons take precedence and are more likely to be influenced by communitarian, relationship-based, and ends-focused values.

Third, there are relationships among some of the various demographic variables and attitudes toward affirmative action and the various rationales offered for it. But with the exception of political ideology, these factors are not nearly as important as membership in an ethnic or gender group; membership in a traditionally excluded group is more important to respondent attitudes than are the various demographic variables, with the occasional exception of political ideology.

Finally, the fourth descriptive question was, Since the affirmative action controversy raises all the major normative ethical questions of distributive justice, what impact might the affirmative action controversy have on the Liberal culture and its norms of distributive justice? My impression is that for all the controversy over affirmative action, the issue probably will have very little impact on the direction of the culture. Most respondents did not demonstrate any significant critical distance from the dominant norms of distribution in the Liberal culture. Even when the problems and inegalitarian consequences of these principles were carefully explained during the interviews, those who found something wrong with such consequences still did not envision an alternative. In my view, limits to growth, grounded both in the scarcity of resources and the perennial limit of preferred positions, will increase the hardships borne by those who lose out in market competition and make these hardships more obvious. But even as this occurs, it appears that few of the respondents have any idea which norms of distributive justice are really morally right or good, and many do not even know what alternatives there may be. In the absence of such a recognition, it is hard to see how the issues raised by the affirmative action controversy will have a decisive cultural impact.

Affirmative action is a confusing issue because—for many if not most of the respondents—the fundamental issues posed by the problem of distributive justice remain shrouded (see also Hochschild 1981, 283).

Normative Ethical Arguments

The descriptive data also provide insight for the normative ethical analysis of affirmative action. I begin by explaining why an examination of group attitudes is relevant to a normative ethical analysis of this issue. I then reexamine each of the four major normative ethical approaches to affirmative action in light of the descriptive data. My purpose is not to resolve all the tensions and conclude with a comprehensive moral argument about affirmative action. Rather, I will suggest which arguments about affirmative action find the least and the most support, and, overall, which lines of argument about affirmative action seem to be the most compelling.

The Contribution of Descriptive Ethics to Normative Ethical Argument

Descriptive data are relevant for the normative ethical analysis of affirmative action for two reasons. First, many arguments about affirmative action depend on perceptions about social facts and about the consequences of affirmative action. Different types of empirical research, including research into attitudes, can illuminate the accuracy of such perceptions. Second, there is a widely shared premise in the Liberal culture that the legitimacy of a government and its social policies depends on the consent of the governed—through a social contract. Given this premise, research into attitudes toward government policies is certainly relevant to the moral evaluation of such policies. Even with Rawls's social contract, arrived at in the original position (where people negotiate over the contract without knowing their actual positions in society), one can argue that attitudes examined through empirical research can provide insight into what moral intuitions people would bring into the original position.

Beyond this obvious point, for those who value the principle of consent, it is especially important to consider the views of those who have been traditionally and systematically excluded from the culturally established processes by which the social contract is decided. Here is a central reason this research is important: women and nonwhites have been excluded from participation in negotiations over U.S. norms of distributive justice. Therefore, it is morally right to give their voices a special place in normative ethical debates about these norms. This is true in part because such norms address the means by which their exclusion is to be remedied. This is not to say that the views of excluded persons are, necessarily, ethically correct, any more than it would be good moral reasoning to say that the views of the majority constitute that which is ethically correct. But certainly normative ethical discourse ought to bring all voices into the discussion of any moral controversy, and particularly those voices that have been excluded from negotiations over the social contract.

Part of the value of this research is that it has listened to traditionally excluded voices. It has tried to bring such voices into the normative ethical debates over affirmative action. Beyond this, given the exclusion of such voices and the moral imperative to reverse this exclusion, arguably, social policy ought to place greater weight on the views of those traditionally excluded than on the views of those already enfranchised. Some would say that such an argument is antithetical to the idea of a social contract grounded in the consent of a *majority* of a society's members, because it would give more weight to one individual's views than to another's. But in negotiations over the social contract, the voices of white men (and especially rich white men) have always weighed more heavily than those of women and nonwhite men. Therefore, the intent of the best social contract theory is preserved by adding weight to traditionally muted voices. This intent is reflected in the idea that the legitimacy of government depends on the individual's right to consent to the moral norms reflected in government policies.

My premise here is that although what people agree to in a social contract may not always be morally right or promote the Good, such agreements place a strong burden of proof upon those who take moral exception to them, as long as the validity of the contract itself is not in question. The validity of any social contract is in question to the extent it can be shown that persons affected by such a contract were excluded from its creation. *Actual consent* (rather than consent in a hypothetical original position) ought to be a key factor in evaluating public policies such as affirmative action. Presumably, in a society that values self-rule, all citizens would (periodically) vote and endorse the basic tenets of that society.

The Four Major Normative Ethical Approaches

The normative ethical analysis in chapter 2 illustrates that the affirmative action controversy is grounded in competing attitudes toward principles of distributive justice and differing perceptions about a wide range of facts. It concludes that much of the controversy boils down to which individuals, the disadvantaged or the dominant, ought to take precedence in the Liberal culture; and whether individual interests ought to take precedence over the general interest. The analysis in chapters 4 and 6 parallel the discussion in chapter 2 and finds confusions and tensions along the same lines as with the arguments of the social philosophers.

The moral issues underlying the affirmative action controversy are complex. These issues have not been resolved in the Liberal culture, and it is not possible to resolve here these tensions. Instead, it is time to focus on the specific points where the descriptive ethical analysis provided by this research illuminates the four major types of approaches to the affirmative action issue. This focus allows some tentative conclusions about which arguments about affirmative action, in light of this research, are most plausible. The descriptive data are most illuminating in showing the *weaknesses* of certain arguments, or at least how little support certain arguments enjoy. These data are not by nature capable of *proving* the validity of any particular approach to affirmative action.

LIBERTARIAN AND CONSERVATIVE ARGUMENTS

As shown in chapter 2, libertarians and conservatives tend to disapprove of affirmative action. For several reasons, however, their arguments against affirmative action do not find much support in these data. First, libertarians (and two interview respondents) believed that the use of racial classifications in public policies, including in affirmative action policy, posed a great threat to individual liberties. For individuals from groups who have been persecuted because of their race, these fears do not necessarily represent a conservative response designed to protect the privileges of the dominant group. Nevertheless, such sentiments often do degenerate into fallacious, slippery-slope thinking, suggesting that the use of such classifications inevitably jeopardizes fundamental civil liberties.

Certainly, these data show that few, even among those who disapproved of affirmative action, perceived affirmative action as having the insidious purpose or consequence of excluding and depriving white men of their fundamental liberties. I do not assume, however, that this perception is necessarily *accurate*. Nevertheless, such perceptions can help us evaluate the accuracy of the claim that affirmative action does erode such liberties. Those who experience an aggressive affirmative action program firsthand are well placed to offer testimony as to the actual effects of the policy—and few conclude it violates fundamental rights.

While fears about the use of racial classifications may be well founded historically, the Supreme Court—by insisting that policies using racial classifications must serve some "important" state purpose (in other words, a "morally permissible" state purpose)—has provided a commonsense safeguard, which can prevent the use of racial classifications from sliding down the slippery slope to Holocaust-style or lesser horrors. (A Jewish respondent felt that a Holocaust was the ultimate danger behind all racial classifications; the lesser horror would be a permanent distribution of preferred positions by some racial proportionality formula.) But any public policy ultimately relies on group classifications, and any public policy affects different groups differently, so it strikes me as naive to suggest that racial classifications themselves can and must be avoided. It is better to recognize the existence of groups, and to justify and calculate the effect of policies on them, than to ignore them (see Garet 1983).

Second, the libertarian tendency to see affirmative action as a scheme to alter distributive outcomes (thus violating entitlement rights) finds little encouragement in these data. Few respondents endorsed such a rigid, exceptionless view of justice. This was true even among opponents of affirmative action. Of course, that few respondents endorsed a libertarian view begs the question as to whether the libertarian entitlement theory is nevertheless right. These data show that few were sympathetic to an exceptionless libertarian approach. In ethical discourse, then, this finding goes first to the issue of the feasibility of implementing libertarian ideals. But this finding also addresses the normative ethical question; we should take seriously the testimony of ordinary people who have experienced affirmative policies firsthand when they say they do not believe it deprives white men of their fundamental liberties. To not do so does not take seriously enough the contextual nature of ethical discourse. Further, to take the principles articulated by social philosphers over the commonsense evaluations of those experiencing such policies may lead to a harmful abstractionism in ethics. (Daniel Maguire [1982] calls such abstractionism the "intellectualist fallacy.")

The arguments of conservatives in the Liberal tradition fare no better in light of these data. Conservatives tend to oppose affirmative action on the ground that it violates their view of justice as distribution according to purely procedural equal opportunity. Although these data show that most individuals endorsed the equal opportunity norm in the abstract, they also show that there was enough ambivalence and countervailing sentiment in favor of supplementing such a principle with concern for outcomes that pure equal opportunity is not the decisive standpoint from which most people evaluate affirmative action.

LIBERAL APPROACHES

When illuminated by these data, the arguments of liberals fare better than the arguments of libertarians and conservatives. The liberal version of the equal opportunity principle based on Liberal equality found greater support than the conservative or libertarian versions. Liberal equality insists that equal opportunity refers not only to equal legal access to market society but also to actual equal life chances to develop and succeed according to one's natural gifts. This shifts the focus from law to social conditions and insists that the disadvantaged receive sufficient help to ensure their equal access to market society.

Many respondents recognized the common sense behind this approach, which insists that the legitimacy of the equal opportunity principle depends on the actual equal opportunities that people have. Many of those who favored affirmative action recognized that policies such as affirmative action are needed to give the disadvantaged a fair chance for positions. Even some of those who were opposed to or very ambivalent about affirmative action recognized that something had to be done to enhance actual opportunities for all (like improving education). This recognition contributed to the willingness of some respondents to "live with" such policy. These data suggest that most respondents were sympathetic to the idea that if the equal opportunity principle was a good principle, it ought to be reflected in social reality.

Another area where liberal arguments fared better than libertarian and conservative ones was on the question of whether affirmative action was needed for women and nonwhite men to be seriously considered for jobs. Most respondents recognized that women and nonwhite men do not receive equal consideration. This is strong testimony indeed, because it comes from ordinary working people who listen daily to their co-workers' attitudes, and not from philosophers who have little contact with ordinary working people. My impressions from observing attitudes in the workplace for many years lead me to a similar conclusion—a conclusion put simply by one of my black respondents, who stated that without affirmative action the department would still be "lily white." And it would also have virtually no women rangers, lifeguards, managers, or maintenance workers.

MARXIST APPROACHES

This research found little support among respondents for jettisoning the equal opportunity principle entirely, as some Marxists would like to do. It did, however, find that a number of respondents were suspicious of this principle, and even more who voiced strong socialist sentiments in favor of greater substantive equality in society (while avoiding, or being timid about, using the term *socialism*). Beyond this, however, this research does little to illuminate a Marxist perspective on affirmative action. This is in part because a Marxist could either approve or disapprove of such policy depending on the relative orthodoxy and pragmatism of his or her overall political strategy. However, while the focus of a Marxist view of justice is not on distribution, affirmative action, with its redistributive effect, does have significant affinity with the communitarian sentiments and the concern for substantive justice found in Marxist thought and in perspectives indebted to Marxism.

CONSEQUENTIALIST APPROACHES

The many consequentialist approaches to affirmative action vary according to which specific concept of the Good is taken as an end. Some are grounded in civic republican concepts of the Good (concern for social order, community, the commonweal, and sometimes social and economic equality). Others conceive of the Good in terms similar to the key tenets of Liberalism. While there may be different versions of the Good with different consequentialist theories, when it comes to the consequences of affirmative action policy, many of the same disputed facts are important to these different consequentialist theories. Of the four approaches to affirmative action, consequentialist arguments are best analyzed by the descriptive data, because consequentialist arguments are especially fact-dependent, and because these data explore the respondents' perceptions about many key facts.

There are essentially four major areas of consequentialist argument against and for affirmative action. I begin with the arguments

of those who claim that affirmative action has negative consequences. When we examine the consequentialist arguments against
and for affirmative action, these data provide, on balance, more evidence of positive than negative consequences resulting from such
policy. While there is probably at least some truth to each of the
assertions of fact made by opponents of affirmative action, the critical question is, Are the perceptions of such opponents accurate
enough to justify the conclusion that affirmative action is morally
wrong? Again, the aim of this section is not to resolve these points
definitively, but rather to begin to suggest which fact-dependent arguments against and for affirmative action seem to be strongest.

Some opponents of affirmative action argue that discrimination
in the United States is in retreat; therefore affirmative action is unnecessary, and only "protective" antidiscrimination measures are
morally acceptable. However, the perceptions of the respondents,
who are average working people, contradict this analysis. Perceptions about the facts, or the consequences of affirmative action,
simply may be inaccurate. But certainly the perceptions of ordinary people, who observe daily their workplace realities, ought to
be taken seriously, and what they report should be discounted only
with good cause.

Most respondents saw discrimination as prevalent in society
and in their workplace. Only white men were inconsistent on this
point. They admitted to the existence of discrimination but did not
think it was prevalent or affected chances within their own organizations. On this issue, where large majorities of nonwhites and
women assert that prejudice was prevalent both in society and in
their own workplace, I would submit that these traditionally excluded individuals are better situated than white men to evaluate
the prevalence of discrimination.

Furthermore, large majorities of all groups except white men
thought that without affirmative action, women and nonwhite
men would not get serious consideration for jobs. And in the interviews, some respondents, particularly women, emphatically stated
that white men would not willingly give up their monopoly on
power. These data (as well as a great deal of economic and sociological data elsewhere), suggest that it is an overstatement to assert
that discrimination is on the wane.[7]

Other opponents argue that affirmative action leads to increasing prejudice and discrimination against women and nonwhite
men, and that this in turn exacerbates tensions and hostilities between such groups and white men. The data suggest that this may
be true for some (one respondent said, for example, that affirmative

action's hiring of people who are not really motivated to do the job has given him a prejudiced attitude toward minorities).

This certainly is an area worthy of concern, but the data do not confirm this nightmare scenario of increasing hostility among groups. To be sure, hostility among groups who presumably benefit from affirmative action could perhaps occur as a result of affirmative action policies. Occasionally, particularly in the interviews, nonwhites would express the belief that white women benefited from affirmative action more than persons from their own group. Some native Americans suggested that, given their small numbers, after a couple of token hires, parity for native Americans was reached and the pressure to hire persons from their group dissipated, thereby allowing white women and other minorities to benefit much more than native Americans. But these observations were not made in a hostile manner, vilifying individuals from the groups that may have benefited disproportionately. Rather, such criticisms were directed at specific problems in the overall affirmative action program.

From the interviews, specifically regarding attitudes toward distributive justice, I gathered that most individuals had already acquiesced to, accommodated to, or resigned themselves to their place and prospects within the market society. This acceptance of one's place and rewards within the equal opportunity culture carried over even to a majority of white men, even some who believed that their prospects had been limited by affirmative action. Most people, even those opposed to affirmative action, could live with it. This finding is, I think, generalizable to the culture at large. As a result, the affirmative action controversy is not, I believe, fueling dramatic changes in attitudes toward distributive justice in the United States.

In summary, in a Liberal culture, distributive outcomes by and large are perceived to be legitimate. I found little evidence that people were preoccupied with overturning such outcomes. There is another reason some people seemed to accept their place in the division of labor, even when they thought their own chances for advancement were reduced by affirmative action; they believed that, without such policy, there would likely be much greater intergroup tension and, possibly, even social instability: a common rationale among whites who identified themselves as conservatives but who nevertheless endorsed affirmative action.

But finally, the most important reasons that affirmative action does not exacerbate hostility among groups is, first, that prejudice is decreasing, in part because affirmative action forces people with diverse backgrounds to work together; and second, that the majority of people, even those opposed to affirmative action, were not so mean-spirited that they bore a grudge against the particular woman or nonwhite man who took advantage of an opportunity provided by affirmative action. Many disliked affirmative action, but animosity toward the policy was not transferred to those who benefited from it. My impression from the interviews—from undercurrents of racism detected in the attitudes of some of the respondents—is that the few individuals who suggested that affirmative action might have made them prejudiced probably already were.[8]

The most prevalent fact-dependent argument against affirmative action uncovered by the research is that unqualified people are being hired and promoted, leading to declining productivity and efficiency. This is a plausible argument. These programs are costly. And such arguments are supported by some anecdotal evidence. Some respondents gave examples of unqualified people being hired and exceptionally well-qualified people being left out. This also is an area worthy of concern.

Yet most women and nonwhite men did not see this as a problem. And quite a few respondents, including some white men, suggested that the opposite was true: productivity was enhanced by the talents of those hired because of affirmative action efforts. While there were occasional complaints about unqualified women and nonwhite men being hired, there were also complaints about unqualified and unmotivated white male workers—thus it is difficult to know how many such complaints are really the result of affirmative action. I found no compelling evidence that affirmative active has created a serious decline in productivity.

Finally, there is the fact-dependent argument that affirmative action stigmatizes women and nonwhite men, causing them psychological harm, by leading everyone to think that they cannot compete on their own merits. If true, this would be a strong argument against affirmative action. The data show this as a common refrain among opponents of affirmative action. But the interviews and my workplace observations suggest that affirmative action causes little if any psychological harm to women and nonwhites; and if there were, such harm may be due to the constant repetition of this argument itself, which could raise doubts about one's own capabilities. Women and nonwhites often related stories about how they have to prove themselves much more than any white man. My data also suggest that the pressure women and nonwhite men felt from this kind of argument was probably the major reason some of them opposed affirmative action—they resent the stigma it carried and the implication that they got where they were only because of their ethnicity or gender.

The argument that affirmative action stigmatizes those it intends to help certainly raises a serious problem for proponents of affirmative action. But one must evaluate the extent of such stigmatizing effects and weigh them against the positive effects of the policies. Serious though these reservations may be, they are not decisive. First, women and nonwhites have always suffered the stigmatizing effects of prejudice and discrimination—and the alternative to affirmative action would overall be fewer jobs and fewer promotions. This hardly would promote the self-esteem and self-confidence these individuals need to compete in a market society.

Second, my overwhelming impression from the interviews is that while there is a constant refrain from some opponents of affirmative action that people are getting jobs regardless of merit, and while many of those from groups targeted for affirmative action concede that this may sometimes be true, affirmative action opens doors to advancement that were previously closed and has thereby *enhanced* the self-esteem and self-regard of numerous women and nonwhite men. Even among those affirmative action hires who thought they may not have been the best qualified when they secured a position, after succeeding in that position, they recognized that they did have the talent to perform well in that role. To oppose affirmative action because some women and nonwhites may not have enough "merit" for many positions could play into the hands of those who, with conscious or unconscious racist or sexist intent, wish to reserve positions for those from their own preferred group. There is a fine line between saying that unqualified people are being hired and saying that individuals from these groups are not able to perform these jobs. Moreover, through sensitivity training, where people are exposed to how language such as, "She only got the job because of affirmative action" can affect an individual, it may be possible to reduce the negative psychological impact of affirmative action policies.

One final insight from the interviews puts to rest the objection that affirmative action can cause irreparable psychological harm to those it purports to help and suggests, on the contrary, that affirmative action can promote psychological health. Several beneficiaries of affirmative action related how, before affirmative action, they had no self-esteem, locked as they were in dead-end jobs—but now they were meeting increasing challenges and responsibilities.

This is true also of many rank-and-file women and nonwhites who found a sense of accomplishment in public service, even when they did not think they were likely to be promoted. So while the danger of further stigmatizing women and nonwhites by preferential policies is real, and while some of these people have accepted the argument that affirmative action negatively reflects on their capabilities and achievements, and while the majority also recognized that they had to do more to prove themselves than their white male colleagues, nevertheless, they knew they could do the job, and went about proving this to those around them. Overall, many have felt prejudice anyway, so this new form of prejudice, in the suggestion that they could not do the job, does not seem so different. In light of this research, it seems, at best, quite patronizing to oppose affirmative action because it might cause feelings of inferiority in women and nonwhite men. At worst, it is a wolf's argument in sheep's clothing.

Beyond the question as to whether affirmative action psychologically harms women and nonwhite men lies the question as to whether affirmative action reinforces white male beliefs in the inferiority of racial minorities and women. My impression is that affirmative action, by exposing white men to diverse race and gender co-workers, reduces their belief in the inferiority of nonwhites and women. When strong affirmative action programs integrate a workplace, these data suggest, white men increasingly recognize the same range of talents among nonwhites as among themselves. Sometimes their comments acknowledging the competence of a woman were grudging. Sometimes the competent woman or nonwhite man was seen as an exception. But through white men's exposure to such persons, anomalies to their prejudiced assumptions mount, gradually overturning prejudiced assumptions, except among the mean-spirited.

In summary, the descriptive data do not support the most common consequentialist arguments against affirmative action. Instead, at significant points, these data suggest that affirmative action has positive consequences.

The preceding synopses of the ways this research illuminates the major arguments over affirmative action leaves unresolved many fundamental issues, including the fundamental tensions within the Liberal culture over whether disadvantaged or privileged individuals ought to take precedence. Nor does it solve the problem over the proper relationship between individual interests and the general interest. It does suggest that, among all the possible arguments for and against affirmative action, proponents have perceived more accurately the problems that have created the need for such programs, as well as the current obstacles to equal opportunity in the workplace.

Practical Implications for Organizations

This research documents diverse attitudes toward affirmative action: hostility, fear, ambivalence, confusion, as well as strong support. Overall, the research found strong support for affirmative action among women and nonwhite men. White men, on the other hand, narrowly approved of affirmative action in the abstract and of "protective" affirmative action practices, but narrowly opposed preferential affirmative action practices. Put differently, within this particular work force, affirmative action enjoys a high level of support among women and nonwhite men, and broke even, more or less, among white men. Although many criticized the ideas behind and practices of the Parks Department's program, many of these same individuals nevertheless have hired women and nonwhite men, helping the department in its efforts to meet its affirmative action goals. Thus, the department's affirmative action program probably has enough support to succeed. At the very least, many individuals are willing to cooperate and not sabotage the program.

The willingness of some opponents to cooperate, however, cannot be taken for granted. There are specific things any agency can do to maximize cooperation and minimize hostility toward affirmative action programs. The following recommendations suggest some ways organizations can enhance the support and cooperation their affirmative action efforts receive.

First, organizations should be consistent and honest about the nature of their programs. Some of the disillusionment and hostility toward affirmative action was expressed by those who felt that the department told them that affirmative action was to promote a protective form of equal opportunity, while in fact the program led to preferential treatment of women and minorities. There is still a tendency within the department to soft pedal the preferential nature of the program. This is counterproductive, because the goals and timetables, and the resulting pressure on supervisors to hire women and minorities, inevitably are perceived as preferences. Therefore, organizations implementing preferential affirmative action should stress that they want qualified (or well-qualified) individuals, not necessarily the best qualified. It should be stressed that affirmative action programs exist as a result of the absence of equal opportunity in market society, and that such programs are supposed to be remedial and temporary.

Some will object to this first suggestion, which I make reluctantly. Nevertheless, I think it is justifiable. As the analysis in chapter 2 indicates, and as some of the respondents suggested, it is possible to argue that being nonwhite or female can be a legitimate job qualification. (For example, minority Park Rangers may be better able to enforce the law among minority visitors and enhance the respect such visitors have for the department's mission.) But even among those who agreed that race or gender could legitimately be considered a job qualification, there was still a sense that if nonwhite or female applicants were less qualified in the traditional experience areas, to hire such individuals would be to treat them preferentially.

Thus, while some may think the department needs more nonwhite and female employees, the equal opportunity ideology of hiring the best qualified remains so pervasive, and the traditional view of what counts as merit so dominant, that it is very difficult to convince people to include gender or ethnicity as a real, valid job qualification. Since people are unlikely to view race or gender as a job qualification of the same level as education and job experience, and because people naturally compare (traditional) job qualifications, most are likely to continue to think that the department's program involves preferential treatment. Since this perception is very unlikely to be overturned, there are more effective ways to promote cooperation with and to defend affirmative action programs than by trying to overturn such a deeply held premise. Despite this judgment, personally, I think the argument that race and gender can legitimately count as merit is a good one, and should be included, along with other arguments, in affirmative action training.

Second, the department should do more to address complaints about declining employee quality. For example, the backgrounds of new employees could be published (for example, ranger trainees) to counteract the perception that unqualified individuals are being hired; and supervisors should be encouraged to introduce new employees to the rest of the staff, explaining their backgrounds and qualifications, as part of a new employee's orientation process. This may not alleviate the complaint that the best qualified are being passed over, but it could mitigate the more damning complaint (and misperception) that unqualified people are being hired.

Third, the department should make sure that information about promotions is systematically and broadly disseminated. This could counter the misperception that only women and nonwhite men are promoted—replacing anecdotal information with more complete, accurate information.

Fourth, since the promotions of some white men will be slowed or halted as a result of affirmative action (there is, after all, a finite amount of room at the top, and less room for white men than existed in the absence of affirmative action), more needs to be done to recognize and reward the efforts and accomplishments of individual employees. This is, of course, simply good managerial practice and should be followed not just as a means of enhancing the morale of white men. But it deserves mention, because the lowering of morale due to affirmative action is a serious concern—if not addressed, it could result in declining productivity. (The failure to address morale problems can enhance the central consequentialist argument against affirmative action.) This research, however, provides no compelling evidence that affirmative action has so lowered morale that it has reduced productivity; nevertheless, this possibility should be taken seriously.

Fifth, answers to two survey questions make it clear that department employees need more affirmative action training. To the statements, *The Parks Department provides adequate explanation of the reasons for its human rights and affirmative action policies* and *The department provides adequate training for its employees concerning its human rights and affirmative action policies*, most employees did not agree (statements 43 and 44, table 3).

Training ought to recognize that no one rationale for affirmative action is going to make sense for everyone. Owing to the dominance of Liberalism, rationales grounded in Liberal principles tend to be more readily accepted. Nevertheless, training should not presume to offer *the* moral rationale for affirmative action. The training should *not* begin by stating that the purpose is to explain why affirmative action is morally right. Rather, a training module on the rationales for affirmative action should stress that the aim of the training is to understand the historical context and what types of moral reasoning have led to affirmative action law and policy. The best way to convey this material is to structure the training so that, as much as possible, the trainees themselves come up with the moral reasons behind affirmative action law and policy. Then the trainer can show that there are only a few rationales for affirmative action and can then superimpose a more sophisticated and coherent explanation of these rationales. With this kind of approach, where the participants themselves bring forth the basic reasons, the entire training module will be more relevant to the average trainee.

The overall goal of such training should be more modest than that of convincing people that affirmative action is morally right (although some may come to this conclusion). Rather, the primary purpose of such training should be to nurture tolerance in opponents of affirmative action and a willingness to live with these programs. Stated differently, the goal should be to create space within an organization where its affirmative action goals can be implemented without excessive resistance. Such a space can be increased by creating or enhancing ambivalence (and thus tolerance) in the minds of those predisposed to dislike affirmative action. Such ambivalence and tolerance can be enhanced if people are exposed to the strongest moral arguments for affirmative action, even though they may not be convinced by them.

While it is good to allow training participants to bring forth the basic arguments about affirmative action, some arguments can be stressed more productively than others. For example, while the idea of compensatory justice may come up, it should not be emphasized. Since this type of idea is the source of much of the animosity toward affirmative action, the trainer could gain some trust with those hostile to affirmative action by acknowledging and explaining the serious problems in applying principles of compensatory justice to the affirmative action issue. It could even be suggested that compensatory notions provide a relatively weak rationale for affirmative action. (Many white men, particularly those with little education, would probably tune out anyone who suggests that they are somehow responsible for the wrongs done previously by their forefathers.) Furthermore, arguments against affirmative action should not be suppressed. Rather, they should be acknowledged, taken seriously, and then juxtaposed with the arguments most closely related to and opposing these arguments. This could provide a context for explaining the different versions of equal opportunity and how some of the disagreement over affirmative action results from some persons referring to equal opportunity in terms of legal access, while others refer to equal opportunity in terms of overall life chances.

Beyond providing some idea of which arguments to de-emphasize, these data also suggest that certain arguments are worth stressing. One of the major disputes about fact had to do with whether women and nonwhite men would receive serious consideration for jobs right now in the department (two-thirds of white men thought they would, while over two-thirds of women and nonwhite men thought they would not). Since so much contemporary debate about affirmative action is in terms of whether it ensures a fair chance for jobs, this is probably the most important issue the training program should address. Persons well trained in conflict resolution might encourage the expression of such different views and the experiences that have led to them. White men could be given a unique chance (perhaps through a role-reversal exercise) to see why women and nonwhite men thought the hiring process is unfair. Although some will still believe that the impressions of women and nonwhites are inaccurate or even paranoid, others might be convinced that, indeed, women and nonwhites would not receive serious consideration without affirmative action.

As with other arguments, the trainer can then superimpose some theory and research that explains why women and nonwhite men tend not to receive the same consideration for jobs and do not actually have opportunities equal to those of white men. Appendix C is a training model that provides an overview of the social prerequisites for equal opportunity (understood as equal life chances). It can facilitate discussion among participants about what is needed in society to achieve equal opportunity. This model can be quite successful in illustrating the strength of an argument for affirmative action based on Liberal equality.

A second argument that should be stressed is that, given changing demographics, the marketing of the organization will increasingly depend on a work force that reflects the diversity of the public. Discussion in this area could provide an opportunity to suggest that in the light of rapidly changing demographics (characterized by increasing proportions of racial minorities), race or gender could be considered critical to the success of the organization, and therefore could be seen as a valid job qualification. The emphasis, however, should be on how the organization *needs* racial and gender diversity because of its dependence on the public, rather than on the argument about what counts as a meritorious job qualification.

The third argument is grounded in reflection on the potential social benefits (compared to the costs) of such policies. The rates of approval among respondents were roughly equal between the statements that affirmative action is morally right and that affirmative action benefits society. And this research, while finding strong individualism, also found significant concern for the common good and the welfare of groups in society. People clearly thought that public policy should focus more on groups than on individuals. And even some self-identified conservatives thought that affirmative action was justified because it preserves social stability and helps preserve America's market society.

Responses such as these, along with my impressions from the interviews, lead to the conclusion that one of the strongest potential bases for supporting affirmative action can be found in a commonsense, societywide, cost-benefit analysis of the pros and cons of affirmative action. Again, these costs and benefits could be brought out largely by training participants themselves, and then could be supplemented by the trainer. An effective wrap-up of the discussion could stress how affirmative action is but one policy among many possibilities that could enhance opportunities and substantive equality in the culture (thus appealing to those with different social ends in mind). The trainer could suggest, for example, that when organizations and individuals participate in such policies, they promote the greatest good, even if, occasionally, they do so at some cost to the individual or to the productivity of the organization. The trainer could also suggest that while all may not agree, the very real pain that accompanies such programs is the price of promoting such consensus values as the individual quest for success and the overall well-being of democratic institutions. (If some well-known conservative employee suggests that affirmative action is the price for social stability, that is sure to carry more weight with like-minded participants than a similar suggestion from someone associated with a liberal program such as affirmative action.) Just as individual self-interest has coexisted and competed with patriotic notions requiring self-sacrifice, the more patriotic streams of the culture could provide some basis for white men to accept some individual sacrifice. However, white men clearly will not willingly accept such sacrifice when they think it is due to some wrong for which they are not responsible.

The sometimes competing and incompatible ethical perspectives recommended to convince workers of the moral case for affirmative action may seem Machiavellian. Some may even think that such an approach may wrongfully treat persons instrumentally, as means to an end—the end of supporting affirmative action. On the contrary: exposing people to the widest range of moral discourse about affirmative action actually respects individuals, by providing them with a context within which to grapple with the difficult moral issues posed by the affirmative action controversy. In the long run, when social conditions permit such a dialogue, most people of good will see that preferential affirmative action is, on balance, morally reasonable and permissible as public policy—and that there is more than one path of moral reasoning toward such a conclusion.

APPENDIXES
NOTES
GLOSSARY
REFERENCES
INDEX

APPENDIX A

Interview Guide

THE INTERVIEWS began with a narrative dealing with an example related to affirmative action. The narrative was read to the interviewee. Questions were interspersed at certain points during the narrative. After the narrative, additional questions were asked. They are listed below in the order they were asked, if the interviewee did not spontaneously deal with them in response to the narrative. A second narrative section describes the typical ways ethicists analyze affirmative action and asks for reactions. This is followed by some final questions.

First Narrative and Questions

A black woman sued an employer when she did not get a job. This woman had been rated well qualified, and she said that she had been discriminated against because of her race and sex. The Federal Equal Employment Opportunity Commission joined her lawsuit and, as evidence of discrimination, pointed out that while black women made up 15 percent of the surrounding community, less than 1 percent of the work force were black women. Do you think this kind of statistical evidence is a good way to measure discrimination? If not, what kind of evidence is needed to show discrimination and to trigger responses to discrimination?

In this case, the employer offered to begin a recruitment program targeting black women. The EEOC, however, would not accept this offer, and so the employer made a stronger settlement offer, agreeing to give the woman a job and to hire 25 percent black women until they were represented in the employer's work force in the same proportion as the surrounding community. Do you think it is fair to use goals as a response to a perception of discrimination?

Several months after this agreement was implemented, a black woman was given an entry-level job over a white man who had scored two points higher on the exam (both were considered qualified). Was this fair? Why or why not? [If interviewee uses "best qualified" idea she or he is asked]: How easy is it to determine who is best qualified?

Do these cases remind you of stories about discrimination that you have heard about in your workplace? Do they remind you of things you feel strongly about?

Additional Questions

1. How common is racial and sexual prejudice in our society today? How about in the department? Do these prejudices result in a lot of discrimination?
2. To you personally, what does affirmative action mean? In your view, what is affirmative action supposed to accomplish?
3. What is involved in the department's affirmative action programs? Is this the right approach to promote the purpose of affirmative action? Do you approve of some types of affirmative action programs? What types of measures, if any, do you approve of in affirmative action policies? What else is good and bad about affirmative action?
4. Is affirmative action the best way to deal with discrimination? Why not just prohibit discrimination and prosecute those who discriminate? Wouldn't this be enough?
5. What do, or would, your parents think about affirmative action?
6. Have you ever been held back or helped by affirmative action? If so, do you think this was justified? Can you give me some examples of people who have been helped or hurt by affirmative action? Was this justified?
7. What sort of society or workplace does affirmative action produce? In what ways does affirmative action benefit or harm society and the workplace? Does it increase or decrease racial and sexual tensions?
8. Have there been times when you have felt isolated? What keeps you in the department?
9. What are the moral values which you believe are important? [If interviewee did not know how to answer, the following examples were given]: For example, truth telling; treating others as they want to be treated; acting to enhance one's own positive feelings and the positive feelings of others.
10. In what ways do your moral values support or contradict affirmative action policies?
11. Affirmative action proponents and opponents base their cases on moral values and arguments. What is your understanding of the moral values that affirmative action is based on? What do you think about these values?

Second Narrative and Questions

I'd like to describe four common ways people talk about the morality of affirmative action, and you can tell me whether any of these make sense to you. For example,

1. Some people say that equal opportunity and hiring based on merit is the best moral principle and that affirmative action should be judged by whether it promotes equal opportunity. Some then argue that it helps opportunities, others says it violates equal opportunity. Is equal opportunity a good principle? Does affirmative action promote it or hinder it? Do you think people can make it if they try hard enough? What are the obstacles to achieving equal opportunity?

2. Some people say that it is wrong to require people today to pay for past discrimination, and that to do so violates people's rights. What do you think? Others say that compensating people for disadvantages they have suffered due to discrimination is morally right. These people say it is O.K. to expect white males to provide the compensation, because they are the beneficiaries of past discrimination through inheritance, superior education, greater opportunities, and so on. What do you think?

3. Some people say that even if you get rid of racism and sexism by making equal opportunity real, you still end up with too much inequality. Instead of domination by white men, you end up with domination by those who happen to be born especially gifted. These people complain that even if we got equal opportunity, only the elites would change. Instead of rule by white men, the rulers and the rich will be those who won the crapshoot of life—and were lucky enough to be born smart, good-looking, or with special talents. Those with few gifts end up falling through the cracks and end up in poverty. These critics conclude that equal opportunity only insures the right to become unequal, but does nothing about inequality itself. These critics say some principle beyond equal opportunity is needed to reduce how big the winners win, and how badly the losers lose, in the merit competition. Does this make any sense to you? [This question often had to be explained and rephrased before the interviewee could understand it.]

4. Finally, others say that affirmative action should be judged not by ideal equal opportunity but on whether it promotes the common good: some say it promotes the total good of society, others say it harms the overall good of society. Is this a good way to judge affirmative action? [If the answer is yes]: Is affirmative action good or not?

Final Questions

[If the following questions had not already been dealt with, they concluded the interview.]

12. Certain arguments about affirmative action involve moral values that are grounded in and depend on religious beliefs. How would you describe your religious beliefs?

13. How do your religious beliefs influence your moral values? [If example was needed, mention was made of how Catholic bishops have issued statements making moral judgments about nuclear war and the economy.]

14. How do your religiously based moral values then influence your views about affirmative action? [For example, if the interviewee is Christian], Does the golden rule say anything about affirmative action?

APPENDIX B

Survey Questions

[Boxes to the right of these questions permitted answers of *strongly agree, agree, disagree,* and *strongly disagree.*]

1. Racial or sexual prejudice is very common in our society today.
2. Racial or sexual prejudice in the Department of Parks and Recreation is very common today.
3. Civil rights leaders are pushing too fast.
4. Civil rights leaders are pushing in the wrong direction.
5. Affirmative action is needed as a remedial effort to overcome the effects of discrimination.
6. Without affirmative action, women and minorities would not get serious consideration for many DPR jobs.
7. In general, I approve of using hiring goals to try to make the DPR's work force as ethnically and sexually diverse as is society.
8. In the DPR, affirmative action goals have become quotas, which mandate hiring precise numbers of women and minorities.
9. In general, I like the DPR's focused recruitment of minorities and women.
10. Overall, I approve of the DPR's Women in Trades program.
11. In general, I approve of the DPR's discrimination complaint process.
12. It is good that the DPR has equal employment opportunity counselors available to advise employees of their rights to a discrimination-free workplace.
13. In general, I approve of the DPR's sexual harassment policy.
14. In general, I approve of the DPR's use of supplemental certification.
15. It is good that the DPR is required to try to recruit persons on welfare.
16. I approve of the DPR's effort to provide "reasonable accommodation" for disabled employees.
17. The DPR provides an adequate *explanation of the reasons* for its human rights and affirmative action policies.

18. The DPR provides adequate *training* for its employees concerning its human rights and affirmative action policies.
19. Women and minorities tend not to be interested in State Park jobs.
20. It is especially hard to dismiss poor DPR employees when they are members of groups targeted for affirmative action.
21. Affirmative action makes it too hard for DPR employees to transfer to better locations, because such positions tend to get filled by minorities or women.
22. Affirmative action reduces the quality of DPR employees.
23. Affirmative action makes it more difficult for the DPR to carry out its mission.
24. Doing well financially is more important to me than overcoming financial inequalities in society.
25. I am more concerned with the overall social good than with my own personal advancement.
26. A good family life is more important to me than making a lot of money.
27. In general, when making public policy, it is best to look more at how policy affects groups than at how such policy affects any single individual.
28. In general, I think affirmative action is a morally right public policy.
29. Affirmative action policy should be implemented because it is required by law or departmental policy, and ethical concerns are not very relevant.
30. Affirmative action law is wrong and should be changed.
31. Affirmative action law is wrong and should not be obeyed.
32. Instead of stressing affirmative action, we should just prohibit discrimination and prosecute those who discriminate.
33. Compassion and caring should be a basis for public policies.
34. Compassion and caring tend to lead to support for affirmative action.
35. White males should be willing to be satisfied with fewer job opportunities so that others may have a chance to succeed.
36. Affirmative action violates the rights of individuals who happen to be male and white.
37. Despite barriers to success such as discrimination, almost anybody can succeed if she or he tries hard enough.
38. Other groups (e.g., the Irish, the Jews) have overcome discrimination without help from preferences, so it would be unfair to give preferences to today's women and minorities.
39. White males have benefited from past discrimination.
40. Assuming white males have benefited from past discrimination, white males should agree that preferential treatment of victims of discrimination is appropriate compensation.

41. Affirmative action helps many who do not need help.
42. Improving education is the best way to overcome discrimination.
43. More public money should be given to improve education.
44. Money used to support affirmative action could better be used for other purposes.
45. Naturally talented people are entitled to better jobs than those who are less talented.
46. Naturally talented people are entitled to get higher salaries than those who are less talented.
47. We need public policies to reduce inequality of income between talented and less talented people who try equally hard.
48. Affirmative action broadened to include all disadvantaged people would be a morally acceptable way to reduce inequality of income.
49. I can tell whether affirmative action is right or wrong without thinking about the effect of affirmative action on society.
50. On balance, affirmative action benefits society.
51. Overall, the workplace is better because of affirmative action.
52. In the long term, affirmative action will reduce tensions between racial groups and between gender groups.
53. My religious beliefs have a strong effect on the way I evaluate public policies.
54. My religious beliefs lead me to disapprove of affirmative action.
55. My religious beliefs lead me to approve of affirmative action.
56. Equal opportunity, hiring based on merit, is a very good moral principle.
57. Affirmative action undermines equal opportunity, hiring based on merit.
58. Affirmative action promotes equal opportunity, hiring based on merit.
59. It is usually possible to identify the "best qualified" applicant.
60. It is morally right always to hire the "best qualified" applicant.
61. When hiring, it is morally acceptable to consider the following when evaluating merit:
    a. education
    b. experience
    c. interest
    d. disability
    e. job performance
    f. seniority
    g. moral character
    h. military service
    i. gender
    j. race/ethnicity
    k. religion
    l. personality

Please give written comments to the following questions:

62. How do you define affirmative action?
63. How do you feel about the department's affirmative action program?
64. Regardless of how you feel, what would make the department's affirmative action program more effective?
65. In your own words, write why you think affirmative action is either morally right or wrong.
66. State *how* your religious beliefs do or do not influence your view of affirmative action.

Please circle the letter in front of the best answer:

67. My age is _____ .
68. If I had to label myself politically, I would say that I am (a) extremely conservative (b) conservative (c) middle of the road (d) liberal (e) extremely liberal.
69. Generally speaking, I consider myself to be (a) upper class (b) upper middle class (c) middle middle class (d) lower middle class (e) upper working class (f) middle working class (g) lower working class (h) lower class.
70. I am (a) Catholic Christian (b) evangelical/fundamentalist Christian (c) Protestant Christian (d) Jew (e) Hindu (f) Buddhist (g) Muslim (h) other: _____ .
71. I participate in religious services (a) at least once a week (b) once a month (c) once a year (d) rarely (e) never.
72. For most of my life I have resided in (a) the East (b) the Midwest (c) the South (d) California (e) the West (excluding California).
73. I have a disability (a) yes (b) no.

APPENDIX C

A Training Model for
Equal Employment Opportunity

The following model takes Liberal equality as its premise. Therefore, the underlying question is, What is necessary for individuals to have equal life chances to compete in market society? The model provides a given and asks two questions, allowing trainees to develop their own answers. The facilitator then puts these answers into categories and juxtaposes what is needed in the workplace with similar requirements for society at large. (This is easily done with two easels, which can be prepared beforehand with reminders of the material to be covered.) Answers not brought up by the trainees themselves can be brought up by the facilitator, who can then ask for examples. The discussion arising from these questions will increase appreciation of how hard it is to make equal opportunity work and help explain how affirmative action is part of a strategy to enhance equal opportunity. The examples given in the model can be changed to fit the particular organization.

Given   *There is a cultural consensus affirming the principle of equal employment opportunity, based on merit.*

Question 1   *What is required at the department level to actualize such a principle?*

- Nonprejudiced persons to do the hiring and promotion.
- Nondiscriminatory job requirements: eliminate nonrelevant job requirements such as advanced educational degrees, which are possessed primarily by groups that are not disadvantaged.
- Nondiscriminatory hiring, promotion, and firing procedures: eliminate word-of-mouth recruitment, interviews held far from minority communities, advertisements appearing only in the Anglo media, and interviews that discourage women and minorities through inappropriate or illegal questions or statements; create job ladders for job classifications disproportionately occupied by disadvantaged groups.
- Equal, groupwide, or rough parity of educational experiences and opportunities, to enable similar proportions of different groups to meet relevant job requirements.

213

- Equal cultural experiences or opportunities, since persons who have never experienced a park, or seen rangers as role models, are unlikely to pursue such a career path.
- Equal nutritional and psychological environments, since opportunity and human development requires that certain biological and emotional needs be met.
- Participation in decision making, which helps to develop human capabilities and enables ability to be recognized.

Question 2 *What is required at the cultural level to support such a principle?*
Possible Answers

- A nonprejudiced society, which does not perpetuate stereotypes.
- Public and private sectors committed to identifying vestiges of discrimination institutionalized through nonrelevant job requirements.
- Public and private sectors committed to recruiting all groups and eliminating obstacles in hiring promotion and firing. Long-term equal opportunity in the culture is necessary to prevent firings based on seniority from disproportionately affecting disadvantaged groups.
- Equalizing educational and cultural experience disparities, which requires one of the following public policies. (1) Redistribution of economic resources, so that all will have equal access to education and to exposure to diverse opportunities or vocations. (Our culture has not decided to move in this direction.) (2) Limiting the educational/cultural opportunities of the economically and socially privileged by bringing their opportunities down to the level of nonprivileged groups. (This also is not seriously considered within our culture.) Implementing public policies and encouraging or mandating similar policies for the private sector to improve the educational and cultural experiences of disadvantaged groups, until rough parity is reached. (Attempts in this direction, especially with regard to education, include Head Start programs, federally insured student loans, and federal and state monetary assistance to relatively poor school districts. Broadening overall cultural experiences is more difficult to address without overcoming poverty itself, but attempts are being made. For example, the community services branch of the Parks Department's Human Rights Office arranges park experiences for inner-city children, which exposes them both to the park and to park employee role models.)
- Equal nutritional and psychological environments. Redistribution is again seldom considered, and would not in itself provide an adequate emotional environment. No one considers depriving privileged children of adequate nutrition and emotional support to provide for the disadvantaged. We might implement public policies (and encourage or mandate similar policies for the private sector) to

make nutritional and emotional environments adequate for human development. (We have made attempts in these areas: Aid to Families with Dependent Children and food stamps, prenatal medical and nutritional services, child abuse laws and enforcement, including removal of children from abusive situations, and child abuse prevention programs within community mental health departments.)

- Participation in the decisions that affect one's own life, as both a means and an end in the development of human capabilities.

Evaluation

Some analysts insist that redistribution is an essential element of any program designed to create equal employment opportunity. At this time, however, given the lack of support for programs of redistribution, those who support equal employment opportunity logically turn to various other policies to improve the opportunities of disadvantaged individuals.

NOTES

Chapter 1. The Cultural and Legal Context of Affirmative Action

1. There is, of course, another type of conservatism, which comes out of the civic republican tradition (Aristotle, Machiavelli, Luther). This conservatism places the good of the community over that of the individual and judges actions based on the extent to which they promote some particular concept of the overall common good. Republican thought values social stability and the preservation of social institutions. (While tending to be conservative, republican notions of substantive justice and public virtue can also be used to promote social reform.) Because of its focus on ends, this type of conservatism is discussed under consequentialist ethical theory.

2. These theorists agree that scarcity prevents Liberalism from being able to deliver the promised goods because, contrary to the assumption of Liberalism, economic growth and an increase in positional goods is not consistently possible. They disagree, however, on which type of scarcity is the more fundamental. Hirsh believes that the most important limits are social, that even during periods of economic growth, competition for positional goods increases because positional goods remain "confined to a fixed size" (1977, 27, see also 16–54). Daly emphasizes the scarcity of available energy as the key limit to economic growth and sees all scarcity, including that of positional goods, as grounded in this more fundamental scarcity (1980, 1–82; see also Rifkin, 1980, 33–60, 99–122). Like Hirsh, Thurow doubts that resource scarcity is the key limit (1980, 111–14). He asserts that the real problem is Liberalism's optimistic belief that economic growth can overcome the nature of market competition, which always produces both losers and winners. He concludes that this naivete prevents Liberalism from establishing principles of distribution by which the losers in market competition are given adequate provision (1980, 18, 180–95).

3. Hirsh wants a morality beyond just "to the self-interested victor belongs the spoils, as long as the competition is fair, as guaranteed by

217

equal opportunity." He wants to reduce the stakes of competition in order to preserve individual competition. He notes that self-interest does not lead to more resources for all (1977, 187) and suggests that enlightened self-interest can lead to people acting *as if* the common good comes first (1977, 179, my emphasis). This enlightened self-interest can create a rationale for reducing the stakes of competition. Hirsh does not challenge liberal premises about self-interest and the ultimate desirability of competition; he simply wants to limit its more destructive consequences.

4. Some conservatives, however, think affirmative action is not necessary, because although inequality of opportunity still exists, the trajectory of U.S. history shows that equality of opportunity is increasing and that progress is satisfactory without recourse to unfair policies such as affirmative action (Glazer 1975).

5. See Burstein (1985), Kellough (1989), Feagin and Feagin (1978, 12–42), Jaynes and Williams (1989), and Shulman and Darity (1989) for a variety of analyses of structural and economic elements of discrimination, and Blanchard and Crosby (1989) for psychological aspects.

6. Fullinwider, who sees little difference between "quota-type" and "goal-type" affirmative action, calls protective affirmative action "nondiscriminatory" affirmative action. He believes that this kind of affirmative action "has a value which is not threatened by any legal decision against preferential hiring" (1980, 170f.).

7. For a good example of this argument, see McIntosh (1988).

8. A similar point is made by St. Antoine (1976). While he supports preferences, he calls disingenuous government disclaimers which deny that affirmative action involves preferences.

9. Fullinwider also frames the issue in a helpful, non-question-begging way. He says first, that there is no significant difference between quota-type and goal-type affirmative action (1980, 162–70). I think this part of his argument is overstated—I observed a relevant difference between having to hire a specific number of a specific group and making a good faith effort to hire the same number—particularly on the psychological impact and perception of the program within an institution. But he helpfully notes that the critical question is: Do abuses resulting from goal-type (preferential) affirmative action outweigh abuses resulting from current, systemic discrimination? He concludes that critics of quota-type (preferential) affirmative action cannot prove their burden: that the abuses resulting from such affirmative action outweigh the abuses of current discrimination (177–80). He also notes, accurately, that the courts have blurred the distinction between protective and preferential affirmative action (161).

10. Some of the following borrows from Burstein (1985, 19–32). For details on the legal background, see Greene (1989, 15–162), Brest and Levinson (1983), Brest (1976), Fiss (1976), Fullinwider (1980, 124–80), Gunther (1975), Burstein (1985, esp. chap. 2), and U.S. Congress (1990). See Benokraitis and Feagin (1978, chap. 2) for a discussion of the birth of affirmative action law.

11. Now codified as 42 U.S.C., secs. 1981–82 (1970), this act deals specifically with contracts, and there is disagreement about how broadly the act should be interpreted. The act states: "All persons . . . shall have the same right . . . to make and enforce contracts . . . and to the full and equal benefit of all laws and proceedings for the security of persons and property as is enjoyed by white persons" (Burstein 1985, 19).

12. The 1990 decision in *Metro Broadcasting v. FCC* (89–453) ruled that discrimination favoring minorities (by preferring minorities applying for broadcast licenses) was justifiable given the government's "important" interest in diversifying the spectrum of thought carried over the air. As discussed later, articulation of a nonremedial rationale for preferential treatment may become very important to affirmative action law.

13. Title VII reads "It shall be an unlawful practice for an employer— (1) to fail or refuse to hire or to discharge any individual or otherwise to discriminate against any individual with respect to his compensation, terms, conditions, or privileges of employment, because of such individual's race, color, sex, or national origin." The 1964 act applied to the federal government and its contractors. In 1972, the act was amended to include state and municipal governments. The act did not mention the disabled, who recently have been protected from job discrimination through the Americans with Disabilities Act of 1990 (signed into law 26 July 1990). This act also requires most facilities and transportation systems to accommodate the disabled.

14. The law recognizes three broad types of civil remedies (responses to a proven wrong done or harm brought upon some individual): "damages, restitution, and equitable relief." "Damages" generally refer to monetary payments. "Punitive" damages are monetary awards designed to punish the wrongdoer and deter others from similar acts—such awards are tied to the assets of the perpetrator. "Compensatory" damages aim to "make whole" economically the wronged party. Usually they involve monetary payments for things such as back pay (for example, for a person denied a promotion due to discrimination), but they may also provide monetary compensation for pain, suffering and emotional distress. "Restitution" refers more to situations: in employment law, e.g., putting parties in positions they would have held in the absence of discrimination—putting them in their "rightful place." With "equitable relief" the courts require that a wrongdoer stop the prohibited behavior. The court may order a variety of other measures to stop present harms and insure that such harms do not recur. Violations of these orders constitutes contempt of court and triggers further enforcement actions. When passing antidiscrimination law, legislators have generally avoided allowing punitive damages and compensatory damages for intangibles such as pain and suffering.

15. Title VII also states that a court may require a discriminating employer to stop the offending practice and may "order such *affirmative action* as may be appropriate, which may include, but is not limited to, reinstatement or hiring of employees, with or without back pay . . . or any

other equitable relief as the court deems appropriate" (42 U.S.C. 2000e–2005[g], my emphasis).

16. For more on the 1972 act, see Bureau of National Affairs (1973) and Jaynes and Williams (1989, 228).

17. Glazer 1975, 48. Glazer criticizes this move as initiating a process where, by 1971, with the creation of a category of "affected class," equal opportunity (the goal of the 1964 civil rights legislation) had been redefined "against its plain meaning, not as opportunity but [as] result" (1975, 49). Glazer contests the assumption that disproportionate representation is strong evidence of discrimination. Others, including Fullinwider (1980, 161), assert that Johnson's and the Labor Department's moves shifted the notion of equal protection in Title VII from the prevention of discrimination to restitution, and that the courts have had to blur the distinction between prevention and restitution in order to support Johnson's order and Labor Department implementation strategies.

18. On this point, the *Bakke* ruling returned to *McLaughlin v. Florida.* One key to the *McLaughlin* ruling was its insistence that there must be "congruence" between the aim of the race-dependent decision and the means chosen—and there must not be other reasonable means available (Brest 1983, 444–47).

19. For discussion of two lower court decisions that preceded the *Weber* ruling, one which mandated the achievement of proportional representation (*Boston Chapter, NAACP v. Beecher*), the other which endorsed racial quotas in a case involving a city fire department (*Germann v. Kipp*), see Fullinwider (1980, 129–34).

20. Sandra Day O'Connor, writing for the majority, stressed that Fourteenth Amendment rights inhere in the individual and argued that without judicial inquiry into the justification for such programs, there was no way to tell if such race-based classifications were benign. She raised a common objection to such programs, the "danger of stigmatic harm" and of promoting "notions of racial inferiority and . . . politics of racial hostility" (*New York Times*, 24 April 1989).

21. *Fullilove* endorsed a set-aside program because it was narrowly tailored to a specific remedial purpose, which was within the power of Congress to address (as a coequal branch of the federal government charged with providing for the "general welfare"). See Greene (1989, 80–86) for a detailed discussion of *Fullilove* and how it framed many of the issues again addressed in the *Croson* decision.

22. Wards Cove Packing Company was sued for discriminating against minorities by restricting them to low-paying jobs. Plaintiffs provided evidence that they were concentrated in lower paying jobs, that white nepotism and word-of-mouth hiring was prevalent, and that the work force was segregated. They produced a letter from a company foreman to a college student seeking work which read, "Our cannery labor is either Eskimo or Filipino, and we do not have the facilities to mix others with these groups." Under *Griggs* such evidence would have shifted the burden of

proof to show job relatedness to *Wards Cove*, and the plaintiffs probably would have won. With the *Wards Cove* decision, the plaintiffs needed further evidence to prove their case (see Alleyne 1989).

23. This interpretation of the ruling was written by Catherine M. Wynne (attorney with the Office of the General Counsel of the Trustees of the California State University System) for Mayer Chapman, vice chancellor and general counsel to the trustees, dated 20 June 1989; author's copy.

24. See U.S. Congress (1990) for a discussion of *Wards Cove* and *Martin v. Wilkes*. This Senate report includes arguments against the enactment of various provisions of the Civil Rights Act of 1990 and provides a good introduction to controversial issues in the bill.

25. Several other rulings are related indirectly to affirmative action policies by their overall effect making it harder for Title VII plaintiffs to prevail, thereby reducing pressures on employers to implement affirmative action programs.

The decision in *Price Waterhouse v. Hopkins* (88–1167), for example, set forth guidelines for "mixed motive" cases where there were both valid and discriminatory reasons for a personnel decision. The Court decided that the plaintiff must show that gender (or race) was a "substantial" motivation in the decision, and only then does the burden shift to the employer, who can still prevail by showing the same decision would have been reached in the absence of discrimination.

This ruling would have been overturned had the Civil Rights Act of 1990 been enacted. The bill declared illegal all intentional discrimination and mandated court remedies. The presence of additional, valid motives for a decision can affect the remedy ordered (for example, no back pay could be ordered if someone would have been dismissed anyway in the absence of discrimination). This would not preclude other remedies and damages, such as for pain and suffering. See U.S. Congress 1990, 7–8, 22–24.

A series of rulings, *Crawford Fitting Co. v. J. T. Gibbons, Inc.* 482 U.S. 437 (1987), *Independent Federation of Flight Attendants v. Zipes* (88–608) (1989), *Evans v. Jeff D.*, 475 U.S. 717 (1986), and *Marek v. Chesny* 473 U.S. 1 (1985), restricted the fees attorneys could collect representing plaintiffs in discrimination cases. Critics of these rulings complained that these rulings made the civil rights attorney an "endangered species." (See statement by Richard Larson before the Committee on Labor and Human Resources, 101st Congress, 7 March 1990, on behalf of the Mexican American Legal Defense and Education Fund, on the Civil Rights Act of 1990). These rulings also would have been overruled by the Civil Rights Act of 1990. For the Senate's rationale, see U.S. Congress 1990, 7–8, 33–35.

Meanwhile, *Lorance v. AT&T Technologies* (87–1428) (1989) "held that the statute of limitations for challenging discriminatory seniority plans begins to run when the plan is adopted, rather than when the plan is applied to harm the plaintiff." This ruling effectively precluded many plaintiffs from challenging such plans (U.S. Congress 1990, 7, 27–29). The Civil Rights Act of 1990 also would have overturned this ruling.

Finally, in *Patterson v. McLean Credit Union* (87–107) (1989), the Court held that the statutes under the Civil Rights Act of 1866 (which in recent times had been interpreted broadly to prohibit racial discrimination and harassment in many areas), should be interpreted narrowly, and applied only to hiring, not to discrimination in promotions or on-the-job racial harassment (U.S. Congress 1990, 6). (This act was never used to provide compensatory or punitive damages for women.) The Civil Rights Act of 1990 would have overturned this ruling also, ensuring that the 1866 act would be interpreted broadly to preclude racial harassment or discrimination in all contractual relationships. The act included compensatory and punitive damages as possible remedies and also provided similar remedies for women under Title VII. For the Senate's rationale, see U.S. Congress (1990, 11–14). The overturning of *Patterson* was another of the least controversial elements of the vetoed 1990 legislation—few argued that racial harassment after hiring was less pernicious than during it.

26. Judging from the logic of *Metro Broadcasting*, I would have expected the current Court to endorse Johnson's executive order on the same grounds—the executive branch as a coequal partner in government. But future decisions will depend on a Court without Justice Brennan.

27. Several realms of society, such as private clubs, are not prohibited from discriminating in areas other than employment, such as member admissions.

Chapter 2. An Ethical Analysis of Affirmative Action

1. Two of the four theorists chosen to represent the different approaches are twentiethth-century figures (Robert Nozick and John Rawls), and two of the theorists are nineteenth-century figures (Karl Marx and J. S. Mill). These figures were chosen for heuristic not historical purposes: partly because they are among the better known representatives of their traditions; partly because most modern utilitarians and Marxists go back to Mill and Marx; partly because the dialogue between Nozick and Rawls provides a clear focus on the critical ethical issues that underlie the affirmative action controversy; and partly because, in my judgment, the writings of Nozick and Rawls are more easily understandable to modern readers than are the writings of their philosophical predecessors, T. H. Green, F. H. Bradley, Kant, Rousseau, Locke, Hobbes, and others.

2. Nozick buttresses his autonomy principle with Kantian absolutism: "Individuals are ends and not merely means; they may not be sacrificed or used for the achieving of other ends without their consent. Individuals are inviolable" (1974, 31). "Moral side constraints" (constraints on actions based upon the rights of some, which place on others a corresponding duty to respect such rights) ought not be violated even if such a violation were "to lessen their total violation in society" (1974, 29).

3. Notions of compensatory justice were first articulated by Aristotle. Some liberal theorists argue for affirmative action based on principles of compensatory justice, but I have chosen to discuss the notion of compensatory justice here under conservative analyses of affirmative action because the conservative critique of this rationale is, in my judgment, compelling. This will allow us to turn to more plausible rationales as we proceed.

4. Sher defends this principle against theorists such as Nagel (1977) and Schaar (1974), arguing that people intuitively find distributions based on fair competition and merit acceptable (1977, 53n6).

5. The purpose of the thin theory of the Good "is to secure the premises about primary goods required to arrive at the principles of justice. Once this theory is worked out and the primary goods are accounted for, we are free to use the principles of justice in the further development of what I shall call the full theory of the good" (1971, 396).

6. On this point he responds to the objections to the equal opportunity principle raised by John Schaar (Rawls 1971, 107n), which are discussed later under Marxist analyses of affirmative action.

7. For a full theory of protective affirmative action, see Fullinwider's theory of "nondiscriminatory affirmative action" (1980, 170–76).

8. Thomas Nagel makes complementary critiques of the equal opportunity principle, while stressing the injustice of the schedule of rewards attached to talents (1977, 8–11).

9. MacIntyre asserts that Mill's proof has a more modest purpose than is usually implied by the term *proof*. He argues that Mill does not commit the naturalistic fallacy—deriving a value from a fact—rather, he is using a factual assertion that all people seek pleasure and avoid pain to make an ad hominem argument against those who deny that the end is pleasure. MacIntyre says the real problem is the haziness of Mill's central concept of pleasure: Mill means by it either (1) anything people aim at (which is a "vacuous tautology" and does not advance Mill's argument) or (2) sensual pleasure—but not all people desire it—for example, Puritans (1966, 239–40).

Chapter 3. Research Theory and Methodology

1. Also important in this issue is the criticism that it is inappropriate to generalize about individualism on the basis of a research sample that included primarily middle-class white men (as in Bellah et al., 1985).

2. Research indicates that eliminating neutral categories probably produces more accuracy in attitudinal responses (Blackstrom and Hursh-Cesar 1981, 137–39).

3. For most statistics, N = 30 is probably adequate, and it is even possible to speculate about relationships down to a dozen individuals (Blackstrom and Hursh-Cesar 1981, 382).

Chapter 4. Impressions from the Workplace and Interviews

1. My impressions here, as a white male, may be limited. I often heard things which would not have been said in the presence of a woman or a nonwhite man. Similarly, I might have been less likely to hear women and nonwhites express approval of affirmative action. Nevertheless, there are some who are very hostile to affirmative action. For example, on the survey's fill-in section, 6 percent of the respondents, when asked how they felt about the department's affirmative action program, wrote either that "it stinks," "it sucks," or "it's a sham."

2. While there have been some periods where several promotions in a row have gone to nonwhite or female candidates, and while there have been a couple of entry-level ranger training courses where very few white men other than those with military preference points have been hired, the perception that affirmative action "precludes" white men from entering or promoting within the department is inaccurate. However, it certainly is true that *some* white men, who otherwise would have been hired or promoted were not, and most department employees have plenty of anecdotal information to this effect.

3. During discussions within the department about affirmative action curriculum development, I pointed out that there has to be some moral fairness principle implicit in any view of what is reasonable, arguing that it would be unwise to concede the moral high ground or to stop attempting to convince employees that affirmative action is morally right. The extent to which ethics will be a part of the department's affirmative action effort is still unresolved. Some of those who embrace technocratic values (such as implementing existing policy as efficiently as possible) work hard to eliminate discussion of the moral dimension of affirmative action from affirmative action training.

4. For example, some evaluations of a training session that included a module I had developed on the ethics of affirmative action contained objections to the ethics part of the curriculum. However, some supporters of affirmative action said it was helpful to know some of the moral rationales for affirmative action, because they did not know what to say to those who argue that affirmative action is unfair. Another example is the reticence of many supporters of affirmative action to speak up in defense of preferential affirmative action. Some people, including some within the affirmative action bureaucracy, avoid characterizing affirmative action as preferential treatment, even though certain aspects of the affirmative action program are clearly preferential to white women and nonwhites.

5. I broadly divided interviewees' responses into views about affirmative action's impact on either the individual or society, rather than into the four main ways social philosophers approach the issue, discussed in chapter 2. It is easier to discuss the sentiments expressed in the interviews in these two categories. Nevertheless, the arguments articulated by the

social philosophers do find expression in this research, as will gradually become apparent.

6. About 10 percent of the respondents wrote on the fill-in section of the survey that affirmative action was either "reverse discrimination," "discrimination," or commented, "two wrongs don't make a right." This *two wrongs* phrase was also voiced by a white woman.

7. That affirmative action reduces the incentive of white men as well as others to improve themselves is a common complaint about affirmative action. One white man, after being passed over for a promotion in favor of a Hispanic candidate, complained that he had worked hard and put in lots of his own time to improve the park, and that this was not being recognized. He said that since all this effort did not help his chance of being promoted, he would now be "an eight-to-fiver."

8. Quite often respondents would endorse some version of the American Dream during one part of the interview, and contradict it in another. For example, an Asian woman said she believed hard work produces success, but when asked about how she felt about rewards being distributed based on the arbitrary distribution of natural talents, she said, "Well, life is not fair." An Asian man said that hard work usually leads to success and that discrimination is not prevalent, but he also stated that sometimes affirmative action is needed "in order to get your foot in the door."

A white female clerical worker said that, with the exception of the issue of equal pay for women, the only discrimination going on in society is against white men and that hiring the best qualified is the only morally right way to distribute rewards. She then denied, however, that the American Dream is real (saying that luck is critical) and added that she preferred distribution based on more socialist-type principles. Along similar lines, a white male maintenance worker strongly endorsed the American Dream, asserted that the biggest factor in success is effort, but remained resigned to inequalities in society, recognizing that luck and natural talents limit what people can achieve.

Many times, respondents would articulate sentiments that to social philosophers seem to be mutually exclusive and contradictory. The reasons for these contradictions are complex and varied. Some of the confusion must be due to the complexity of the issue itself. Other contradictions were probably caused by countervailing pressures, such as the perception that affirmative action has both personal and social costs and benefits. Other contradictions resulted from unresolved tensions among the competing moral values expressed in a Liberal culture. For example, individualistic values, such as those sympathetic to competition and acquisition, coexist with values such as community, neighborliness, and patriotism, which obviously can involve self-sacrifice for the commonweal.

Not all who think the American Dream is intact, that unbounded opportunities still exist, or that a "welfare ethic" accounts for much human failure in society, oppose affirmative action. I have heard such sentiments among different ethnic and gender groups.

A few examples include: a white male maintenance worker who asserted that affirmative action gives people something for nothing, "and that's why generation after generation live and die on welfare." He continued that many women and minorities are not even interested in Parks Department jobs or in a long-term career. When they are given jobs without working to get the qualifications, "Its just like anything else, when you hand something over to someone, it loses its value. I don't care, if they handed gold out on the corners, it would lose its value." A Hispanic male maintenance manager thought that affirmative action benefits society and has been helpful in racially integrating the department. But he also asserted that minorities who fail usually bring it upon themselves with attitudes such as, "Because you are a minority they owe you something."

A black female maintenance worker strongly believed that discrimination was real, and she approved of the specifics of the affirmative action program. But at the same time, she insisted that with hard work and a good attitude a person could overcome discrimination by winning over prejudiced people. "People are like this—a person, no matter . . . how prejudiced they are, they see you trying, whether they like you or not, they'll help you in a roundabout way. And if you continue to prove yourself, and you get what it takes to get you up there, and you climb and strive and work for it, believe it or not they'll help you instead of kicking you. . . . If you earn respect, you'll get it." She went on to lament the attitudes of some young people who think they "automatically are going to have a job because of EEO [equal employment opportunity] and AA [affirmative action]. . . . That's not being realistic . . . and it sickens me to death. [Some young people think], 'I don't have to worry because I'm a certain race.' No way! Some people are not trying! Nothing."

9. One alternative to affirmative action was never spontaneously offered: redistributing wealth, which is, arguably, the key building block of opportunity. However, some agreed with this idea when it was suggested during the interview.

10. The language of one white, female manager provides a good example of those who recognize that affirmative action does, for a time, compromise on the equal opportunity principle. Her response is interesting because until this point in the interview, she was so strongly in favor of the equal opportunity principle, that I had the impression that, for her, this principle was inviolable: "Well, I think equal opportunity is absolutely what we want. And affirmative action, the reason it's there is that we haven't had equal opportunity. . . . And affirmative action is the pendulum having to go way over here [gestures], so we end up here, where we really need to be. And I don't know of any way, or any social change, where you don't take a pendulum swing for a period of time. . . . And I think [affirmative action] promotes [equal opportunity]. . . . [It] does hammer away at the barriers . . . but I'm not sure the powerful are ready for it."

A middle-aged, white, male ex-military officer also strongly insisted that equal opportunity is what we want. But he called himself a pragmatist and said that there are no moral absolutes, he said that affirmative action is morally acceptable only for a while, not much more than ten more years. He added that one positive result of affirmative action is that it reduced nepotism within the department.

11. A black man insisted that, without affirmative action, the department would still be "lily white." One of the first women rangers noted that without affirmative action she would not have been there.

12. A good example here is from a white, male maintenance worker, who felt that affirmative action had become a numbers game, which "totally blows the whole concept" of fair employment and equal rights. He felt that too often unqualified people were being hired. Nevertheless, he thought that sometimes affirmative action helps the workplace, if qualified people are hired. For example, it would be O.K. to hire black workers "as long as they are close" to white workers in their qualifications. So, although he used language grounded in pure equal opportunity notions, in practice he hedged: he was willing to put up with preferences for nonwhites and women, if they were qualified enough to do the job.

13. "Compensating people for [the] past don't appeal to me at all. It's like trying to make amends, and you can't make amends. What you do is put the pieces together and you look forward, and you go on." She discussed the reparations awarded World War II Japanese internees: "Why can't they pick up the pieces and go on like everybody else. Why go into the taxpayer money?"

14. Another black, female maintenance worker shared the overall premise of this woman: an individualistic self-sufficiency ethic, a strong endorsement of the reality of the American Dream, a rejection of preferences for women and nonwhites. She also stressed that education and competition are the keys to the good society. Although less strongly, she also hedged when thinking concretely about how affirmative action preferences could help people like her: "I don't think that extra points and all should have anything to do with [hiring people]. I think qualifications, only, should. On the other hand, the person who is looking forward to these points, for being a minority or for being in the service, it's a help to them." Here, without abandoning the equal opportunity rhetoric, she seemed torn between equal opportunity and the benefits of affirmative action to her group.

15. This man insisted that affirmative action was supposed to increase the number of female and nonwhite applicants; but after this, the "best qualified" were to be hired. But at the same time, he did not trust white men to define "best qualified." He also denied the myth of opportunity found in American Dream rhetoric.

16. One Hispanic man said compensation is right because it is "our turn." Another Hispanic man said that while affirmative action is unfair, it is necessary to compensate minorities for previous wrongs at the point of hiring. Another Hispanic man endorsed redistribution and compensation. One black respondent said that somebody has to pay for discrimination. Although he was uncomfortable with the fact that it falls on individual white males, not the group as a whole, he added that he did not

know how to prevent this. Somebody had to pay, because in the past, it was the minorities and females who paid.

One white woman explicitly said that equal opportunity must be overridden to rectify past discrimination and added that sometimes the individual has to suffer for the common good. Another said that white men have a collective responsibility for discrimination and to rectify injustices. Another said that excessive emphasis on the individual is not good and argued that compensation may be an evil that works toward a greater good. Another agreed, adding that compensation prevents revolution. Two white women were quite ambivalent, saying that both those who make and reject compensatory arguments are right. Both native American interviewees rejected an individualistic approach to public policies, grounding their views in concern for their ethnic group, their priority on the social whole, and communitarian native American values. They both suggested that whites have a collective responsibility for discrimination and that compensation, therefore, makes sense. An Asian respondent reluctantly endorsed compensatory ideas, saying that compensatory programs are "sad," but necessary to right wrongs.

17. This problem has been highlighted recently in a "futures" report prepared by and for Parks Department management to guide the department's long-range strategies.

18. This pattern is similar to that of social philosophers: those who place a premium on the individual against the group tend to oppose affirmative action.

19. My impression is that many ambivalent supporters recite the dominant cultural credo in favor of merit hiring and equal opportunity, but there is an often unconscious belief among nonwhites and women that this principle does not always work for them, and so it is balanced by expressions of concern for their group or for the society at large.

20. The apparent exception to this is with those, I think a minority, who maintain the fiction that affirmative action does not involve preferences and is actually equivalent to pure equal opportunity. Rarely do proponents of affirmative action insist that affirmative action is justified only if it promotes the hiring of the best qualified.

21. I was surprised by how many interviewees, when presented with arguments about equal opportunity from a Marxist perspective (as summarized in chapter 2), which questions distributions of jobs and rewards according to natural talents, expressed sentiments in favor of such arguments or spontaneously expressed socialistic ideas. For example, one interviewee expressed sympathy for New Zealand style socialism, another voiced support for socialism, another said she likes the idea of socialized medicine, while still another said she would be willing to give up a bathroom and a bedroom if it would solve the homeless problem. After such expressions of egalitarian values, the interviewee often either seemed to apologize for voicing such heretical ideas, or expressed despair about the possibility of implementing such ideas in the United States.

Chapter 5. Survey Responses: Approval and Disapproval of Affirmative Action

1. Zero-order gamma is −.14; first-order gamma is −.23.

2. Correlation, tau-c = −.09, p ≤ .05)

3. Correlation, tau-c = −.15, p ≤ .01.

4. While the small number of Asian women respondents (N = 10) urges caution, differences between Asian men (N = 28) and Asian women were common. The difference between Asian men and women seen here was revealed in answers to many of the survey questions, with Asian men often more supportive of affirmative action than Asian women. With other subgroups, the opposite was usually true, with women more supportive. In the next two chapters, differences between men and women within ethnic subgroups are discussed. However, there were few respondents among Asian, black, and native American women (N = 10, 7, and 6, respectively), so one must be cautious in making inferences.

5. Correlation, tau-c = −. 13, p ≤ .001.

6. Correlation, tau-c = −.14, p ≤ .001. The following number represent those who identified themselves as conservative, moderate, or liberal in each of the four main research groups. White men: 41, 69, 44. White women: 20, 41, 33. Nonwhite men: 29, 49, 44. Nonwhite women, 8, 27, 13. Compared to figures in a national election study published in 1986 by the Center for Political Study, University of Michigan, these figures suggest that the institutional context for this research is slightly more liberal than the population at large.

7. These figures deserve mention, because responses in which black women are more inclined than black men to favor affirmative action and its premises are a pattern for many questions.

8. Correlation, tau-c = −.102, p ≤ .01.

9. Correlation, tau-c = −.09, p ≤ .05.

10. There were only nine respondents under thirty years of age.

11. Correlation, tau-c = −.09, p ≤ .01.

12. Correlation, tau-c = .26, p ≤ .001.

13. Correlation, tau-c = .285, p ≤ .001.

14. Correlation, tau-c = .13, p ≤ .01.

15. Low numbers of respondents, ranging from lows of about eight for evangelical subgroups, urge caution.

16. Responses are missing for about 20 percent of those who returned questionnaires. I coded up to two definitions for each respondent, which is why the responses summarized total to slightly more than 100 percent.

17. Correlation, tau-c = −.14, p ≤ .01.

18. Correlation, tau-c = .13, p ≤ .01.

19. Correlation, tau-c = −.29, p ≤ .001.

20. Correlation, tau-c = .17, p ≤ .01.

21. Correlation, tau-c = .22, p ≤ .001.

22. Zero-order gamma, .24, first-order gamma, .42.

23. Correlation, *tau-c* = −.07, *p* ≤ .05.
24. Correlation, *tau-c* = −.08, *p* ≤ .05.
25. Correlation, *tau-c* = −.19, *p* ≤ .001.
26. Correlation, *tau-c* = −.10, *p* ≤ .01.
27. Correlation, *tau-c* = −.15, *p* ≤ .01.
28. Correlation, *tau-c* = −.20, *p* ≤ .001.
29. Correlation, *tau-c* = −.13, *p* ≤ .01.

Chapter 6. Survey Responses: Moral Arguments About Affirmative Action

1. Correlation, *tau-c* = −.12, *p* ≤ .01.
2. Correlation, *tau-c* = .10, *p* ≤ .05.
3. Correlation, *tau-c* = .13, *p* ≤ .001.
4. One of the weaknesses of survey research is the inability to probe in depth, to sort out nuances in respondent attitudes. This must be kept in mind throughout the analysis of conservative and libertarian approaches to affirmative action. Their responses are lumped together by the limitations of survey research. For example, conservatives may not see autonomy as an absolute human right grounded in inviolable principle, but their tendency is to protect the individual against the interests of the state—and this is what makes libertarians and conservatives more similar than different, and part of what separates conservatives and libertarians from those who in common parlance are called liberals.
5. Correlation, *tau-c* = .25, *p* ≤ .001.
6. Correlation, *tau-c* = .16, *p* .001.
7. Correlation, *tau-c* = −.10, *p* ≤ .01.
8. The compensatory argument for affirmative action is also made by analysts who are not conservative or libertarian, and so the discussion here is relevant to subsequent discussion of liberal, Marxist, and consequentialist approaches to affirmative action.
9. Conservatives disagreed more than moderates and liberals (*tau-c* = −.13, *p* ≤ .01).
10. The gender gap continues: women differed from men (*tau-c* = .10, *p* ≤ .05).
11. Correlation, *tau-c* = −.18, *p* ≤ .001.
12. Correlation, *tau-c* = .15, *p* ≤ .001.
13. Correlation, *tau-c* = .09, *p* ≤ .05.
14. Correlation, *tau-c* = .09, *p* ≤ .05.
15. Correlation, *tau-c* = −.10 *p* ≤ .05.
16. Correlation, *tau-c* = −.16, *p* ≤ .001.
17. Correlation, *tau-c* = −.14, *p* ≤ .001.
18. Correlation, *tau-c* = .09, *p* ≤ .01.
19. Correlation, *tau-c* = .13, *p* ≤ .01.

20. In debates over the Civil Rights Act of 1990, the equivalent notion to the idea that equal opportunity is the axial moral principle upon which to base all hiring decisions is the appeal to color-blind hiring. My overall perception from both the qualitative and quantitative phases of this research is that many respondents recognized the complexity of the ethical dimensions of the affirmative action issue. This recognition is reflected either in confusion or in a conscious perception of multiple, sometimes competing, ethical concerns (beyond equal opportunity or color blindness), which also ought to be considered when reflecting morally about this issue.

21. This is one of two survey questions related to perceptions about the effect of affirmative action on equal opportunity. The other stated, *Affirmative action undermines equal opportunity, hiring based on merit.* The question regarding whether affirmative action promotes equal opportunity was posed in negative and positive forms because agreement with one does not necessarily mean disagreement with the other. Responses to both question indicate that virtually the same ratios who *disagreed* that affirmative action *promotes* equal opportunity *agreed* that affirmative action *hinders* equal opportunity.

22. Correlation, *tau-c* = −.19, *p* ≤ .001.

23. Correlation, *tau-c* = −.19, *p* ≤ .001. These differences are enhanced when controlling for race (zero-order gamma is −.11, first-order gamma is −.24).

24. Correlation, *tau-c* = −.18, *p* ≤ .001.

25. Correlation, *tau-c* = −.23, *p* ≤ .001.

26. Correlation, *tau-c* = −.13, *p* ≤ .001.

27. Correlation, *tau-c* = −.08, *p* ≤ .05.

28. Correlation, *tau-c* = −.18, *p* ≤ .001.

29. Correlation, *tau-c* = −.10, *p* ≤ .01 (regarding best jobs); correlation, *tau-c* = −.09, *p* ≤ .01 (regarding higher salaries).

30. Correlation, *tau-c* = −.07, *p* ≤ .05.

31. Correlation, *tau-c* = .09, *p* ≤ .05.

32. Correlation, *tau-c* = .12, *p* ≤ .01.

33. Correlation, *tau-c* = .10, *p* ≤ .05.

34. Correlation, *tau-c* = −.16, *p* ≤ .001.

35. Correlation, *tau-c* = −.18, *p* ≤ .001.

36. Correlation, *tau-c* = .27, *p* ≤ .001.

37. Correlation, *tau-c* = .15, *p* ≤ .01.

38. Correlation, *tau-c* = .25, *p* ≤ .001.

39. Correlation, *tau-c* = −.26, *p* ≤ .001.

Chapter 7. Conclusions and Implications

1. Rawls calls his version *democratic equality.* This version attempts to resolve the problem related to the meritocratic implications of Liberal

equality. But, as I argued in chapter 2, Rawls's preferred concept of democratic equality does not sufficiently alter the equal opportunity principle to prevent meritocracy. While he identified the problem, he does not provide a solution to the moral problem of meritocracy. My view is that Schaar's critique is better and even more fundamental. But Scharr also provides no specific way out. Like Marx, he leaves it for history to work out the specifics of what might replace Liberalism's equal opportunity principle.

2. This point, of how socially constructed ideas come to appear to individuals as inexorable facts, is derived from the sociology of knowledge's notion of reification—the apprehension of human phenomena as if they were things (Berger and Luckmann 1967, 88–89).

3. There is some debate over the value that civic republicanism places on social and economic equality. Certainly Aristotle was no egalitarian. But recently some have suggested that "classic republican theory from Aristotle to the American founders rested on the assumption that free institutions could survive in a society only if there were a rough equality of condition, that extremes of wealth and poverty are incompatible with a republic" (Bellah et al. 1985, 285; see also Sullivan 1982, 8–9, 175). While Bellah and Sullivan may overstate the egalitarian sentiments of republicanism, here I refer to those forms of civic republicanism that do value social and economic equality.

4. Since beginning this research project, I have paid strict attention to the rhetoric of distributive justice throughout U.S. culture. On the basis of these observations, I have concluded that the dominant view of distributive justice is some version of a primarily procedural notion of equal opportunity. In fact, with the notable (and relatively recent) exception of Jesse Jackson, seldom are non-Liberal distributive norms expressed. Even with the outpouring of concern for homeless people, the majority of the concern focuses on getting these people "back on their feet" so they can again compete in market society. In light of this admittedly anecdotal evidence about how little concern is expressed for substantive justice, I was surprised to find as much ambivalence about formal equal opportunity as I did.

5. After initially analyzing the empirical findings, I spoke with several native Americans about the results (Suzanne Guerra, Mark Thompson, and José Rivera). I am indebted to them for most of these reflections on native American culture's impact on attitudes. Among their comments were: The hunter-warrior is given an individual name, which reflects his individual achievements and expectations. Native American women's names tend to reflect other virtues, such as endurance, character, and nurturing capabilities, rather than individualistic achievement. Native American men are especially concerned that they make it on their own; they want no hint of special preference, and this type of individualism may be grounded in the native American (male) ethic of personal achievement. Given the low social position of most native American men in the Liberal culture, their intense hostility toward affirmative action may be grounded

in feelings of low self-esteem and resentment of suggestions that they have received special treatment.

6. My conclusion replicates part of the findings of Jennifer Hochschild's important qualitative interview study of the attitudes of white men and women toward distributive justice. She found that, with regard to economic equality, most people strongly believed that widespread inequality was acceptable and that wealth is earned, while at the same time, through helplessness, anger, inconsistency and confusion, they expressed ambivalence about economic inequality (1981, 237–59). My research found similar ambivalence, expressed in similar ways. But I also found this ambivalence greater among nonwhite men and women as well as among white women, than among white men. (I put off reading Hochschild's study until my analysis had been largely completed. The parallels between many of the attitudes of her and my respondents are striking and provide evidence that these data can be generalized.)

7. Of course, some argue that inequalities of income (and even wealth) are due not to discrimination but to cultural factors, and that discrimination is declining as a factor in economic inequalities (e.g., Sowell 1984, 1981a, 1981b). However, Shulman and Darity argue well against such claims (1989). A study of blacks in U.S. society provides much information on issues related to affirmative action. See especially Jaynes and Williams on the effectiveness of affirmative action policies (1989, 315-17) and on the attitudes of white men toward affirmative action (150, 153–54, 376–79). Morrison and Von Glinow provide a good summary of current research, which shows that women and minorities encounter a "glass ceiling" that limits their advancement in organizations in U.S. society (1990, 200–08). Other recent studies relevant to these issues include Blanchard and Crosby (1989), and Kellough (1989).

As one respondent indicated, and Wasserstrom (1977) argues, one way discrimination is perpetrated is by the dominance of elite white men over the means of production—which includes the production of the idea of what counts as *merit*. By framing merit in terms of experiences and education to which white men have greater access, the merit ideal can perpetuate discriminatory effects. For an interesting case study regarding the discriminatory effects of concepts of merit, see Heins (1987); for a more comprehensive study of similar issues, see Gottfried (1988).

8. Kellough challenges the assumption that conflict over policies like affirmative action is necessarily bad. It "may not be undesirable since it draws attention to problems of minority and female under-representation, and as a result, it helps to keep that issue on the public agenda" (1989, 115).

GLOSSARY

AFFIRMATIVE ACTION. A continuum of different responses to discrimination, from measures designed primarily to prevent discrimination (such as *protective affirmative action*) to measures designed to increase the numbers of women and nonwhites in a work force through the preferential treatment of such individuals (*preferential affirmative action*).

CIVIC REPUBLICAN. See *republican*.

CONSERVATIVE. Those persons and ideas on the right wing of philosophical Liberalism. Conservatives and liberals share the central tenets of philosophical *Liberalism*, but conservatives, more than liberals, tend to approve of *pure equal opportunity* and *protective affirmative action*, while liberals are more likely to also endorse *preferential affirmative action*.

DEONTOLOGY. One of the two major branches of normative ethical theory, the opposite of *teleology*. Deontology insists that the rightness or wrongness of actions can be determined intrinsically, without reference to ends.

EQUAL OPPORTUNITY PRINCIPLE. One of the central tenets of *Liberalism:* the idea that everyone ought to be given a fair and equal chance to compete for preferred jobs and salaries and that such jobs and salaries ought to be distributed according to *merit"* where the best qualified candidate is hired.

FORMAL EQUALITY (sometimes called procedural equality). The extent to which procedures are provided equally for all. For example, is due process provided to all? Or do all persons have equal legal access to certain benefits? Here, equality is a principle, in the sense of a rule of action. Compare with *substantive equality*.

LIBERAL. Those persons and ideas on the left wing of philosophical Liberalism. Liberals share with conservatives the central tenets of philosophical *Liberalism* but differ in significant ways. See *conservative*.

LIBERALISM. The enlightenment philosophy that is the dominant social philosophy in the United States. Its key tenets are shared by liberals, con-

235

servatives, and libertarians. These tenets include: rights inhere to the individual; people are self-interested, acquisitive, maximizing consumers (usually unchangeably so); people compete in political and economic markets and are entitled to *equal opportunity* in this competition (so philosophical Liberals embrace capitalism); and this competition produces, at best, a good society or, at least, the best society people are capable of producing. Philosophical Liberals believe that the *Liberal culture* is characterized usually by economic growth and political freedom.

LIBERAL CULTURE. The dominant U.S. culture, in which there is an overwhelming consensus in favor of principles grounded in philosophical *Liberalism*, such as the *equal opportunity principle*.

LIBERTARIAN. Ideas or people belonging to the right wing of philosophical *Liberalism*. These ideas place a premium on autonomy, where any teleological, ends-focused distribution of jobs or salaries is seen as a violation of individual rights, as taking from one individual to give to another. Libertarian thought therefore tends to embrace pure equal opportunity, while rejecting *preferential affirmative action* as well as many measures undertaken with *protective affirmative action* in mind.

MERIT. Job qualifications, especially specific job-related education, training, skills, and experience. The idea of merit is less concerned with a person's long-term potential than with current levels of skill and achievement.

NATURAL TALENTS. Innate abilities inherited through one's genes.

PREFERENTIAL AFFIRMATIVE ACTION. Measures designed to increase the numbers of women and nonwhites in a work force by giving them preference. Such action usually involves statistical measures to determine proportions of different groups in a work force, and hiring and promotion goals to increase the representation of women and nonwhites.

PROTECTIVE AFFIRMATIVE ACTION. Measures designed to eliminate intentional and nonintentional personnel practices that have the effect of discriminating against women and nonwhite individuals, short of extending preferential treatment. This type of affirmative action is compatible with the idea of *pure equal opportunity*.

PURE EQUAL OPPORTUNITY. The *equal opportunity principle*, with the added understanding that this principle ought to be inviolable: people have the right to be treated as individuals in every instance, and people ought never be treated based on their membership in any racial or gender group. Proponents of this concept of *equal opportunity* tend to be *conservative* or *libertarian* in philosophy.

REPUBLICAN. Persons and ideas from the civic republican tradition (whose major figures include Aristotle, Machiavelli, and Luther). Republican thought places the good of the community over that of the individual and values social stability and the preservation of social institutions. However, republican notions of substantive justice and public virtue (understood as that which benefits society as a whole and increases happiness in society) can also promote social reform.

SUBSTANTIVE EQUALITY. Equality among people as to their material condition, including material goods and positions. Here, equality is a value, in the sense of a desired good or a condition worth pursuing. Compare with *formal equality.*

TELEOLOGY. One of the two major branches of normative ethical theory, the opposite of *deontology.* Teleology judges the rightness or wrongness of action by reference to ends (to some concept of the Good). Therefore, the consequences of actions and the goals sought are most important in determining what actions are right or wrong. Teleological theory, by justifying actions by reference to ends, ultimately places relatively greater importance on ends than on means. (Although, rule teleology emphasizes rules of action, the rules must still serve the ends.)

REFERENCES

Alleyne, Reginald. 1989. Smoking Guns Are Hard to Find. *Los Angeles Times*, 12 June.

Beauchamp, Tom L. 1977. The Justification of Reverse Discrimination. In *Social Justice and Preferential Treatment*, ed. William T. Blackstone and Robert P. Heslep. Athens: University of Georgia Press. (Also in *Social Ethics: Morality and Social Policy*, ed. Thomas A. Mappes and Jane S. Zembaty. New York: McGraw-Hill, 1977, 1982.)

Beauchamp, Tom L., and LeRoy Walters, eds. 1982. *Contemporary Issues in Bioethics*. 2d ed. Belmont, Calif.: Wadsworth.

Becker, Howard S. 1970. *Sociologial Work: Method and Substance*. Chicago: Aldine.

Bedau, Hugo. 1972. Compensatory Justice and the Black Manifesto. *Monist* 56: 20–42.

Bellah, Robert, et al. 1985. *Habits of the Heart*. Berkeley and Los Angeles: University of California Press.

Benokraitis, Nijole V., and Joe R. Feagin. 1978. *Affirmative Action and Equal Opportunity: Action, Inaction, Reaction*. Boulder, Colo.: Westview.

Berger, Peter, and Thomas Luckmann. 1967 [1966]. *The Social Construction of Reality*. New York: Anchor.

Bittker, Boris. 1973. *The Case for Black Reparations*. New York: Vintage.

Blackstone, William T., and Robert Heslep, eds. 1977. *Social Justice and Preferential Treatment*. Athens: University of Georgia Press.

Blackstrom, Charles H., and Gerald Hursh-Cesar. 1981. *Survey Research*. 2d ed. New York: John Wiley.

Blanchard, Fletcher A., and Faye J. Crosby, eds. 1989. *Affirmative Action in Perspective*. New York: Springer-Verlag.

Boxill, Bernard. 1975. The Morality of Reparation. In *Today's Moral Problems*, ed. Richard Wasserstrom, 2d ed. New York: Macmillan.

———. 1978. The Morality of Preferential Hiring. *Philosophy and Public Affairs* 7: 246–68.

Brest, Paul. 1976. The Supreme Court 1975 Term. Foreword: In Defense of the Antidiscrimination Principle. *Harvard Law Review* 90 (1): 1–54.

Brest, Paul, and Sanford Levinson. 1983. *Processes of Constitutional Decisionmaking: Cases and Materials.* 2d ed. Boston: Little, Brown.

Bureau of National Affairs. 1973. *The Equal Opportunity Act of 1972.* Washington, D.C.: BNA.

Burstein, Paul. 1985. *Discrimination, Jobs, and Politics: The Struggle for Equal Employment Opportunity in the United States Since the New Deal.* Chicago: University of Chicago Press.

Campbell, T. D. 1974–75. Equality of Opportunity. *Proceedings of the Aristotelian Society* 75: 51–68.

Chapman, John W. 1967. Natural Rights and the Justice of Liberalism. In *Political Theory and the Rights of Man*, ed. D. D. Raphael. Bloomington: Indiana University Press.

Charmaz, Kathy. 1983. The Grounded Theory Method: An Explication and Interpretation. In *Contemporary Field Research*, ed. Robert M. Emerson. Boston: Little, Brown.

Cohen, Carl. 1975. Race and the Constitution. In *Today's Moral Problems*, ed. Richard Wasserstrom, 2d ed. New York: Macmillan.

Cohen, Marshall, Thomas Nagel, and Thomas Scanlon, eds. 1977. *Equality and Preferential Treatment: A Philosophy and Public Affairs Reader.* Princeton, N.J.: Princeton University Press.

Daly, Herman E., ed. 1980. *Economics, Ecology, Ethics: Essays Toward a Steady-State Economy.* San Francisco: W. H. Freeman.

Davidson, Kenneth. 1976. Preferential Treatment and Equal Opportunity. *Oregon Law Review* 55: 53–83.

Dworkin, Ronald. 1977. *Taking Rights Seriously.* Cambridge, Mass.: Harvard University Press.

Ely, John Hart. 1974. The Constitutionality of Reverse Racial Discrimination. *University of Chicago Law Review* 41: 723–41.

Emerson, Robert, ed. 1983. *Contemporary Field Research.* Boston: Little, Brown.

Feagin, Joe R., and Clairece Booher Feagin. 1978. *Discrimination American Style: Institutional Racism and Sexism.* Englewood Cliffs, N.J.: Prentice-Hall.

Feinberg, Joel. 1964. Wasserstrom on Human Rights. *Journal of Philosophy* 61: 641–45.

———. 1966. Duties, Rights, and Claims. *American Philosphical Quarterly* 3: 137–44.

———. 1973. *Social Philosophy.* Englewood Cliffs, N.J.: Prentice-Hall.

Fiss, Owen. 1971. Theory of Fair Employment Laws. *University of Chicago Law Review* 38: 235–314.

———. 1976. Groups and the Equal Protection Clause. *Philosophy and Public Affairs* 5: 107–77.

Frankena, William K. 1973. *Ethics.* Englewood Cliffs, N.J.: Prentice-Hall.

Freeman, Alan. 1978. Legitimizing Racial Discrimination Through Antidiscrimination Law: A Critical Review of Supreme Court Doctrine. *Minnesota Law Review* 62: 1049ff.

Fullinwider, Robert K. 1980. *The Reverse Discrimination Controversy: A Moral and Legal Analysis.* Totowa, N.J.: Rowman and Littlefield.

Garet, Ronald R. 1983. Communality and Existence: The Rights of Groups. *Southern California Law Review* 56: 1001–75.

Gewirth, Alan. 1978. *Reason and Morality.* Chicago: University of Chicago Press.

Gilligan, Carol. 1982. *In a Different Voice.* Cambridge, Mass.: Harvard University Press.

———. 1983. Do the Social Sciences Have an Adequate Theory of Moral Development? In *Social Science as Moral Inquiry,* ed. N. Haan, R. N. Bellah, P. Rabinow, and W. Sullivan. New York: Columbia University Press.

Glazer, Barney G., and Anselm L. Strauss. 1967. *The Discovery of Grounded Theory: Strategies for Qualitative Research.* Chicago: Aldine.

Glazer, Nathan. 1975. *Affirmative Discrimination: Ethnic Inequality and Public Policy.* New York: Basic Books.

Goldman, Alan H. 1977. Affirmative Action. In *Equality and Preferential Treatment,* ed. Marshall Cohen, Thomas Nagel, and Thomas Scanlon. Princeton, N.J.: Princeton University Press.

———. 1979. *Justice and Reverse Discrimination.* Princeton, N.J.: Princeton University Press.

Gottfried, Francis. 1988. *The Merit System and Municipal Civil Service: A Fostering of Social Inequality.* New York: Greenwood.

Goulding, Martin P. 1981. From Prudence to Rights: A Critique. *Human Rights: Nomos XXIII,* ed. J. R. Pennock and J. W. Chapman. New York: New York University Press.

Greene, Kathanne W. 1989. *Affirmative Action and Principles of Justice.* New York: Greenwood.

Greene, Maxine. 1976. An Approach to Compensatory Justice. In *Social Justice and Preferential Treatment,* ed. William T. Blackstone and Robert Heslep. Athens: University of Georgia Press.

Greenhouse, Linda. 1990a. Justices Bolster Race Preferences at Federal Level. *New York Times,* 28 June.

———. 1990b. The Dispute over Quotas. *New York Times,* 21 July.

Gross, Barry R. 1978. *Discrimination in Reverse: Is Turnabout Fair Play?* New York: New York University Press.

Gunther, Gerald. 1975. *Cases and Materials on Constitutional Law.* 9th ed. Mineola, N.Y.: Foundation.

Gutman, Amy. 1980. *Liberal Equality.* London: Cambridge University Press.

Heins, Marjorie. 1987. *Cutting the Mustard: Affirmative Action and the Nature of Excellence.* Boston: Farber and Farber.

Held, Virginia. 1973. Reasonable Progress and Self-Respect. *Monist* 57: 1.

Heslep, Robert D. 1977. Preferential Treatment in Admitting Racial Minority Students. In *Social Justice and Preferential Treatment,* ed. Heslep and William T. Blackstone. Athens: University of Georgia Press.

Hirsh, Fred. 1977. *Social Limits to Growth*. Cambridge, Mass.: Harvard University Press.

Hochschild, Jennifer L. 1981. *What's Fair: American Beliefs About Distributive Justice*. Cambridge, Mass: Harvard University Press.

Holloway, Francis A. 1989. What Is Affirmative Action? *Affirmative Action in Perspective*, ed. Fletcher A. Blanchard and Faye J. Crosby. New York: Springer-Verlag.

Hook, Sidney. 1977a. Discrimination, Color Blindness, and the Quota System. In *Reverse Discrimination*, ed. Barry Gross. Buffalo, N.Y.: Prometheus.

——. 1977b. Discrimination Against the Qualified? In *Social Ethics: Morality and Social Policy*, ed. Thomas A. Mappes and Jane S. Zembaty. New York: McGraw-Hill.

Jaynes, Gerald David, and Robin M. Williams, Jr., eds. 1989. *A Common Destiny: Blacks and American Society*. Washington, D.C.: National Academy Press.

Kann, Mark E. 1982. *The American Left: Failures and Fortunes*. New York: Praeger.

Kellough, J. Edward. 1989. *Federal Equal Employment Opportunity Policy and Timetables: An Impact Assessment*. New York: Praeger.

Kilborn, Peter. 1990. Labor Department Wants to Take on Job Bias in the Executive Suite. *New York Times*, 30 July.

Lebacqz, Karen. 1981. Preferential Treatment—Women and Minority Groups: Recent Ethical Studies. *Religious Studies Review* 7: 97–107.

Lewis, Neil A. 1990. Ruling on Minority Broadcasting Seen as Aiding Affirmative Action. *New York Times*, 4 July.

Lofland, John. 1971. *Analyzing Social Settings*. Belmont, Calif.: Wadsworth.

Lowi, Theodore J. 1979. *The End of Liberalism*. New York: Norton.

Lyons, David. 1978. Rights, Utility, and Racial Discrimination. In *Philosophical Law*, ed. Richard Bronaugh. Westport, Conn.: Greenwood.

McIntosh, Peggy. 1988. White Privilege and Male Privilege: A Personal Account of Coming to See Correspondences Through Work in Women's Studies. Working Paper 189. Wellesley, Mass.: Wellesley College Center for Research on Women.

MacIntyre, Alasdair. 1966. *A Short History of Ethics*. New York: Macmillan.

MacPherson, C. B. 1967. *Natural Rights in Hobbes and Locke. In Political Theory and the Rights of Man*, ed. D. D. Raphael. Bloomington: Indiana University Press.

——. 1977. *The Life and Times of Liberal Democracy*. Oxford: Oxford University Press.

Maguire, Daniel C. 1980. *A New American Justice*. Garden City, N.Y.: Winston.

——. 1982. The Feminization of God and Ethics. *Christianity and Crisis*. 42 (4): 59–67.

Mappes, Thomas A., and Jane S. Zembaty, eds. 1977. *Social Ethics: Morality and Social Policy*. New York: McGraw-Hill.

Martin, Rex, and James W. Nickel. 1980. Recent Work on the Concept of Rights. *American Philosophical Quarterly* 17 (3): 165–80.

Mill, J. S. 1957 [1861]. *Utilitarianism,* ed. Oscar Priest. Indianapolis: Bobbs-Merrill.

Morrison, Ann M., and Mary Ann Von Glinow. 1990. Women and Minorities in Management. *American Psychologist* 45 (2): 200–08.

Nagel, Thomas. 1977. Equal Treatment and Compensatory Discrimination. In *Equality and Preferential Treatement,* ed. Marshall Cohen, Thomas Nagel, and Thomas Scanlon. Princeton, N.J.: Princeton University Press.

Neill, Marshall A. 1977. Majority Opinion in DeFunis v. Odegaard. In *Social Ethics: Morality and Social Policy,* ed. Thomas A. Mappes and Jane S. Zembaty. New York: McGraw-Hill.

Newman, Jim D. 1989. Affirmative Action and the Courts. In *Affirmative Action in Perspective,* ed. Fletcher A. Blanchard and Faye J. Crosby. New York: Springer-Verlag.

Newton, Lisa H. 1977. Reverse Discrimination as Unjustified. *Social Ethics: Morality and Social Policy,* ed. Thomas A. Mappes and Jane S. Zembaty. New York: McGraw-Hill.

Nickel, James W. 1972. Discrimination and Morally Relevant Characteristics. *Analysis* 32: 113.

―――. 1975. Preferential Policies in Hiring and Admissions: A Jurisprudential Approach. In *Today's Moral Problems,* ed. Richard Wasserstrom. New York: Macmillan.

Nozick, Robert. 1974. *Anarchy, State, and Utopia.* New York: Basic Books.

Okin, Susan Moller. 1981. Liberty and Welfare: Some Issues in Human Rights Theory. *Human Rights: Nomos XXIII,* ed. J. R. Pennock and J. W. Chapman. New York: New York University Press.

O'Neill, Onora. 1979. How Do We Know When Opportunities Are Equal? In *Feminism and Philosophy,* ed. Mary Vetterling-Braggin, Frederick A. Elliston, and Jane English. Totowa, N.J.: Littlefield, Adams.

Pear, Robert. 1990a. Courts Are Undoing Efforts to Aid Minority Contractors. *New York Times,* 16 July.

―――. 1990b. How '89 Ruling Spurs New Suits on Civil Rights. *New York Times,* 15 October.

Raphael, D. D. 1967. *Political Theory and the Rights of Man.* Bloomington: Indiana University Press.

Rawls, John. 1971. *A Theory of Justice.* Cambridge, Mass.: Harvard University Press.

Rifkin, Jeremy. 1980. *Entropy: A New World View* New York: Viking.

Savage, David G. 1986. Affirmative Action Faces Test on Women's Status. *Los Angeles Times,* 10 November.

―――. 1987a. Court Extends Racial Quotas to Promotions. *Los Angeles Times,* 26 February.

―――. 1987b. High Court Backs Job Preference for Women. *Los Angeles Times,* 26 March.

———. 1988a. Split Court Reopens '76 Rights Case. *Los Angeles Times*, 26 April.

———. 1988b. Statistics Held Proof of Bias in Workplace. *Los Angeles Times*, 30 June.

———. 1989a. Minority Quotas Curbed by the Court. *Los Angeles Times*, 24 January.

———. 1989b. Justices Set Guideline on Job Bias. *Los Angeles Times*, 2 May.

———. 1989c. Job Bias Suit "Death Knell" Seen in High Court Ruling. *Los Angeles Times*, 6 June.

———. 1989d. Late Challenges to Minority Job Benefits Upheld. *Los Angeles Times*, 13 June.

Schaar, John H. 1974. Equality of Opportunity and Beyond. In *Up the Mainstream: A Critique of Ideology in American Politics and Everyday Life*, ed. Herbert G. Reid. New York: David McKay. (Also in *Equality: Nomos IX*, ed. J. R. Pennock and J. W. Chapman. New York: Atherton, 1967.)

Schuman, Howard, Charlotte Steeh, and Lawrence Bobo. 1985. *Racial Attitudes in America*. Cambridge, Mass.: Harvard University Press.

Schwartz, Bernard. 1988. *Behind Bakke*. New York University Press.

Sher, George. 1977. Justifying Reverse Discrimination in Employment. In *Equality and Preferential Treatment*, ed. Marshall Cohen, Thomas Nagel, and Thomas Scanlon. Princeton, N.J.: Princeton University Press. (Also in *Philosophy and Public Affairs* 4 [1975]: 159–70.)

Shulman, Steven, and William Darity, Jr. 1989. *The Question of Discrimination: Racial Inequality in the U.S. Labor Market*. Middletown, Conn.: Wesleyan University Press.

Simon, Robert L. 1977. Preferential Hiring: A Reply to Judith Jarvis Thomson. In *Equality and Preferential Treatment*, ed. M. Cohen, T. Nagel, and T. Scanlon. Princeton, N.J.: Princeton University Press.

Skelton, George. 1987. California's Affinity for GOP Is Growing, Poll Says. *Los Angeles Times*, 15 December.

Sowell, Thomas. 1981a. *Ethnic America*. New York: Basic Books.

———. 1981b. *Markets and Minorities*. New York: Basic Books.

———. 1984. *Civil Rights: Rhetoric or Reality?* New York: William Morrow.

St. Antoine, Theodore. 1976. Affirmative Action: Hypocritical Euphemism or Noble Mandate? *University of Michigan Journal of Law Reform* 10:28–43.

Strike, Kenneth. 1976. Justice and Reverse Discrimination. *University of Chicago Law School Review* 84: 516–37.

Sullivan, William. 1982. *Reconstructing Public Philosophy*. Berkeley and Los Angeles: University of California Press.

Taylor, Paul. 1973. Reverse Discrimination and Compensatory Justice. *Analysis* 33 (4): 177–82.

Thalberg, Irving. 1973–74. Reverse Discrimination and the Future. *Philosophical Forum* 5 (Fall–Winter): 300.

———. 1977. Visceral Racism. In *Social Ethics: Morality and Social Policy*, ed. Thomas A. Mappes and Jane S. Zembaty. New York: McGraw-Hill (excerpted from *Monist* 56 [1977]: 1).

Thomson, Judith Jarvis. 1977. Preferential Hiring. In *Equality and Preferential Treatment*, ed. Marshall Cohen, Thomas Nagel, and Thomas Scanlon. Princeton, N.J.: Princeton University Press, 19–48. (Also in *Philosophy and Public Affairs* 2 [1973]: 364–84.)

Thurow, Lester C. 1980. *The Zero-Sum Society.* New York: Penguin.

Tipton, Steven M. 1982. *Getting Saved from the Sixties: Moral Meaning in Conversion and Cultural Change.* Berkeley and Los Angeles: University of California Press.

Tucker, Robert C. 1978. *The Marx-Engels Reader,* 2d ed. New York: Norton.

U.S. Congress. Senate. 1990. *Report Together with Minority Views: The Civil Rights Act of 1990.* 101st Cong., 2d sess., S. Rpt. 101–315.

Velasquez, Manuel G. 1982. *Business Ethics.* Englewood Cliffs, N.J.: Prentice-Hall.

Vlastos, Gregory. 1962. Justice and Equality. In *Social Justice*, ed. Richard B. Brandt. Englewood Cliffs, N.J.: Prentice-Hall.

Wasserstrom, Richard. 1964. Rights, Human Rights and Racial Discrimination. *Journal of Philosophy* 61: 628–41.

———. 1977. The University and the Case for Preferential Treatment. In *Social Justice and Preferential Treatment*, ed. W. T. Blackstone and R. D. Heslep. Athens: University of Georgia Press.

Wasserstrom, Richard, ed. 1975. *Today's Moral Problems.* New York: Macmillan.

Yankelovich, Daniel. 1982 [1981]. *New Rules.* New York: Bantam.

INDEX

AA. *See* Affirmative action

Actual consent, 187

Affirmative action (AA): ambivalence toward, 89, 99; confusion about, 89, 98; controversy over, 10, 12, 76–78, 88–89, 120–33; and culture, 185; and disadvantaged people, 69, 162; as distributive justice, 11; goals and timetables for, 27; and liberalism, 8–10; as moral issue, 76, 94, 98, 120–33; protective, 12, 13, 43; psychological responses to, 89–99, 192–95; social costs of, 67, 176; strongest advocates of, 109; training for implementing, 199–202; and U.S. history and culture, 67, 77, 78, 96, 145, 174, 218n4; variables affecting attitudes toward, 174–75; and white males, 139–40, 143–46, 148–49; and women, 8, 13, 77–78, 156–58, 187. *See also* Distributive justice; Justice, theories of

Affirmative action, survey of attitudes about in CSDPR

———— descriptive analysis of data: and communitarian v. individual sentiments, 176, 179, 180; and compensatory justice, 176–77; and consequentialist rationales, 177–79; and demographic factors, 174–75; and distributive justice, 174, 184–86; and equal opportunity principle, 150, 152–54, 176, 180, 181; and ethics, 179, 180–81, 182–83; and socialist concepts, 178

———— and moral arguments, 150, 152–54; consequentialist, 163–68; conservative and libertarian, 139–50; liberal, 150–58; Marxist, 159–61

———— normative analysis of data: and consequentalist arguments, 196; and conservative and libertarian arguments, 188–90; and equal opportunity principle, 190–91; and Marxist ideas, 191; and distributive justice, 193; and organizational productivity, 194; and psychological effects, 89–99, 192–95; value of descriptive data to, 186–87

———— and perceptions: of affirmative action laws, 124–27; of civil rights leaders, 115, 120; of ethics, 127–28; of hiring goals, 129–32

———— research methods used in, 8, 75–87, 172–73, 230n4

———— variables in survey sample: age, 115, 123, 126, 129–30, 132; ethnicity and gender, 115, 122, 129, 131–32, 134; political ideology, 120, 122–23, 125, 129, 132, 134; race and gender, 121, 124–25, 129, 131–32, 133–34; religion, 123, 125–26, 130, 132, 135; social class, 115, 125–26

Albermarle Paper Co. v. Moody (1975), 23

American Dream, 106, 146–50, 179–80, 225n8, 227n14

Americans with Disabilities Act of 1990, 31

Antidiscrimination law: as alternative to affirmative action, 102; beneficiaries of, 32; and compensatory principle, 44, 223n3; court cases defining, 18; and disability, 31; enforcement of, 104, 144; future of, 17, 21; and pain and suffering, 219n14; and relation to affirmative action, 29; and results-oriented remedies, 23; and the workplace, 19. *See also* Justice; Law

Bakke v. Regents of the University of California (1978), 24–25
Beauchamp, Tom C., 34–36
Becker, Howard, 83
Bedau, Hugo, 45
Bellah, Robert, 77, 232n3
Benokraitis, Nijole V., 218n10
Blacks: and equal opportunity, 104; and preferential treatment, 13; support for affirmative action among, 175. *See also* Race
Blackstone, William T., 12, 44
Blackstrom, Charles H., 80
Bobrow, Davis, xii
Brennan, William, 33
Brest, Paul, 17, 18, 25, 46
Burstein, Paul, 17
Bush, George, 17

California State Department of Parks and Recreation (CSDPR): affirmative action policy in, xii, 5–6, 199; affirmative action program in, 88–90; demographic makeup of, 84; Human Rights Office of, 92; ideological composition of, 86–87. *See also* Affirmative action, survey of attitudes about in CSDPR
California State Personnel Board, 14, 75
Charmaz, Kathy, 79
Civic republican tradition: and consequentalism, 66–67; as conservativism, 43, 217n1; ethical perspectives in, 181; and social and economic equality, 232n3
Civil rights, 86, 114–20, 221n25
Civil Rights Act of 1866, 16–17
Civil Rights Act of 1964, 19–20: Title IV of, 19, 20, 22, 24, 26–27, 29–30, 219nn13, 14, 222n25
Civil rights bill of 1990, 17, 27, 221n25, 231n20
Cohen, Carl, 67, 68
Compensation, basis of, 46, 145–56, 154–56, 162. *See also* Distributive justice

Compensatory justice, 11, 43–45, 143–46. *See also* Distributive justice
Consequentalism: and affirmative action, 66–70, 110; and the common good, 43; and deontological theory, 36; and equal opportunity, 177–78; false positions of, 67; and the Good, 36, 64, 66–67, 191; and justice, 36, 103; and moral principles, 35; and teleological and deontological arguments, 162–64; and utilitarianism, 63–66; and the workplace, 166–68, 192–96. *See also* Distributive justice
Conservatives: and affirmative action, 56, 69, 116, 139–50; and the American Dream, 147; and equal opportunity, 56; and Kantian ideas, 56; and Liberalism, 56, 69; types of, 43; and U.S. domestic policy, 139
Cost-benefit analysis, and affirmative action, 202
CSDPR. *See* California State Department of Parks and Recreation

Daly, Herman E., 7, 217n2
Democratic equality, and liberal equality, 58
Deontological theory, 104. *See also* Consequentalism; Conservatives
Disability, as cause for discrimination, 31
Discrimination: and adverse impact theory, 24; and the complaint process, 12; in corporations, 41; and disability, 31; and exclusion v. inclusion, 100; intentional and unintentional, 20; perceived decline of, 104; and productivity, 30, 68; and reverse discrimination, 11; systemic, 22. *See also* Antidiscrimination law
Distributive justice, 7, 10, 172, 175–79. *See also* Justice, theories of
Dole, Elizabeth, 32
Dryzek, John, xii
Durkheim, Emile, 76
Dworkin, Ronald, 54–55

Emerson, Robert, 75, 80
Employment tests, 23
Equal employment opportunity, 11

Equal Employment Opportunity Act of 1972, 20, 22

Equal Employment Opportunity Commission (EEOC), 19, 20–21, 23, 205

Equality, 10, 36, 58

Equal opportunity: and affirmative action, 9, 11, 152–54; and blacks, 104; definitions of, 9–11, 36, 180; and distributive justice, 7, 150; as fairness, 54–57; in liberal culture, 7; and merit principle, 7; and morality, 150–52; perceived decline of, 9, 12; and preferential and protective affirmative action, 11, 12, 54–55, 218n9; as productive freedom, 59, 61–63; "pure," 11, 99; and qualifications, 106. *See also* Justice, theories of

Equal Opportunity Employment Committee, 80

Ethics: and affirmative action, 224n3; descriptive, 184–86; and equality, 36–27; and normative principle, 34–37, 187; and qualitative and quantitative methods, 173; as social ethics, xvi; in social science, xi–xiii

Eulau, Heinz, xi

Fiss, Owen, 46

Fourteenth Amendment of the U.S. Constitution, 14–19, 28

Frankena, William K., 34

Freedom, positive and negative, 48. *See also* Justice, theories of

Freeman, Alan, 45–56

Fullilove v. Klutznick (1980), 28

Fullinwider, Robert K., 19, 20, 25, 47–48, 68, 218nn6, 9, 220n17, 223n7

Garet, Ronald R., 189

Gilligan, Carol, 77–78

Glazer, Nathan, 67, 79, 220n17

Goldman, Alan H., 12

Griggs v. Duke Power (1971), 22–23, 27, 30

Green, Maxine, 47, 48

Greene, Kathanne W., 20, 22–23, 24

Greenhouse, Linda, 29

Gross, Barry R., 45, 67

Gunther, Gerald, 17

Hazlewood School District v. United States (n.d.), 23

Heslep, Robert, 12, 45, 68

Hiring, of best qualified, 108, 150–52, 159–61, 197

Hiring goals: attitudes toward, 130; controversy over, 131; at CSDPR, 128; fairness of, 106; pressure to meet, 103, 105

Hirsh, Fred, 7, 8, 217nn2, 3

Hochschilds, Jennifer L., 186, 233n6

Hofferbert, Richard, xii

Individualism: and affirmative action, 109; and compensatory justice, 45–46; rejection of, 77–78, 179; and social goals, 77

Inequality: defense of, 47, 50–53; of income, 68; and Liberalism, 7; of talent, 161; as tyranny of majority, 65

Intelligence tests, 22

Johnson, Lyndon, 21, 22, 24, 31

Johnson v. Transportation Agency (1987), 26

Jones v. Mayer (1968), 17

Justice, theories of

———— Justice as fairness (liberal theory): and affirmative action, 47–49, 51, 55, 58; and equal opportunity, 54–57; and human nature, 50; and individual rights, 47, 54–55; and individual v. society, 48, 53–54, 58; and inequality, 47, 50, 52–54, 58; and market as rewarding talent, 58; and meritocracy, 52; and protective affirmative action, 58; and views of liberty, 48–49, 52, 54, 56

———— Justice as freedom (libertarian and conservative theory): and compensatory justice, 43, 44–46; and distributive justice, 39, 42; and free choice, 42; and individualism, 45–46; and liberalism, 39, 42, 45; and protective affirmative action, 41, 43; and rectification principle, 39–41; and the role of the state, 38

———— Justice as greatest good (consequentalist theory): and affirmative action, 66–69; and consequentalism, 63–69; and utilitarian principle, 63–66, 68

——— Justice as productive freedom (Marxist theory): and affirmative action, 60–61, 66–69; and distributive justice, 60; and equal opportunity, 59, 61–63; and freedom, 59–60

See also Conservatives; Consequentalism; Distributive justice; Equal opportunity; Liberals; Libertarians; Marxism/Socialism

Kann, Mark E., 181–82
Kant, Immanuel, 56, 222n1
Kellough, J. Edward, 233n8
Kennedy, Anthony, 27
Kilborn, Peter, 32
King, Martin Luther, Jr., 123
Korematsu v. United States (1944), 17–18, 19

Law: and adverse impact theory, 24; and affirmative action goals and timetables, 21; antidiscriminatory, 14–16, 18–19, 23, 28, 31–33; and disparate impact cases, 22, 30; and history of affirmative action, 14–33; and individual rights v. common good, 25; and race-dependent decisions, 17–18; and set-aside programs, 28; and systemic discrimination, 22. *See also* individual cases
Lewis, Neil, 32
Liberal culture, 6–10, 172
Liberal equality, and democratic equality, 58, 190, 213
Liberalism: and compensatory justice, 101, 109, 143–46; and democratic equality, 54, 58; and distributive justice, 39, 150; and economic and positional scarcity, 217n2; and equal opportunity, 7, 55, 57, 174, 178; and hiring the best qualified, 106; and human nature, 8; and human rights, 54–55; and merit principle, 160; and opposition to affirmative action, 45–56, 69, 190; and social welfare goals v. individual rights, 8, 10; and

white males, 148. *See also* Distributive justice
Libertarianism: and affirmative action, 45–56, 101, 139–50, 175–76; and American Dream, 147; and compensatory justice, 43; and Liberalism, 69; on compensation and prosecution, 140–41; and conservatism, 58; on domestic policy, 139; and equal opportunity, 56, 148, 177; and individual rights, 41; and Kantian ideas, 56; and legal barriers, 56; and opposition to affirmative action, 45–56, 175–76; and preferential affirmative action, 43; and role of state, 40; views of justice of, 188–89. *See also* Distributive justice
Liberty, 10, 50, 52
Lofland, John, 79–80
Lorance v. AT&T Technologies (1989), 221n25
Lowi, Theodore, 8

MacIntyre, Alisdair, 65, 223n9
McLaughlin v. Florida (1964), 18
MacPherson, C. B., 62
Maguire, Daniel, 25, 189
Market competition, 8, 76–77
Martin v. Wilkes (n.d.), 30
Marx, Karl, 59–63, 76, 222n1
Marxism/Socialism: and affirmative action, 61–63, 69, 191; criticism of, 60–61; and equal opportunity, 59; ethics of, 60, 181; and the Good, 60; influence of among survey respondents, 158–62, 178, 228n21; and Liberal theory, 63; and policy making, 69; and self-interest, 76
Men, white, 13, 45, 174, 176
Merit: and affirmative action, 68, 142–54; as basis for hiring, 228n19; definition of, 107; and distributive justice, 7–8, 39; in market system, 39; and Marxist principles, 160. *See also* Equal opportunity
Meritocracy, 61, 178, 231n1. *See also* Rawls, John
Metro Broadcasting v. FCC (1990), 28, 29, 219n12
Mill, John Stuart, 63–66, 221n1

Nachmias, David, xii
Nagel, Thomas, 223n8
Native Americans: and affirmative action, 157, 175, 183–84, 232n5; differing views among, 183–84; and equal opportunity, 170; influence of Native American culture on attitudes of, 232n5; parity in hiring of, 193; views of compared with those of white men, 183–84
Newman, Jim, 26
Newton, Lisa H., 67
Nickel, James W., 68
Nozick, Robert, 37–43, 46, 51–52, 55, 60, 143, 181, 222n1

O'Connor, Sandra Day, 28, 220n20
Okin, Susan Moller, 59

Patterson v. McLean Credit Union (1989), 17, 222n25
Pear, Robert, 31
Preferential treatment, 11, 12, 54–55, 218n9
Prejudice, 114, 194, 196
Price Waterhouse v. Hopkins, 221n25
Protective affirmative action, 12, 13, 43
Pure equality of opportunity, 11, 99

Quotas, for hiring, 18–19, 32, 91, 103, 129; and admissions policies, 25; as opposed to goals, 121

Race: and affirmative action, 17–18, 25, 31; and gender, 53. *See also* Affirmative action; Blacks; Women
Rawls, John, 47–54, 55, 56, 58, 65, 178, 186, 222n1, 231n1
Reagan, Ronald, 27
Religion, and affirmative action, 123, 125–26, 130, 132, 135
Results-oriented affirmative action, 23, 24
Richard v. Croson (1989), 28

Savage, David, 26
Scalia, Antonin, 27
Scarcity, and affirmative action, 9; and equal opportunity principle,

178; resource and positional, 7–8, 148
Schaar, John H., 61, 178
Schwartz, Bernard, 25
Set-aside programs, 28
Sher, George, 44, 54
Shulman, Steven, 233n7
Simon, Robert L., 45
Skelton, George, 86
Souter, David, 27
Sullivan, William, 67, 232n3

Taft-Hartley Act, 15
Taylor, Paul, 45
Taxes, 110
Thompson, Judith Jarvis, 44
Thurow, Lester C., 7, 8, 50, 53, 217n2
Title IV. *See* Civil Rights Act of 1964
Tucker, Robert, 59

United States v. Paradise (1987), 26
United Steelworkers of America v. Weber (1979), 25, 26
U.S. culture, competing values in, 174; individualism in, 77, 78, 145; and lack of moral language, 96
U.S. history, and affirmative action, 67, 218n4
U.S. Labor Department, 21, 22
U.S. Office of Federal Contract Compliance Programs (OFFCCP), 21

Valasquez, Manuel G., 34

Wards Cove Packing Co., 220n22
Wards Cove v. Antonio (1989), 30–31
Wasserstrom, Richard, 68, 233n7
Watson v. Fort Worth Bank and Trust (1988), 27
Weber, Max, 3, 67
Wolin, Sheldon, xi
Women: and affirmative action, 8, 13, 77–78, 156–58, 187; and available opportunities, 8; benefits of AA to, 156–58; and ethical approach to affirmative action, 77–78; and exclusion of nonwhites from negotiations over distributive justice, 187; nonwhite as most supportive of affirmative action, 174–75

Pitt Series in Policy and Institutional Studies
Bert A. Rockman, Editor

The Acid Rain Controversy
James L. Regens and Robert W. Rycroft

Affirmative Action at Work: Law, Politics, and Ethics
Bron Raymond Taylor

Agency Merger and Bureaucratic Redesign
Karen M. Hult

The Aging: A Guide to Public Policy
Bennett M. Rich and Martha Baum

*Arms for the Horn: U.S. Security Policy in Ethiopia and Somalia,
1953–1991*
Jeffrey A. Lefebvre

The Atlantic Alliance and the Middle East
Joseph I. Coffey and Gianni Bonvicini, Editors

The Budget-Maximizing Bureaucrat: Appraisals and Evidence
André Blais and Stéphane Dion

Clean Air: The Policies and Politics of Pollution Control
Charles O. Jones

The Competitive City: The Political Economy of Suburbia
Mark Schneider

Conflict and Rhetoric in French Policymaking
Frank R. Baumgartner

Congress and Economic Policymaking
Darrell M. West

Congress Oversees the Bureaucracy: Studies in Legislative Supervision
Morris S. Ogul

Democracy in Japan
Takeshi Ishida and Ellis S. Krauss, Editors

Demographic Change and the American Future
R. Scott Fosler, William Alonso, Jack A. Meyer, and Rosemary Kern

*Economic Decline and Political Change: Canada, Great Britain, and the
United States*
Harold D. Clarke, Marianne C. Stewart, and Gary Zuk, Editors

*Extraordinary Measures: The Exercise of Prerogative Powers in the
United States*
Daniel P. Franklin

Foreign Policy Motivation: A General Theory and a Case Study
Richard W. Cottam

"He Shall Not Pass This Way Again": The Legacy of Justice William O. Douglas
Stephen L. Wasby, Editor

Homeward Bound: Explaining Changes in Congressional Behavior
Glenn Parker

How Does Social Science Work? Reflections on Practice
Paul Diesing

Imagery and Ideology in U.S. Policy Toward Libya, 1969–1982
Mahmoud G. ElWarfally

The Impact of Policy Analysis
James M. Rogers

Iran and the United States: A Cold War Case Study
Richard W. Cottam

Japanese Prefectures and Policymaking
Steven R. Reed

Making Regulatory Policy
Keith Hawkins and John M. Thomas, Editors

Managing the Presidency: Carter, Reagan, and the Search for Executive Harmony
Colin Campbell, S.J.

Organizing Governance, Governing Organizations
Colin Campbell, S.J., and B. Guy Peters, Editors

Party Organizations in American Politics
Cornelius P. Cotter et al.

Perceptions and Behavior in Soviet Foreign Policy
Richard K. Herrmann

Pesticides and Politics: The Life Cycle of a Public Issue
Christopher J. Bosso

Policy Analysis by Design
Davis B. Bobrow and John S. Dryzek

The Political Failure of Employment Policy, 1945–1982
Gary Mucciaroni

Political Leadership: A Source Book
Barbara Kellerman, Editor

The Politics of Public Utility Regulation
William T. Gormley, Jr.

The Politics of the U.S. Cabinet: Representation in the Executive Branch, 1789–1984
Jeffrey E. Cohen

The Presidency and Public Policy Making
George C. Edwards III, Steven A. Shull, and Norman C. Thomas, Editors

Private Markets and Public Intervention: A Primer for Policy Designers
Harvey Averch

Public Policy in Latin America: A Comparative Survey
John W. Sloan

Roads to Reason: Transportation, Administration, and Rationality in Colombia
Richard E. Hartwig

Site Unseen: The Politics of Siting a Nuclear Waste Repository
Gerald Jacob

The Struggle for Social Security, 1900–1935
Roy Lubove

Tage Erlander: Serving the Welfare State, 1946–1969
Olof Ruin

Traffic Safety Reform in the United States and Great Britain
Jerome S. Legge, Jr.

Urban Alternatives: Public and Private Markets in the Provision of Local Services
Robert M. Stein

The U.S. Experiment in Social Medicine: The Community Health Center Program, 1965–1986
Alice Sardell